SECRETS
From My
SECRET PLACE

JENNY ELDER

There is a God in heaven who reveals secrets.
Daniel 2:28, NLT

Table of Contents

Dedicated to Mark

S ome men wouldn't like the idea of sharing a bed with his wife and her other lover, but you have been amazingly understanding. I know why you did it—you love Him, too. That is why I am dedicating this book to you.

I am overwhelmed with gratitude that you agreed with the Lord that I was to write this book. Of course, there was no way He would ever bypass you to get to me. He is the One who knit our hearts together in the first place and set you in place over me as my covering.

Thank you for your willingness to lie beside me night after night as I wrote in the dark and listen to the sound of page after page of paper silently floating through the air, never failing to land with a noise on our bedroom floor. Thank you for your patience as the Lord flooded my mind with memories, making me shake our bed with laughter over funny things and wet my pillow with tears over painful places in my past.

I am amazed that never once did you ask me to stop. Without your support there would be no book. I wrote a poem for you to let you know what your love has meant to me.

Down the Halls of Time Gone By

Down the halls of time gone by
Memories ever linger.
Happiness washing over me
Gazing at the ring upon my finger.

You smiled that smile, the spell was cast
My heart beat ever faster.
You gave me your heart—I gave you mine
You've cared for it like a master.

Laughter echoes through the walls
The sound of children playing.
We've had the best, we've had it all
We've done a lot of praying!

Side by side we've seen the world
Rich with vibrant beauty.
We've played, we've danced, we've had our fun
But you never shirked your duty.

Your love took me to soaring heights,
Expanded every border.
Your silent strength always there,
You're my knight in shining armor.

My best friend, my lover,
My hiding place, three in one.
We've walked through hills and valleys
In the brilliance of the Son.

You've always encouraged, "sing your song!"

Even when I sang too long.
Always saying, "try your wings!"
Love like that meant everything.

Transparency has been the key
You've been you, and I've been me.
Nothing between, not big or small
Always dealing with every wall.

When life brought pain and I fell down
You kissed away my sorrows.
Always bright with shining hope
Assuring life would be better tomorrow.

At the end of the day when our time comes
Looking back, what an awesome run
No regrets, nothing to change
Nothing for me to rearrange.

My first love, my last love
And everything in between.
I'll hold to you till the end of our time
Till this earthly life is no longer seen.

Acknowledgements

I want to thank you, Kaye Moreno, for all the hours you spent editing this book and all the encouragement you gave me along the way. I also want to thank Dudley Hall for teaching me and thousands of others through his sermons and his books about the beauty of the grace of God.

I am forever grateful for Robert Morris, Bill Anderson, Jimmy Draper, Doug White, Bobby Treece, Ken Harp, and Tommy Briggs—the pastors I have had in my life who have saturated my soul with the truth of God's Word. I also want to thank many others, including John Sheasby, James Ryle, Mike Bickle, Bill Johnson, T. D. Jakes, James Robison, Peter Lord, Jack Taylor, and Kenneth Hagin for challenging me to leave the wilderness of my life behind and step over into the promised land of life in the Spirit with the Lover of my soul.

Letter from Gigi

The secret things belong to the Lord our God, but those things that are revealed belong to us and our children forever.   Deuteronomy 29:29

To my children, my children's children, and all the descendants who come after me, I wrote this book to you! All of us who travel the road of life have a story to tell, and no two are the same. In the next few pages, I want to share some of my story with you and some of the lessons I have learned along life's way.

I begin with a confession: I have led two lives, one very public and one private. I have been married forty-eight years to your grandfather, Mark Elder, but I have had another lover for forty of those forty-eight years. I know I could have taken my secrets to the grave. It would have been easier to keep many things hidden from the prying eyes of the world, but I have decided to leave some of the most intimate moments of my life with you on this side of the grave.

If you are wondering why I would write something that would expose my private life in such detail, the answer is simple: in case you find yourself longing for the thrill of a lifetime by having a secret love affair with the Lover of your soul, the Lord Jesus Christ, I want to make sure you know exactly what to do in order to make it happen.

The Power of Persuasion

But the Comforter, which is the Holy Spirit, whom the father will send in My name, He shall teach you all things and bring all things, to your remembrance, whatsoever I have said unto you.   John 14:26

In the beginning writing a book wasn't on my bucket list of things I wanted to accomplish. I had no desire to expose the private details of my life, but something happened that made it impossible for me to keep my secrets to myself. The Lord spoke to me and told me He wanted me to write a book in the dark.

My initial response was unbelief. That sounded ridiculous. I didn't think it was possible for someone like me to write a book, but then He turned on His charm using His powers of persuasion which made it impossible for me to refuse His request. I know it sounds strange that He would choose the middle of the night, but nighttime has always been one of His favorite times to spend with me. He likes to have me all to Himself when most of my distractions are sleeping.

Some of you know Him, and some of you haven't met Him yet, but for those who know Him, you understand exactly how persuasive He can be. He assured me I wouldn't have to write the book alone; He would be right there with me every step of the way.

Of course, to strengthen His case about how easy it was going to be for me to write this book, He said, "You don't even have to get out of bed or turn on the light. In fact, you don't even have to open your eyes. Just lean over, pick up your favorite pen that always accompanies the white paper on your nightstand, and write down the memories I will bring to your mind." He knew full well when He made that statement that was exactly what He had watched me do for the last thirty-eight years of my life—write down everything He said to me in the dark.

He said He would do His part if I would do mine. The only thing I would have to do was listen and write. After all those arguments, you can see what I mean about Him being persuasive. What's a grandmother to do when she hears so many clear, sensible reasons for writing a book in the dark?

Of course, as you know, my little chickadees, I am a pushover when it comes to someone presenting their case for what they want me to do for them in such an eloquent manner. Now look what has happened. Your favorite pushover, the one who is such an easy touch, is doing exactly what she had no intention of doing, writing a book in the dark.

In the beginning I was concerned that my memories might fail me, but shortly after my adventure through the nights began, I was relieved to discover they were not stale, but fresh, still alive in my mind just as if I were reliving them all over again. By the way, just in case you find any information that is incorrect, don't blame the Lord. Remember, your grandmother is not infallible. Instead of taking down word for word dictation, which would have been easier, the Lord chose to speak to me by bringing snapshots from my past across the runway of my mind; therefore, the words in this book are my words not His. All mistakes are mine. I take full responsibility for all of them.

Why and How

Nate, Parker, Luke, and Gabe, I am very aware, my little darlings, the fact I wrote this book in the dark is no surprise to you, because all four of you have spent many nights lying beside me, listening to me write, only to wake up the next morning to papers all over the floor, but I have never told you why I write in the dark.

You see, years ago I was sitting on the back row of a Bible conference when I heard a preacher quote Habakkuk 2:2a: *"Then the Lord replied; write down the revelation and make it plain on tablets..."* The preacher just made the passing comment that it was a good idea to always keep paper and pen by our bedside just in case the Lord spoke. I thought that was a great idea, never thinking the Lord would ever actually talk to someone like me.

In the beginning, the only obstacle I encountered was your grand-father. You know how He loves his sleep, so not wanting to disturb him by turning on the light, I learned to lean over in the dark on my left side in a slightly diagonal direction toward the nightstand. I would then get into writing position by extending my left arm toward the paper.

Feeling my way to the top edge of the paper, I would then place my left thumb at the starting point. My thumb's job was always the same. All it had to do was move from the top to the bottom of the paper one space at a time, acting as a guide to mark the starting points for my pen.

The sound of the Lord's voice always triggered my mind to notify my pen to move to the area next to my thumb. I am certain if Newton's first law of physics applied to my pen, which was resting on the middle finger of my right hand being embraced by my right thumb and index finger, he wasn't happy about having to move from his place of rest, but because of Einstein's greatest brainchild, the theory of relativity, we have to give him a little slack. We can't blame the pen if, in fact, he didn't want to move, because the laws of physics apply to everyone. I can certainly relate to how hard it is to move in the middle of the night after being all wrapped up in my warm, comfortable place of rest.

No matter how the pen felt about the initial call each night, the external force being exerted by my fingers was all the incentive he needed to move. Even though he might not have been happy having to cozy up to my thumb, after coming dangerously close to falling off the paper, the invitation being issued by my thumb to come back to its next starting point must have thrilled him because he always headed back quickly, without hesitation. Some may think my pen was the hero of the night, but actually, my thumb, who was always there to rescue my pen on his journey through the darkness, was the true hero of the hour.

Under the Cloak of Darkness

Night after night, writing under the cloak of darkness, I captured my pen between the fingers of my right hand, only allowing it to escape after the papers on my nightstand had been stained by the ink that flowed from its veins. As I pressed my fingertips against the pen, the fragrance of memories from long ago never failed to flood my mind. Each night the Lord and I would go through the same routine. He would nudge me with the sound of His voice. I would roll over, grab my pen, and write the memories.

After numbering each page, I would gently throw them on the champagne carpet that was sprawled out all the way to the very corners of my bedroom floor. Often, when twilight came the next morning, I would carefully retrieve each individual piece of paper, making sure they were placed in their proper, consecutive order.

Of course, after years of practice, hearing the Lord's voice and writing in the dark were not problems, but getting those words off that paper onto the computer was a different ball of wax. I would have gladly paid someone to type my notes, but I thought trying to help them decipher my hen-scratching would be more trouble than it was worth. I am sure the thought has already crossed your mind that I should have saved time by using my computer to type what I was hearing in the first place, but when it comes to typing, your grandmother has internal scars from her past.

As you go through life, you will discover that things you experienced in your past will affect the way you respond to your future. For years I had to hunt and peck my way through term papers on an old black typewriter that had a mind of its own. Every key seemed to try to prevent me from accomplishing my goal by pushing against the pressure of my fingers. If that wasn't bad enough, instead of hitting the backspace key and instantly removing my mistakes, I had to use a creamy white liquid substance called Wite-out.

The problems with Wite-out were twofold. It either ended up smeared on the page covering up letters that didn't need to be covered, or if it did cover the mistake I had to blow on it for at least a minute before it was finally dry enough to resume typing again.

Even though typing on the computer today is a far cry from that old black typewriter, typing is at the top of a long list of things I don't do well. With that being said, I think you can understand why I never tried to change horses in the middle of the stream, trying to do something in the dark that I can't even do that well in the light.

Gigi and Aunt Robin

I have a funny story to tell you about one night that took place years ago when Aunt Robin found out I wrote in the dark. I know all of you would likely agree with L. P. Hartley who said, "The past is a foreign country; they do things differently there." His statement is so true—things from the past were different from the experiences we have today, but keep in mind, being different can be a lot of fun. When we are cruising around town in Grandad's '57 Chevy with the windows rolled down, I notice a lot more laughter floating around in his old car than I have ever heard when we are riding in my air-conditioned BMW.

My blast from the past took place a long time ago when Aunt Robin and I were in our early thirties. We took a trip to Arizona to visit your Uncle Tim and his family. He had purchased a house there in Bisbee and was in the process of remodeling it. While we were there, we slept on the two sofas that were in the family room. When bedtime came, Robin and I talked for a while before drifting off to sleep.

As usual, just like clockwork, the Lord woke me up in the night. Realizing I needed my paper and pen which were in my suitcase in the closet on the other side of the room, I carefully removed my covers, trying to be as quiet as possible, and tip-toed across the room in the dark. As I opened the closet door, I cringed as it made a loud squeaking noise. Thinking I was going to wake Robin, I froze for a few seconds, not moving a muscle until I thought the coast was clear.

Finally, after opening my suitcase, I felt my way through the maze of socks, underwear, t-shirts, and jeans until I reached the writing utensil and white paper which were hiding at the very bottom of the suitcase.

As I made my way back to the sofa, my worst nightmare came true. I hit my big toe on the edge of the sofa's frame. Of course, I wanted to scream, but I knew I couldn't make a sound, so my throbbing big toe and

I got back under the covers, and settled in for some much-needed time with the Lord.

In the meantime, Robin must have heard the squeaking or me writing or the sound of the paper rattling, because at some point she woke up. Not realizing she was awake, thinking I was all alone with the Lord in the stillness of the night, suddenly out of the blackness I was startled to hear a voice saying, "Jenny, what are you doing?"

When I heard the sound of her voice, I almost jumped out of my skin. At first I thought I was hearing the voice of the Lord speaking out loud to me, but then of course, realizing it was Robin, all I could do was laugh. You know how Aunt Robin and I are when we get together, we laugh about everything.

Pillow Talk Notes

Parker, my beauty, I revisited a memory last night that took place when you were just seven years old. You were standing at the foot of my bed staring at papers all over the floor. In my mind's eye I could see you shaking your precious little head that was adorned with those beautiful, dark brown pigtails, saying, "Gigi, look at all of this mess! No one would ever believe this unless they could see it for themselves."

At first I thought you were scolding me about the clutter on the floor, but you removed my concerns when you decided to take pictures as evidence to show your friends that your grandmother could really write in the dark. You then said, "Gigi, instead of throwing these papers away would you save all these pillow talk notes for me. I would like to read them someday."

I couldn't quit laughing because you called them my pillow talk notes, but I assured you that day I would not throw those papers away. So because you asked, when you are ready to read those notes climb the ladder to my third attic, where you will find an old black suitcase filled with your "pillow talk" notes. I hope you can read them, but if not, just remember one of the greatest lessons you can ever learn from me, *"ask and you shall receive, that your joy may be full"* (John 16:24).

The Vision of the Four Strands of Thread

> *And a vision appeared to Paul in the night; there stood a man in Macedonia and prayed him, saying, Come over into Macedonia, and help us.*　　　　Acts 16:9

When the Lord first spoke to me in the night, I asked Him what He had in mind for the book. As soon as I asked the question, a vision of four strands that looked like threads of yarn appeared before me. One was multicolored. One was white. One was a mixture of green and brown, and the last one was a combination of silver and gold. He told me He would take all four strands and weave them throughout the book.

He then took away all the strands except the one that was multicolored. It was the most striking strand of all, consisting of red, orange, yellow, green, blue, and purple. It contained all the colors of a rainbow that graces the sky after a warm summer afternoon rain, reminding all who gaze upon it of His promise to never flood the earth again. He said that strand represented the promises of His Word. He said it was the main, most important foundational thread and He would wrap all the other threads around it.

He said He was going to use portions of His Word I had memorized and taught for thirty years of my life, some things that had been gleaned from other teachers, preachers, and books I had read, and a few things that had been downloaded directly from Him, divine revelation. He assured me He would use whatever He needed in every chapter for His glory.

He then showed me the second white strand of thread. He said it represented our secret life together, my life in the Spirit spent with Him that no one else knew about. When I asked Him why it was white, He said it was the only part of my life that was one hundred percent pure. The outside world couldn't see it. To anyone looking, it was colorless; it didn't exist, but after reading the book one would know it was actually the most important part of my life.

Next, He showed me the third strand, which was a mixture of different shades of brown and one beautiful shade of green. The green wasn't a deep forest green, or a light lime green, but the shade of green we often see worn by parts of the earth covered by well-watered winter rye. The browns were a combinations of light, dark and medium browns just like the different shades of dirt we see around the earth. He said these strands represented my earthly life, the things that took place in my secular life, in the day-to-day events of life lived in the flesh.

He then reminded me of that famous quote made by Tom Hanks in the movie, Forest Gump: "Life is like a box of chocolates—you never know what you are going to get." At that moment a box of chocolates appeared before me as He said, "Jenny, your everyday life has been like this box of chocolates, filled with an assorted array of delicacies."

He said He was going to be sure to include a sampling of pieces from my life that were filled with nuts, the hard, difficult places, the ones that hadn't been as easy for me to swallow as some of the other pieces. He said He didn't want to leave those pieces out because they were the ones He had used to shape me.

When He showed me the dark chocolate pieces in the box, He said He was going to give you a taste of the darkest places in my life, the pieces I didn't like, the pieces I didn't want you to know about, that took place in the dark. I tried to tell Him it was best to let sleeping dogs lie, but He assured me He could use anything for His glory, even my sins.

I was so glad He softened the blow by showing me several of my favorite pieces of chocolate, the ones I love the most. You know what I am talking about—the ones with the melt-in-your-mouth milk chocolate outer coating which covers up the even more delightful milk chocolate surprise hidden away in the center just waiting to be embraced by our taste buds with explosions of ecstasy. I call them my double-your-pleasure, double-your-fun pieces. He said not to worry. He would be sure to share some of the savory parts of my life with you, parts that were full of flavor.

He then held up the forth strand. It was a mixture of silver and gold. I could see it glisten as the light of the glory of His presence illuminated it. He said this was the strand that He would use to add strength to the weaving. He said the world's movies, songs, stories, and famous sayings were some of the things that generated their silver and gold. He planned to use them to illustrate spiritual truths.

He said He planned to pull out of me some of the things I had experienced in the world He could use for His glory. He said He would take some things from movies I had seen, some from songs I had heard, and some things from books I had read. At first I was surprised that He would use things from the world until He reminded me of the parables. He said using the world's stuff to help us understand His stuff is nothing new.

The Cracked Pot

> *Then I looked, and I saw a hand stretched out to me. In it was a scroll which He unrolled before me.* Ezekiel 2:9

He then showed me another vision. It was His nail-scarred hand in an open position extending down toward me. Of course, He knows I have a soft spot for His scars. I knew He wanted me to agree to the idea of writing the book, but there was one huge problem: I had just heard Him say three times He was going to use things from my life for His glory, and I couldn't possibly see how He could use anything from my life because it was so full of flaws.

As quickly as I had that thought I was reminded of the story I had often told others about the water boy and his cracked pot. The water boy lived on a beautiful mountain in India. It was his responsibility to go to the river every day and get the water that was needed for the master's house. He had a long, strong pole that he carried on his shoulders, behind his neck, which he used to balance the two huge pots, one on each end of his pole.

He was so proud of his pots. In his eyes they were perfect. Every day he put the empty pots on the pole and made his way down the path to the river. He loved making the trip because it was so peaceful along the quiet, well-worn trail.

One day he heard the pot that he always carried on his left side crying. When he asked what was wrong, the pot said he thought it was time for the water boy to get rid of him because he was cracked. The pot said, "I don't understand why you even bother to carry me. Every day you make your way to the river; you fill me and your other perfect pot with water and by the time we get back to the master's house all the water has fallen out of me. I am useless. For the wellbeing of the house, you need to get another pot to replace me."

The water boy smiled. He said to the cracked pot, "Have you ever noticed all the flowers that line the path from the river bank to the master's house?" The cracked pot assured him that he had. He said, "I planted those flowers there because I knew I could use you to water them every day as we made our way back to the main house. It was never my plan to use you for the needs of the house. I had a different plan in mind for you. You see, one of my jobs is to put a beautiful floral arrangement on the master's table every day, and it is because of you that his table is adorned with beauty."

As I remembered the story the Lord said, "Jenny, I can use you, flaws and all, for my glory even as the water boy used the cracked pot." As I thought about the idea of writing the book, I knew if it were up to me it would be impossible, but I also realized with Him all things were possible.

The moment I agreed to write this book, He expanded the vision of His hand and I saw my right hand, my writing hand, reaching up toward His. He then took my hand in His and said, "It is time to begin." British singer Adele sings a song that is one of my grandson Gabriel's favorites called, "Rolling in the Deep." Not the words of the song, but the four words in its title describe exactly how I felt as I wrote in the dark. I was "rolling in the deep."

Something's Gotta Give

The movie, "Something's Gotta Give," was released in 2003 and stars Jack Nicholson and Diane Keaton. One memorable scene showcases Diane, who portrays an author, sitting at her computer typing about events that had taken place in her life. At one point she became so overwhelmed with emotion that she started laughing, screaming, and crying all at the same time.

Was it a dignified, ladylike sound? Absolutely not; it was the sound that someone would make when every bottled up emotion held captive in the confines of a soul are finally given the freedom to escape, rushing out randomly with no restraint whatsoever, all at the same time. There were times sitting at my computer typing the notes I had written in the night, when just like Diane, I couldn't contain myself. I sat at my computer and laughed and cried all at the same time. If the truth be told, I am glad you weren't there because it was anything but dignified.

The Truth, The Whole Truth, and Nothing but the Truth

In closing, I have one last thing to say to you, my precious children. For the first few years of your life, as you well know I told you many fairy tales full of frivolous follies. I told you story after story that didn't have one ounce of truth in them. I hope you respond to the stories in this book, which are stories of some of the things that took place in my life, like you responded to the fairy tales—but I must warn you there is one big difference. These stories are not fairy tales. Everything I wrote in the dark, which has been brought to the light through this book, is the truth, the whole truth, and nothing but the truth.

The Secret Keys to the Path of Lovesickness

And you shall love the Lord your God with all your heart, and with all your soul, and with all your mind, and with all your strength.   Mark 12:30

I heard the call. It was a sound from heaven, and I knew who was speaking. There was no doubt about it—it was Him. I recognized His voice because I had heard it once before after I was born again when He said, "You are Mine." Then, it was just a faint whisper but nevertheless I heard Him.

I thought that would be the first and last time I would ever hear His voice until I got to heaven. It had been some time, and now to my surprise He was calling me again. This time it was different—He was calling me to come to a place I had never been before.

I knew what He wanted. I had read about it in His Word. He wanted me to love Him with all of my heart, and with all of my soul, and with all of my mind and with all of my strength. I loved Him, but I didn't love Him the way He wanted to be loved. I loved Him with some of my heart, some of my soul, some of my mind, and some of my strength. But He wanted all of me, not just part of me.

Every time I heard Willie Nelson sing "All of Me," I thought about Him. That's what He wanted me to give Him—all of me. To tell you the truth, when it came to our relationship, I was at a place in my life where I was just going through the motions, but my heart was far from Him. I don't know if He thought I was cold or just lukewarm, but I was definitely indifferent.

I knew who I was. I had read about it in the Bible. I was His bride and He was my Bridegroom.

> *...Come here, I will show you the bride, the wife of the Lamb*   Revelation 21:9b

The problem was, instead of acting like His bride, I acted like the friend of the bridegroom who was sitting on the sidelines watching Him from a distance.

And now He was calling again. At first, His call was easy to ignore. I was too busy living my life. I didn't have time for Him. I felt like I was in a tug of war being pulled by the world and the things of the world from one side and by His still, small but strong voice from the other side. I had made a commitment to Him, but I couldn't decide where I really belonged. I knew He wanted passion in our relationship, but there was no passion coming from me.

The lyrics of an old song written by Elvis Presley, "Burning Love" say "I'm just a hunka, hunka burning love." I suspected that song described how He felt about me. I was also pretty sure that was how He wanted my love to be toward Him. He was calling again. I had once heard someone call Him the "hound of heaven," and that is exactly who I felt like He was.

He was after me. He was relentless. He wanted me to love Him with a passion, and He wasn't giving up. The longer I listened, the louder His call became. He kept on keeping on until I could feel the beginnings of desire for more of Him stirring in my spirit, but I had questions: How could I ever get to the place in my life where I loved Him with that all-consuming kind of love? Was it even possible?

How Can I Get There?

> *He brought me into the Banqueting House, and His banner over me was love. Sustain me with raisins. Refresh me with apples, for I am lovesick.*   Song of Solomon 2:4-5

How can I get there? That was the question I asked in response to His call. I still remember the day I was reading the Bible and came across Song of Solomon. In the second chapter of the book I read about a woman who loved her king so much she was lovesick. Lovesick—wow! I paused at that word long enough to drink in the fact that she must have really loved him if she was lovesick.

As I pondered that word, the Lord spoke to me and told me the path I would have to travel to the place where I was lovesick was the same secret path this woman took in Song of Solomon that took her to the place of becoming lovesick. What secret path, I asked myself?

It was hard for me to believe He would use my least favorite book in the Bible, the book that made no sense to my natural mind, to speak to me about how to get to the place that I could love Him the way He wanted to be loved. I had read in I Corinthians 1:27 *that God had chosen the foolish things* to *confound the wise*, and without a doubt this book sounded like foolishness to me.

In fact, the first time I read Song of Solomon, I was appalled. I thought someone had made a huge mistake. Surely the Lord had better things to do with His time than talking about kissing and breasts. I was certain that this song should have never been included in the Bible. My natural mind was offended, and I avoided this book for several years.

We have all heard the saying, "Hindsight is 20/20." It's true. It is always easier to look back on a situation with greater clarity than when we are in the process of going through it. I can see now, when I entered into this song I was like a young child taking her first baby steps. I tried to walk through it, but staggered and fell as the gravity from my lack of spiritual knowledge pulled me down.

This song didn't fit into the framework of my preconceived ideas of how God spoke. How could a love relationship between a King and an ordinary woman, who ultimately became His bride, possibly have anything to do with me? How could these words teach me anything about my Lord?

Little did I know the day would come when these words which I so easily rejected would miraculously, by the power of the Holy Spirit, come alive and speak to the deepest recesses of my soul. In those early years I would have never believed that words which were so foreign to my way of thinking would be one of the things used by the Holy Spirit to usher me into a place of intimacy with the Lord Jesus Christ that I never dreamed possible.

All Scripture is Inspired by God

One day as I was reading God's Word in 2 Timothy, six words jumped up off the page and spoke to me loud and clear.

All scripture is inspired by God...　　　　2 Timothy 3:16a

Those words began to resonate within my soul over and over. "All scripture is inspired by God. All scripture is inspired by God. All scripture is inspired by God." As I rehearsed that verse, I thought about the book that couldn't possibly have been written by Him, the Song of Solomon.

I suddenly realized that Solomon may have been the one whom God used to write it down, but if all scripture is inspired by God, this song came from His heart, not Solomon's. I tucked that thought away in the forefront of my mind, still puzzled at His purpose in writing such a song. After rereading Song of Solomon, I began to see a current of truth starting in Genesis and running all the way through the book of Revelation that was the very same current of truth running strongly just under the surface of the Song of Solomon.

Over a period of time, I began to see that one of the main methods He uses to teach His people is symbolism. When He walked on the earth, He told stories about everyday circumstances that took place in the lives of the people. He would then take those natural stories which included situations the people were familiar with and use them to explain spiritual truths. He called these stories parables.

After reading through many of the thirty-nine parables, I could see that they were full of symbolic imagery. In the book of Matthew, we find several parables. Matthew said one day Jesus was sitting by a lake and when a large crowd gathered around Him, He got into a boat and pushed out a little way while all the people stood on the shore to listen to what He had to say. I would have loved to be one of those people standing in that crowd listening to the sound of His voice as He shared stories with them.

He began His time with them talking about the parable of the sower. I am sure the people in the crowd, especially the farmers, could relate to exactly what He was saying.

> *Then he told them many things in parables, saying, "A farmer went out to sow his seed. As he was scattering the seed, some fell along the path, and the birds came and ate it up. Some fell on rocky places, where it did not have good soil. It sprang up quickly, because the soil was shallow. But when the sun came up, the plants were scorched, and withered because they had no root. Other seed fell among thorns, which grew up and choked the plants. Still other still other seeds fell on good soil, where it produced a crop-a hundred, sixty or thirty times what was sown. Whoever has ears to hear, let him hear.*
>
> Matthew 13:1-9

Later, He told the disciples the meaning of the parable.

> *When anyone hears the message about the kingdom and
> does not understand it, the evil one comes and snatches
> away what was sown in their heart. This is the seed sown
> along the path. The seed falling on rocky ground refers to
> someone who hears the word and at once receives it with
> joy, but since they have no root, they last only a short time.
> When trouble or persecution comes because of the word,
> they quickly fall away. The seed falling among the thorns
> refers to someone who hears the word, but the worries of
> this life and the deceitfulness of wealth choke the word
> making it unfruitful. But the seed falling on good soil refers
> to someone who hears the word and understands it. This is
> the one who produces a crop, yielding a hundred, sixty or
> thirty times what was sown.*   Matthew 13:18-23

In the same chapter, I read the parable of the tares and the wheat,
the parables of the mustard seed, the leaven, the hidden treasure, the
dragnet, and the pearl of great price. In other passages, He told parables
about the new wine in old wineskins, the fig tree, the lost coin and the
lost sheep. These people were not only farmers but shepherds and fish-
ermen, and He used the things from their everyday lives to help them
understand His Kingdom.

He also used figurative language in other passages of His Word, like
the book of Revelation and portions of the major and minor prophets. The
book of Hosea was a natural story about a man who married a woman,
a harlot, who went after other lovers. God used the things Hosea went
through to help His people understand how He felt as Israel, His bride,
played the harlot, forsaking Him for all their other lovers.

In Galatians 4: 22-31, He used the natural story about Abraham's
two sons, Isaac and Ishmael and their mothers Sarah and Hagar to explain

the differences between the old covenant and the new covenant. He ended up saying,

> *Now all this is an allegory; these two women represent two* *covenants.*   Galatians 4:24a

When I looked up the meaning of the word "allegory," I read that an allegory is "a story in which people, things and happenings have hidden or symbolic meanings." I closed the dictionary that day with one question running through my mind. Could Song of Solomon be an allegory?

The Lord continued to reinforce the truth that using symbolism was one of the main ways He taught. He even chose to use symbolic imagery as He communicated with His people through dreams and visions. Jesus, the master storyteller, the greatest Teacher who ever lived painted pictures with His words, using symbolism to help the people have a clearer understanding of spiritual truths. With this knowledge ringing loud in my spirit, I turned to Song of Solomon.

The King

Reading the book once again, I discovered that the king in this song was not only a shepherd and a friend, but he became the bride's beloved, as well as her bridegroom. Who else did I know in the Word who was my King, my Shepherd, my Friend, my Beloved, and my Bridegroom? Could this male figure in the Song of Solomon be a picture of Jesus?

Just an Ordinary Woman

The female lead in this song was just an ordinary woman who was seeking a closer relationship with her king. We never hear her name, but we do hear her referred to as the Shulamite (Song of Solomon 6:13). He also called her "my love," "my Dove," and "my Bride." Was there any mention in the Word of a king who had a bride? Of course, the Word of

God has made it clear. All of us who have been born again, both male and female, are the bride of the King of Kings, the Lord Jesus Christ.

> *For you are all the children of God by faith in Christ Jesus.*
> *For as many of you as have been baptized into Christ have*
> *put on Christ. There is neither Jew nor Greek, there is nei-*
> *ther bond nor free, there is neither male nor female: for ye*
> *are all one in Christ Jesus.*   Galatians 3:26-28

Who did I know in the Word in whom the Dove, His Holy Spirit resided? Who did I know without a shadow of a doubt that Jesus loved? This woman was actively, aggressively pursuing her beloved.

She wasn't satisfied with a causal relationship or business as usual. She went through many experiences of seeking and finding until she finally became one with her beloved, entering into a place of rest. Could she be a picture of those in the body of Christ who are seeking after a deeper, more intimate relationship with the Lord? In this song the King compared his love to a garden.

> *A garden enclosed is my sister, my spouse, a spring shut*
> *up, a fountain sealed. Thy plants are an orchard of pome-*
> *granates, with pleasant fruits, camphire with spikenard.*
> *Spikenard and saffron, calamus and cinnamon with all*
> *trees of frankencense; myrr and aloes, with all the chief*
> *spices. You are a garden, A WELL OF LIVING WATER,*
> *Awake north wind; and come thou south; blow upon my*
> *garden, make my garden breathe out fragrance.*
>   Song of Songs 4:12-16

This garden, which was a picture of the king's bride, was full of spices and fruit. He called for the wind to blow upon His garden so all who came near could smell the fragrance that came from the beauty of his garden.

Could this woman represented by a garden be a picture of the Bride of Christ who is full of the fruit of the Spirit (Galatians 5:22)? Could the fragrance that came forth from this garden be a picture of the fragrant aroma that comes forth from the Bride of Christ that is carried to the world by the Wind of His Spirit?

> *For we are a sweet fragrance of Christ unto God, among those who are being saved and among those who are perishing. To the latter it is an aroma from death to death; to the former it is an aroma from life to life.*
> 2 Corinthians 2: 15-16

Amazingly, there was also "living water" in this garden. Oh, my heart, living water! Could she be a picture of the Bride of Christ who has LIVING WATERS flowing from her innermost being?

> *He who believes in Me, as the Scripture said, from his innermost being will flow rivers of LIVING water.* John 7:38

The Daughters

The third group of singers in this song was the daughters of Jerusalem. They spent their time talking about the king, but never experiencing a relationship with him for themselves. They admired him from afar. Could they be a picture of those of us in the body of Christ who, like me, had never moved past loving their Lord from a distance, always observing but never entering in?

The Keys

Was this story an allegory of the Lord Jesus Christ and His Bride? I was intrigued with this thought. I realized that the Lord was beginning to remove the veils from my eyes in order to bring me into the book that

I had so blatantly ignored. He had whetted my appetite. I realized that the Holy Spirit was beginning to interpret this portion of His Word for me, and I wanted to know more.

I also knew that in addition to the Holy Spirit I had another resource I could rely on, the literal Word of God. I could use the Word itself to reveal the meaning of its own symbols. I could use scripture to interpret scripture. I could take the Word with me on every step of my journey and make sure everything I was about to discover lined up with the entirety of the Word of God.

I finally came to the realization that I had two powerful keys in my possession that could help me unlock the mysteries that were hidden in this book — the Word, and the Spirit of the Living God. With these keys firmly attached to my spiritual belt, I was finally ready to explore Song of Solomon and uncover the unexpected treasures that were sitting silently on white pages all dressed up in black just waiting for me to find them. I was ready to open my heart to hear the Lord speak in a way I had never heard Him speak before.

The Divine Love Affair

The secret path — where was it? I had no idea. With my natural eyes I knew I could never find it, but when I was finally ready for the Holy Spirit to remove the veils that were blurring my vison, He lovingly and graciously took me down the same road the Shulamite took. This was the same road, by the way, that many other lovesick brides have traveled, and the same, seemingly impossible thing happened to me. I became lovesick, too.

You can't take someone somewhere you have never been before, but if you have been there, you can show others the way. To all my descendants and my fellow travelers on the road of life who find themselves hearing the call, feeling the Divine drawing to come to the deep, I am writing this book to show you one of the paths that can take you to the place of intimacy with your Bridegroom.

As I retrace my steps, reliving my memories, I want to share some of the secrets I discovered on my path. I also want to share secrets from the "secret place" that He used to change me forever, but most of all, I want to tell you about my love affair with the King. I realize that intimate moments between two lovers are best kept private, left behind closed doors, but my Lover, the Lover of my Soul, has given me permission to share some of our love story with you.

I want to tell you how He wooed me into the divine romance. I want to tell you how He manifested Himself to me through dreams and visions and drenched me with fresh revelations of His amazing love. I want to tell you how He whispered sweet nothings in my spiritual ears, caressing my soul with words of love. I want to tell you how He brought me to the place where I finally realized that His desire was for me (Song of Solomon 7:10).

I want to reveal to you why I took a chance on the path to the high places, where the revelation exploded in my spirit that "my Beloved is mine and I am His" (Song of Songs 2:16), and I was never the same again. I want to tell you how He wined me and dined me. I want to explain how He got me drunk on the New Wine of His Spirit and filled me up with the rich meat of His Words until I came to the same place in my life that the Shulamite came to in hers.

I was unashamedly, overwhelmingly, exploding with love for my King, the Lord Jesus Christ. I was *"LOVESICK!"*

Simmering on the Back Burner

The Lord used some of the secrets hidden in Song of Solomon to unleash an unbridled, holy passion in my life for Himself. I believe He has had this book simmering on the back burner for years, but He is moving it to the forefront for such a time as this. He has put all the ingredients in this song to take His Bride from a surface kind of love all the way to the deep.

This book is by no means an extensive study of the Song of Solomon. Daniel 2:28b NLT, tells us, *"...there is a God in heaven* that *reveals secrets."* As you soak in some of the secrets hidden in this song, I pray they will swell in you as they did in me until they ultimately usher you into a place of intimacy with the King that you have never been before. I pray that you will have an encounter with Jesus and enjoy the revelation of His presence on every page.

As we begin our time together along the secret path, I have just two requests. First, fasten your spiritual seat belts. Buckle up and hang on because we are going for a ride. The journey you are about to take with me that took me to the place I now call a close encounter of the third kind, the Holy Ghost kind, is full of surprises. Expect the unexpected.

Secondly, I pray as you turn each page you will remember to:

Eat, friends, and drink deeply oh lovers.

Song of Solomon 5:1

1

The Secret Entrance

The song of songs, which is Solomon's. Let him kiss me
with the kisses of his mouth: for thy love is better than wine.
Because of the fragrance of thy good ointments thy name
is as ointment poured forth, therefore do the virgins love
thee. Draw me, we will run after thee.

Song of Solomon 1:1-4

Reading the first few words in Song of Solomon through the magnifying lens of the Holy Spirit helped me find the entrance to the path that many lovers take to the place of becoming lovesick. I could tell from the opening words of the Shulamite, the leading lady of the song, that something within her had been stirred.

I caught a glimpse of what was in her heart as she revealed the fact that she wanted the king's kisses. "Let him kiss me with the kisses of his mouth!" She didn't ask him to shake her hand, or to give her a pat on the back. A casual relationship with the king didn't interest her. She obviously wanted more than that. She wanted intimacy, and she wasn't shy about letting him know exactly that.

She described how she felt about his name by likening it to the smell of a fragrant oil being poured out, and when she asked him to draw her to himself, with her next breath, she let him know all he had to do was say the word, and she would start running after him. As I continued to read the song I realized that DESIRE for intimacy with her king consumed her. I could hear the longing, the yearning in her words to experience more of him.

The desire she experienced is a great spiritual picture of the desire that overcomes many of us in the kingdom of God today. There often comes a time when just like this woman, we have an encounter with this life-changing emotion called spiritual desire. Many times we can't adequately describe it because it isn't something tangible we can see with our eyes or touch with our hands, but many of us know exactly how it feels.

We come to the place in our lives where we suddenly realize that something in our relationship with our King is missing. We are no longer satisfied with where we are on our spiritual journey. We know there is more, and we want it.

When David found himself in a place where he longed for more of God, he said, "*As the deer pants for the water brooks, so pants my soul for You, O God*" (Psalms 42:1). He likened the overwhelming desire that burned within his soul to the experience of a deer who is so thirsty for water that he is actually panting.

 Isaiah also hungered for God. He said, "*My soul yearns for you (O Lord) in the night, yes, my spirit within me seeks you earnestly'* (Isaiah 26:9a).

Paul used other words to express his desire, "*I count all things to be loss in view of the surpassing value of knowing Christ Jesus my Lord, for whom I have suffered the loss of all things and count them but dung in order that I may gain Christ*" (Philippians 3:8). After Paul, who set out to persecute Christians, had an encounter with the Lord on the road to Damascus, he was so filled with desire to know the Lord Jesus Christ that he compared everything else in his life to dung. Wow! What desire!

Most of us have experienced a spiritual desire for more at different stages of our lives and can attest that it is a crying out from the recesses of our souls for a closer relationship with Jesus. The pathway to the place of lovesickness always begins with this gnawing, craving sensation called desire that will ever beckon us to take our relationship with the Lord to a more intimate place. Does the Lord really want to have intimate relationships with His people? He tells us in the book of Proverbs that He does.

> *He is intimate with the upright.*   Proverbs 3:32 NASB

What Triggers Desire?

We will never know what caused desire for intimacy with the king to rise up in the heart of the Shulamite. Possibly, she wanted to be with him because of his position. Maybe she was attracted to his appearance, or his riches, or it could have been because she could see in him the possibility of a great love. We can only speculate what was actually in her heart, but we do know for sure from the words that came out of her mouth that the desire for a closer relationship existed.

In our lives today there are many things that trigger desire for our King. Sometimes the sparks of desire for more begin to flicker in our soul while listening to an anointed sermon. Sometimes it is ignited while reading the Word, and truth suddenly rises up off the page and becomes revelation. Sometimes desire erupts when a friend simply tells us of an encounter they have had with Him through a word, a dream, or a vision.

All of us who have had an encounter with desire know it is a strategic place in our spiritual lives because without it we will never take the path the Holy Spirit is calling for us to take in the realm of the Spirit. Paul tells us in Romans 11:36, *"for from Him, and through Him, and to Him are all things. To Him be the glory forever."*

Desire for spiritual things can't be manufactured by man. When we experience a spiritual drawing, we can't take credit for it. It is Him. He is the One who draws us. He is the Lover of our souls, and He wants all of us for Himself. He created us for His pleasure, and He longs for all of us to experience His marvelous, magnificent love and to know it in a way that "surpasses knowledge." In Ephesians Paul writes, *"And that you being rooted and grounded in love, may be able to comprehend with all the saints what is the breadth and length and height and depth, and to know the love of Christ which surpasses knowledge"* (Ephesians 3: 17b-19a).

Knowledge of His love is wonderful, but He doesn't want us to store the fact that He loves us as just another trivial piece of information to be logged in our brains. He wants us to experience His love on a deeper level.

He Won't Allow Desire to Override Our Will

As Christians, when we experience desire, it is the Holy Spirit at work drawing us to enter into a closer relationship with Jesus. We have all watched the power of a magnet drawing metal to itself. There is an invisible force that does the drawing and the metal is drawn until it is left clinging to the magnet. Just like a magnet, the Holy Spirit is the invisible force that draws us to Jesus. He wants to draw us until there is nothing between, and we are left clinging to the Lord Jesus Christ.

He draws us; however, unlike the metal, the choice of what we do with desire and how far we allow Him to draw us is always up to us. The Lord is a gentleman, and He will never override our will. He has given all of us the ability to choose for ourselves the direction our spiritual lives will take. The path each one of us chooses is ours to walk and ours alone.

Our response to the Holy Spirit's call is crucial because it determines what direction our spiritual lives will take. We can give in and go with the flow of the Holy Spirit into the deeper things of God, or we can resist Him. There are many degrees of desire that thrive in the living waters that flow through our spiritual veins. In my life what started off in a small measure ultimately grew from desire into another more intense "D" word, desperation.

In the beginning when I felt the pull of desire beginning to draw me, it felt like there was a slow-moving, lazy river, running at an easy pace within, but it didn't stay that way. Over time, the drawing became like the rapids of the Colorado River, all consuming, moving so swiftly within me that there were times when I felt like His presence would take my breath away. Desire brought me to the place that my heart began to throb for Him in a way I had never experienced before.

I came to the place in my life that I was no longer content to just know about Him. I wanted more than to just read facts about Him in the Word. I wanted more than just information. I wanted more than just another sermon. I wanted more than just another cross to hang around my neck. I wanted more than to just go to church on Saturdays or Sundays. I wanted more than the formalism of religion. I wanted more than to hear other saints tell me about their encounters with Him.

I wanted more. In fact, I wanted a lot more. I wanted a relationship with Him. I wanted Him, just Him, and nothing else was going to satisfy the longing in my soul. I wanted to hear His voice with greater clarity. I wanted to dream dreams and see visions, not just read about them or hear about them from someone else. I wanted to be up close and personal. I wanted to experience the power of His name. I wanted Him to manifest Himself to me just like He told me He would in the book of John.

> *On that day you will realize that I am in my Father, and you are in me, and I am in you. Whoever has my commands and obeys them, he is the one who loves me. He who loves me will be loved by my Father, and I too will love him and SHOW MYSELF to him.* John 14:20-21

That is exactly what I wanted. I wanted Him to show Himself to me. I wanted to experience Him in the cleft of the rock, just like Moses did. I wanted to experience His presence when I was cooking dinner for my family. I wanted to experience His presence when I was cleaning my house. I wanted to experience His presence when I was driving my car. I wanted to experience His presence when I was taking a walk. I wanted to experience His presence when I was waking up in the morning. I wanted to experience His presence when I was going to sleep at night.

I came to the place in my life where I wanted to experience His presence twenty-four hours a day, seven days a week. Just like the Shulamite in Song of Solomon, who wanted the king's kisses, I wanted the kisses of my King, King Jesus. I wanted His oils. I wanted to smell the fragrance of His presence. Bottom line, I wanted intimacy with Him.

I wanted to experience the thrill of life with the King for myself, but at that time I didn't know that this overwhelming feeling of desire would not only consume me, but would ultimately sweep me off my feet and take me past everything that was familiar into fresh revelations of His everlasting love.

Just like the Shulamite, I began my journey to the place of becoming lovesick with desire, but I discovered over the years that desire is not only the entrance to the path of becoming lovesick; it is also the constant companion of every bride who chooses to move closer to the place of loving the Lord with all of her heart, all of her soul, all of her mind, and all of her strength. The Holy Spirit is always enticing us to move forward into all that the Lord has for us.

As I journeyed along my own path carried by desire, I discovered that the more I experienced Him the more I wanted Him. I came to the place that I just couldn't get enough. The more I heard His voice, the more I wanted to hear it. The more I dreamed dreams from the Lord, the more dreams I wanted to dream. The more visions I saw in the realm of the Spirit, the more visions I wanted to see. The more I experienced His love that surpasses knowledge, the more I wanted to experience it.

You may be at a place in your spiritual life where just like me, you feel desire wooing you, calling for you to come closer to your King. If so, there are questions that must be answered. How will you respond to desire? Are you going to quench desire saying no to His advances, or are you going to give in and say yes to all that the Holy Spirit is offering you? The choice is always up to us.

Many times we feel the Lord drawing us, calling for us to enter into a more intimate relationship with Him, but we choose to ignore Him. We are not ready. We brush Him aside, and continue to go on with life as usual. If desire knocks on the door of our souls, and we are not open to His divine wooing, no problem; the Lord will respect our wishes.

We all come from different backgrounds. We have all traveled down different paths to get to where we are in our spiritual lives today. Some of us are satisfied with where we are and some aren't. Some want more and some don't. We are the ones who get to choose what kind of relationship we have with Him. If we want to worship Him from a distance, that is exactly what He will allow us to do. If we want to just to think about Him, read about Him, talk to Him occasionally, and listen to sermons about Him that is our choice.

Will He love us any less if that is what we want to do? Absolutely not. He doesn't play favorites. He loves us all the same. The only difference saying yes to the divine drawing will make in our lives is in what we experience on this side of heaven.

"Draw Me and We Will Run After You"

The first clue that we are well on our way to becoming lovesick is when desire turns into desperation, and desperation has consumed us. What will desperation do? It will bring us to the place that we are no longer able to contain ourselves. It will cause us to become just like the Shulamite who was ready to run after her king.

The Shulamite said to her King, *"Draw me and we will run after you."* She didn't say "draw me, and we will walk after you." She didn't say "draw me, and we will jog along at a slow pace after you." She said, draw me, and when you do we are going to take off running. What passion! What zeal! This woman didn't sit back in the place of passivity saying *"que sera sera*, what will be will be." She was passionate in her pursuit. When desperation takes over, there is no question about it; we feel compelled to run after Him, to seek Him with every fiber of our being.

I have never met a bride who walked in the place of intimacy with the King who was not a runner in the realm of the Spirit. One of the reasons I love this woman so much is because there was nothing nonchalant about her pursuit. She was amazingly aggressive. She knew what she wanted. She wanted intimacy with her king, and she was prepared to go after him.

She knew what her response was going to be from the very beginning. She knew what she was going to do the minute she felt his drawing. She was not going to hesitate. She knew there would be no holding back. She had no intention of letting any grass grow under her feet.

I once watched the runners who competed in the Olympics in London. Before the race began, they got into position. They bent down on all fours and shook their feet. The minute the gun went off, they started running without hesitation. I think that is exactly how the Shulamite must have been positioned in her spirit. The minute she felt His drawing she was ready to take off.

We can all learn from this woman. We need to be just like her as we run after intimacy with our King. It is so important what we choose to run after in our lives because whatever we choose to pursue is probably what we are going to end up with. In the beginning Solomon had a great relationship with the Lord, but eventually he made a huge mistake. He actually went so far away from God that He built altars on the hills of Jerusalem so he and his foreign wives could worship false gods.

In Ecclesiastes 12:8, we hear his words as Solomon looked back over his life, '*it was all vanity.*" It was useless. How tragic it would be to find ourselves at the end of our lives on the highway of regret, with the knowledge that we wasted our time running after the wrong things. We need to make sure the choices we are making right now are the right choices! We need to be make sure what we are running after in life will bring the true satisfaction we are looking for.

The Kite

I have two amazing sons, Kevin and Chris. Time has gone by so quickly. I guess the adage is true, time does fly when you are having fun. It seems like I closed my eyes for just a moment and suddenly two men stood where my little boys use to be. They have given me so much plea-sure and so many reasons to be proud of them, but the proudest moments for me today are the ones when I tell others they are my sons.

When my oldest son Kevin was about ten years old, I asked the Lord to give him a special verse for his life. The verse He gave for Kevin is the same verse all of us need in order to know how to run after Jesus in the realm of the spirit.

The answer to my prayer came on a warm, windy, Sunday afternoon in March. My Mom and Dad lived out in the country about twenty miles away, and it was our weekly ritual after church to come home, change clothes, and head straight for the country. There is something wonderful about leaving the hustle and bustle of city life and entering into miles and miles of nothing but trees and grass and nature. We rolled down our windows when the weather was nice, always eager to inhale the clean smells carried in the uncluttered breezes of the country air.

When the boys didn't have school the next day we stayed late into the night to watch the display of thousands of stars shining like diamonds against the backdrop of the blackened sky. On this particular day the March winds were blowing just right for Kevin and me to fly his new kite. We found the perfect place in an empty field adjacent to my parent's home. Kevin had taken off his shirt and shoes giving his feet the freedom to wallow around in the uncut grassy part of the field.

After I unwrapped the kite, Kevin took it and started running. We watched as it went through the gyrations of dipping and diving until a gust of wind finally caught it just right and carried it to what seemed like its happy place where it floated with ease in the sky. Our time together was one of my favorite memories because I had Kevin all to myself, away from school, friends, and even family. It was just the two of us. He has always been one of my life's greatest treasures, and just being with him taking turns flying that kite was so much fun.

Kevin would hold it for a while and then I would hold it. We were having a relaxing, easy, uneventful Sunday afternoon until suddenly the string holding the kite came unraveled from the stick and the kite started flying unfettered in the wind toward the other end of the field. Kevin immediately took off running after the kite, and I started running right behind him. He ran as fast as he could, never taking his eyes off that kite for one second. It was his goal to catch the kite, and he had no intention of slowing down for anything.

I noticed as we ran that the north part of the field was full of rocks and twigs and stickers, but even though he was barefoot Kevin didn't even flinch. He ran right over every obstacle. He had no intention of letting anything keep him from his goal of catching the kite. When we finally got to the very end of the field, the kite slowed down long enough for Kevin to grab the string. He was thrilled. He reached his goal. He got what he was running after.

On the way back across the field, I noticed that Kevin was in great pain as his focus was no longer on the kite but on the rocks, twigs, and stickers. Later that night the Lord spoke to me and said, "you asked for Kevin's life verse, and today you saw a physical picture of the verse I am giving to Kevin."

Wherefore seeing we also are compassed about with so great a cloud of witnesses, let us lay aside every weight, and the sin which doth so easily beset us, and let us run with patience the race that is set before us. Looking unto Jesus the author and finisher of our faith...

Hebrews 12:1-2a

The Lord said, "Today, Kevin ran the race set before him with his eyes fixed on that kite, and he reached his goal. He got what he was running after. When he is ready to run after Me like he ran after that kite, letting nothing stand in his way, with his eyes fixed firmly on Me, he will reach Me, and I will show Myself to Him." Just like Kevin, we need to assume the position of a runner, girding our loins with spiritual tenacity. The prize that awaits all spiritual runners is far greater than a gold medal to hang around our necks. The prize is intimacy with Jesus, the author and finisher of our faith.

We also need to keep in mind that when we run after Him, we don't have to run in our own strength. It is not a difficult task. The Holy Spirit's job is to draw us closer and closer to Jesus, and when we give Him the go ahead He supplies all the strength we need. He wants us to run after Him until, like the Shulamite at the end of Song of Solomon, we come to the place in our spiritual lives we are not only running after Him, but also running with Him in the realm of the Spirit.

Hide and Seek

> *And you will seek Me and find Me, when you search for Me*
> *with all your heart.*   Jeremiah 29:13

The promise we need to remember when we are running after the Lord in the realm of the Spirit is, if we seek Him with all our hearts, we will find Him. He didn't say we might find Him. He didn't say there was a strong possibility we would find Him. He said if we seek Him we WILL FIND HIM.

Over the years all my children and grandchildren have been hide and seek players. Believe it or not, even at my age, I like to play hide and seek. When my children were little my favorite places to hide were in the dirty clothes hamper and behind the bi-fold doors on top of the washing machine or dryer. As I have gotten older I tend to hide in places that I don't have to curl into a ball to get into.

My youngest grandson, Gabriel, who is seven years old, loves to play games. Every Wednesday is what he calls Gigi day. On Gigi day Gabe spends the day and night with his granddad and me. On those days I drop everything and become a child again, playing games and eating popsicles. Gabe brings such joy into our lives with his sense of humor. He is always laughing and doing things that make us laugh. He is so much fun to be with.

Hide and seek is one of his favorite games. On Gigi day we take turns hiding while the other one races through the house looking in the closets, under the beds, behind the doors, and in every possible hiding place in the house. When it is my turn to hide, I try to hide in a place where I know it will be easy for him to find me. When I hear him getting closer and closer I always feel the excitement building when I know the thrill of him finding me is just around the corner. Sometimes I even jump out of my hiding place to surprise him.

I often wonder if the Lord likes to play hide and seek. He has told us what to do if we want to find Him. All we have to do is seek Him with all of our hearts. There are times when I also wonder if He feels the same excitement I often feel building when He knows the thrill of me finding Him again is just around the corner. Like me with Gabe, there have been many times when He has surprised me, jumping out and showing Himself to me.

The fact that He wants us to find Him is a settled issue, but the question we all have to ask ourselves is, do we want to find Him? If you are encountering desire for the first time, and you are on the fence about what you are going to do, before you make your final decision, may I tell you one important truth that every bride of Christ needs to know? Yes, it is true; if desire is not quenched He will carry you into the deep things of the Spirit, but He will also take you along a path of No Return.

Once you have tasted the joys, the overwhelming delights, the beauty that is on this path, a casual relationship with your Lord will never satisfy you again. Desire is not only a strong catalyst that will cause us to start running after Jesus, but it will also cause us to press in to apprehend the One that has apprehended us. There is a thing called "pressing in," even when you want to give up, that all runners know about. Paul knew the importance of pressing in: "*I press on to take hold of that for which Christ Jesus took hold of me*" (Philippians 3:12).

There were setbacks in his life, but Paul didn't give up. He said, "I press on." He wanted to lay hold of his destiny. He wanted to lay hold of what Christ Jesus had laid hold of him for. The Shulamite in the Song of Solomon also knew about pressing in. She didn't run her race for intimacy with the king perfectly. She had setbacks. It is encouraging for all of us to know that she made mistakes just like we do.

There was a time in chapter five of Song of Solomon where the king knocked, and it was inconvenient for her to respond. She had her own agenda, and he didn't fit into her plans. Her flesh took over, and she missed an opportunity. We all have times where we blow it; however, we can look at how she dealt with her mistake and learn a great lesson. When she fell down in her quest, she didn't stay down. She didn't give up. She realized her failure and was immediately remorseful. She didn't let the setback disqualify her from the prize.

The missed opportunity was actually a blessing in disguise because it caused her to regroup and rediscover what was really important. She got up, dusted herself off, and started after him again. Her apparent failure served her well because the regret of missing an encounter with the one she loved caused her to run after him, pressing in with an even greater fervency on the next leg of her journey.

All of us have times in our lives where we miss the mark. None of us are perfect, but as long as we have breath in our bodies, He gives us the ability get up after a fall, get back in the race, and enjoy the thrill of running after Him again.

The First Time Desire Consumed Me I Needed a Savior

I will never forget the first time I came to the place in my life when desire consumed me. When I was a young girl, our family seldom went to church, but when we did I heard about the Ten Commandments. I decided to memorize them, thinking if I could just keep all of them, I could ensure my place in heaven. There was only one problem. After years of trying, I realized I couldn't do it. If getting to heaven depended on me being perfect, I wasn't going to make it.

I didn't realize that Jesus had fulfilled the law on our behalf and now we were under the New Covenant of grace. The New Covenant didn't say we could sin all we wanted to, but that the Lord would place His

Spirit in all who put their faith in Him, and if we would walk in the Spirit we would not fulfill the lust of the flesh. In hindsight, I am glad I spent so much time trying to keep the law to get to heaven, because with every failure the fact that I was a sinner and needed a Savior became stronger and stronger.

When I was a teenager, our family joined First Baptist Church located right in the middle of downtown Fort Worth, Texas. The main reason I enjoyed going to church was to see my friends. Years later, after I was married, in September of 1972 at the age of twenty-five, a new neighbor who moved into the house across the street invited me to a bible study. Her name was Marilyn Lilly. I had been out of church for several years and really had no interest in spiritual things, but I went because I wanted to get to know her.

I can still remember walking through that crowd of women. Somehow, I knew they had something I didn't have. As I listened to the speaker it was as if she was speaking directly to me. She said that Jesus had died on the cross for all our sins, and if we would just repent, asking Him to forgive us of our sins, and put our faith and trust in Him as our Lord and Savior, He would give us the gift of eternal life. She read the words of Jesus written in red from John 3:3, *"Truly, truly, I say to you, unless one is born again, he cannot see the kingdom of God."*

What did that mean? How could I be born again? That sounded impossible. She said we must be born again not in the flesh, but in the Spirit. I still didn't fully understand what she was talking about. She talked about letting the old life go and being born again by His Spirit allowing a new life in the kingdom of God to begin.

Every time I thought about that verse I knew whatever Jesus meant when He said we must be born again, that experience had never happened to me. She also said when it came to salvation, we couldn't do anything to earn it or deserve it. It was a free gift and all we had to do was receive it by faith.

> *For by grace are you saved through faith, and that not of yourselves: it is the gift of God: not of works lest any man should boast.* Ephesians 2:8-9

When I left the meeting that day I went home and cried for two weeks knowing if I died I would not be going to heaven. I would step into eternity without a Savior. I would exist, but not in heaven. I would exist in a place of eternal punishment. I also knew if I died before receiving this free gift of eternal life, my chances of going to heaven could be gone forever. I didn't really understand what was happening, until I later read the words of Jesus: *"No one can come to Me, unless the Father who sent Me draws him"* (John 6:44).

I was being drawn. The Holy Spirit was convicting me of my sins. Everything in me cried out for a Savior. A memory came across my mind of a pastor at a local Baptist church named Bill Anderson, who had knocked on my door and invited me to come to his church when I was just a teenager. I called him and asked if he would come over and tell me exactly what I needed to do to be saved.

When he arrived I told him I had played church for several years, and I didn't want to do that anymore. After he graciously shared the Word with me, I asked him if I did exactly what the Word told me to do, how would I know for sure, without a shadow of a doubt that when I died I would go to heaven. I loved his answer. He said, "If Kevin, your son, asked you if you were really his mother, wouldn't you pick him up, put your arms around him and assure him you were his mother?" I quickly answered, "Yes."

He said, "That is exactly what the Lord will do for you. There will be no doubt in your mind. You will know because the Holy Spirit will assure you in your inner man that you belong to the Lord." He asked me if I wanted him to pray with me, but I felt like it was something I needed to do all by myself.

That night after dinner I went outside and found a comfortable place to sit on my front porch. I scanned the sky, looking up into the heavens at all the brightly shining stars. Sitting under the beauty of His heavenly creation, I bowed my head with a heavy heart. It was weighted down with the burden of my sins, but after asking Jesus to forgive me, inviting Him to come into my life to be my Lord and Savior, I raised my head with the thrill of knowing my sins had been forgiven and I now had eternal life.

The preacher was right. There was no doubt in my mind. I knew for sure I belonged to the Lord and when I died I was going to heaven.

> *The Spirit himself bears witness with our spirit, that we are*
> *children of God.*   Romans 8:16

I looked forward to the fact that when I got to heaven I would see Jesus. I was thrilled to think about getting to talk to Him and being able to hear His voice all the time in heaven. I looked forward to asking Him all the many questions that were shuttling through the coils of my mind. I thought that knowing Him as Savior was all there was to the Christian walk.

I was baptized by Brother Anderson and still remember the amazing feeling I experienced after coming up out of those baptismal waters. The world looked different to me. It was as if the blues were bluer and the reds redder. I thought everything around me looked so bright and clean, but it wasn't the things of the world that were suddenly clean; I was clean. I had been washed in the blood of the Lamb and I began to see things differently.

On the day I was born again I had no idea the incredible adventure that was in store for me. I had no idea He had written me a love letter. I knew in my head He loved me, but I had no idea about the depth, or width, or height, or breadth of His love. I had no idea He didn't want to wait until I got to heaven to have a relationship with me. I had no idea He wanted to walk through my life with me. I had no idea He had created me for His pleasure and the day would come when I would discover that He took great pleasure in me. I had no idea the One who created me had wed me. I had no idea that I was, *"the Bride of Christ, the wife of the Lamb"* (Revelation 21:9).

Tabernacle of Moses: The Shadow of the Substance

The second time desire consumed me, I was at the beginning of the path to the place of meeting my Baptizer and my Bridegroom. It was a day that started off like many other days. I walked into a Bible study where a woman was teaching about the Tabernacle of Moses. I was disappointed to find out her topic was going to be about that old tabernacle. I couldn't imagine how it could have anything to do with me. To tell you the truth I really wasn't interested in a history lesson. I wanted to learn something fresh and new from the New Testament about Jesus. Little did I know when I sat down that morning, wanting to escape from what I thought was going to be a dull sermon, that what I was about to hear would change my spiritual life forever.

The teacher started off by talking about how important it was to God for us to understand the Tabernacle of Moses by comparing it to His description of creation. God took only two chapters in Genesis to describe creation, whereas, He took fifty chapters from Exodus, Leviticus, Numbers, Deuteronomy, and Hebrews to explain the Tabernacle of Moses.

The teacher reviewed the events leading up to the children of Israel leaving Egypt. God told Pharaoh, through Moses, to let His people go. He wanted to meet with them in the desert. After much opposition, when they finally left Egypt He gave Moses detailed instructions about how to build this meeting place. He didn't give Moses the freedom to build this tabernacle any way he wanted to. Just like an architect who provides the plans for a home, He was the Divine Architect that gave Moses specific instructions for every single detail of that meeting place.

> *And the Lord spoke unto Moses, saying, "Speak unto the children of Israel, that they bring me an offering: of every man that giveth it willingly, with his heart. And let them make me a sanctuary; THAT I MAY DWELL AMONG THEM. According to all that I show thee, after the pattern of the tabernacle and the pattern of all the instruments thereof, even so shall ye make it."*   Exodus 25:1-2, 8-9

The reason God told Moses to build that tabernacle was, He wanted them to make a place for Him to dwell with them. It had to be made exactly as He commanded because that tabernacle was a picture of the true tabernacle in heaven where the Lord Jesus Christ is enthroned as our

High Priest. He didn't want the picture on earth to misrepresent the true tabernacle in heaven. She then quoted a passage in Hebrew:

> *Now the main point of what we are saying is this: We do have such a high priest, who sat down at the right hand of the throne of the Majesty in heaven, and who serves in the sanctuary, the true tabernacle set up by the Lord, not a mere human being. Every high priest is appointed to offer both gifts and sacrifices, and so it was necessary for this one also to have something to offer. If he were on earth, he would not be a priest, for there are already priest who offer the gifts prescribed by the law. They serve at a sanctuary that is a COPY AND SHADOW of what is in heaven. This is why Moses was warned when he was about to build the tabernacle: See to it that you make everything according to the pattern shown you on the mountain.* Hebrews 8:1-5

After establishing the fact that everything in that tabernacle was a copy of the true tabernacle in heaven, she began to talk about the furniture inside it. When she started teaching about this furniture, I would have never believed that what she was about to say would be a catalyst to take me to places in the realm of the Spirit I never even knew existed.

She started by drawing a vertical line on the blackboard and then a horizontal line intersecting the vertical line above the middle section. The picture looked like the shape of the cross Jesus died on.

The teacher then positioned the furniture on the picture of the cross. At the foot of the picture of the cross she drew a picture of the Brazen Altar. Directly above the Brazen Altar, below the horizontal portion of the cross was the Brazen Laver. She said that these two pieces of furniture were in the outer court.

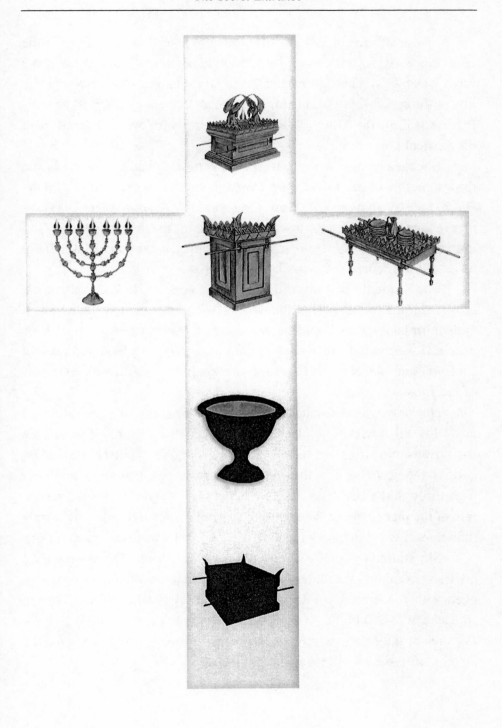

The next three pieces of furniture were placed behind a veil in the Holy Place. At the left end of the horizontal portion of the picture of the cross was the Golden Lampstand. At the right end of the horizontal portion of the cross was the Table of Showbread. In the top center of the Holy Place, she drew the Altar of Incense. It was the third piece of furniture in the vertical portion of the cross.

She then went to the very top of the vertical portion of the cross and drew a picture of the Ark of the Covenant which was separated from the Holy Place by another veil. Wow, God had told Moses to place the furniture in the shape of a cross. It was interesting for me to discover that God used that furniture to draw a picture of the cross on the canvas of that old desert floor hundreds of years before Jesus was ever born.

She suddenly had my full attention. She said He knew about the cross from the foundation of the world. He had a plan, and if we looked with spiritual eyes we could see a picture of Jesus in every piece of furniture. It was as if Jesus were standing in heaven and God had taken a spotlight and placed it on Him, and the shadow on earth was a shadow of the substance, Jesus.

Not only was each picture of furniture a picture of Jesus, she said as we looked at what took place at every piece of furniture we would see the various ministries that Jesus performed, not only while He walked on earth in the flesh, but also the ministries He was performing today in our lives through the power of His Spirit. She said we could also use the picture of the placement of the furniture to gauge where we were in our spiritual lives. I was intrigued. I had no idea where I was in my spiritual life.

She started by briefly discussing the Outer Court. There were sixty pillars surrounding the Outer Court which held the wall of linen curtains; even as there were sixty pillars, in the genealogy of Christ (Matthew 1:1-16; Luke 3:23-38) in the bloodline from Adam to Christ through Joseph. The area of the Tabernacle was comprised of three separate sections, the Outer Court, the Holy Place, and the Holy of Holies.

Outer Court: The Brazen Altar

Exodus 27: 1-8, Exodus 38: 1-7, Leviticus 1:1-13

She then began to describe the first piece of furniture everyone saw when they entered the gate to the outer court, the Brazen Altar. There was no way anyone could get to all the other pieces of furniture without going by this altar. It was made of acacia wood, overlaid with brass. Acacia wood was an indestructible, incorruptible wood that was found in the Sinai desert. This wood was a picture of Jesus. Just like that wood, He withstood death; even death on the cross couldn't destroy Him. He rose from the grave alive, indestructible.

She described this altar in great detail, and then went on to tell us what happened there. When someone sinned, they brought a sacrificial animal to the door of the tabernacle. It had to be a male without defect—a lamb, a goat, a pigeon, a turtledove, or a bull, depending on their wealth. They would stand before the priest laying both hands on the head of the animal. Symbolically their sins were transferred from themselves to the animal. The animal was then killed. The priest sprinkled its blood on the Brazen Altar, and then placed the flayed animal on the altar as an atonement for their sin.

> *Without the shedding of blood, there is no forgiveness.*
> Hebrews 9: 22b

That animal was a picture of the Lamb of God, Jesus, who would one day come and die for the sins of the world. Most of us remember what John the Baptist said when he saw Jesus walking toward him while he was baptizing the masses: *"Behold the Lamb of God who takes away the sin of the world"* (John 1:29).

When he spoke those thirteen words, the Israelites understood exactly what he meant because they understood what happened at the Brazen Altar. Just like the animal sacrifices, Jesus was our sacrifice who took our place, taking the punishment for our sins. His blood was shed at the cross for our sins just like the blood of the animals was shed at the Brazen Altar. I had just recently found the Lamb of God. He was so precious to me. I was so grateful that He loved me so much that He was willing to take the punishment that I deserved. Oh, what love! I was so grateful for forgiveness and for the eternal life that He had so freely given to me.

He made Him who knew no sin to be sin on our behalf, so we might become the righteousness of God in Him.

2 Corinthians 5:21

Outer Court: The Brazen Laver

Exodus 30:17-21, Exodus 38:8, Exodus 40:7; 30-32

She went on to describe the next piece of furniture that was in the outer court which was the Brazen Laver. It was used by the priests to wash themselves. It had two parts. The pedestal was made from solid brass, and on top of the pedestal was the circular brass bowl made from brass mirrors the women brought with them from Egypt. Fresh water was continually poured into the laver. Its purpose was for purification. As the priest washed themselves they could look into the mirrors and see what needed to be cleaned. I could see the picture of "the washing of water with the Word."

Husbands love your wives even as Christ loved the church and gave Himself up for her, to make her holy, cleansing her by the washing with water through the Word.

Ephesians 5:26

I knew as I had been in the Word He had been washing me. He was using His Word to wash away my wrong way of thinking, my wrong habits. As I looked into the Word, just like they looked into those mirrors, I could see myself. I could see where the dirt was. I could see what

Don't stay in outer court — move in

needed to be changed. The Word was washing me and changing me all at the same time. I could see the analogy from this piece of furniture, and I was so glad I was there.

The teacher said it was important to remember that these two pieces of furniture, the Brazen Altar and the Brazen Laver, were in the outer court. She said many Christians stayed in the outer court experience all their lives and never moved past these two stations. She said that the outer court was a wonderful place to be, but there was so much more. I had no idea there was anything more than celebrating what Jesus did on the cross and His precious Word. I listened intently.

Holy Place: The Golden Lampstand

Exodus 25:31-40, Exodus 37:17-24, Leviticus 24:1-4

The next section of the tabernacle was the Holy Place. Only the priests could enter this room. I knew from studying God's word I was now part of His royal priesthood.

> *But you are a chosen people, a royal priesthood, a holy*
> *nation, God's special possession, that you may declare the*
> *praises of him who called you out of darkness into his won-*
> *derful light.*   1 Peter 2:9

Before the priests could enter this room they had to change their garments and be anointed with oil. As they entered the room, on the left side of the Holy Place was the Golden Lampstand. It was made of pure beaten gold with seven branches. It was the priests' job to make sure it was continually filled with olive oil. The wicks were set on fire and they were to burn continually to light the room.

I could immediately see the picture. I realized that just like this Golden Lampstand had been beaten, Jesus had been beaten. Jesus was certainly full of the Oil of the Spirit, and He was the Light of the world. She then said that we were to be just like that lampstand continually being filled with the Oil of the Holy Spirit, on fire, burning with passion for the Lord Jesus Christ. We were to let His light shine through us for His glory. She confirmed her teaching with many New Testament scriptures.

One of the scriptures she used was Ephesians 5:18: *"Be continually filled with the Spirit."* I knew that I had received the Holy Spirit when I was born again. I knew that the Holy Spirit lived in me, but I didn't know if I had ever been filled with the Holy Spirit. I had never heard anything about being filled with the Holy Spirit or being on fire with a passion for Jesus. That was new to me.

Holy Place: The Table of Showbread

Exodus 25: 23-30, Exodus 37: 10-16, Leviticus 23:13, Leviticus 24:5-9, Numbers 28:7-10, 14-15, 24, 31

On the right side of the Holy Place was the Table of Showbread. It was made of acacia wood, overlaid with pure gold. She said the wood was a picture of His humanity and the gold a picture of His divinity. He was both human and divine. Twelve loaves of bread were on the table representing the twelve tribes of Israel. The priests would gather around the table and break the unleavened bread before consuming it.

Leaven was a symbol of sin and there could be no leaven in this bread, even as there was no sin found in Jesus. I could definitely see the picture. He was the sinless son of God who told His followers in John 6 that He was the "Bread of Life." The bread was a picture of Jesus, whose body was broken for you and for me.

> *I am the Living Bread that came down out of heaven.*
> *Whoever eats this Bread will live forever.*   John 6:51

Wine was also on the table. The priests in the Holy Place were instructed to take the wine and pour it out on the earthen floor as a drink offering. I was reminded of the last supper where Jesus used wine to symbolize His blood. I could visualize in my mind's eye that wine falling from the cup on to the earthen floor of that old tent in the desert of Sinai, and only imagine how the blood of Jesus must have looked as it fell from his body hitting the earthen floor of Calvary that He, Himself had created. How wonderful that He willingly shed His precious blood.

I loved the beautiful picture of Jesus that was portrayed at the Table of Showbread. The table was a picture of us. Just like that table was used to put the bread and the wine on display, we were to put Him on display through our lives, lifting Him up for all of the world to see. We were to live our lives in such a way that when others looked at us, they would see Him. That was certainly what I wanted to do. I wanted to be all that He wanted me to be.

Holy Place: The Golden Altar of Incense

Exodus 30: 1-10, Exodus 37: 25-29, Exodus 40: 34-38

The Altar of Incense was placed in the center of the Holy Place in front of the curtain that separated the Holy Place from the Holy of Holies. It was also made of acacia wood and overlaid with pure gold. The priest would throw the sweet fragrant incense on the fire that had been made by the perfumer with the sweet spices according to Gods directions. As the incense hit the fire, you could see the smoke ascending up toward heaven and smell a wonderful fragrant aroma. As she painted the picture of the smoke ascending to the heavens, I could see the picture of Jesus, our Intercessor, the One who ever lives to make intercession on our behalf.

> *Wherefore, He is able also to save them to the uttermost*
> *that come unto God by Him, seeing He ever liveth to make*
> *intercession for them.* Hebrews 7:25

I could see the picture of the smoke as a picture of His prayers ascending into the very heart of His Father. She said that even as Jesus is our Intercessor, we are to be intercessors, sending our prayers to heaven on behalf of others and ourselves.

Holy of Holies: The Ark of the Covenant

Exodus 25: 10-22, Exodus 37:1-9

She finally came to the last room in the tabernacle. It was called the Holy of Holies. There was a curtain separating the Holy Place from the Holy of Holies. It was in this room that God told Moses to place the Ark of the Covenant after the tabernacle was complete. He told him to instruct the workers to make this piece of furniture out of acacia wood and overlay it with pure gold inside and out.

On the top of the Ark of the Covenant was the Mercy Seat which was made of pure gold, and at the two ends of the Mercy Seat were two cherubim which were also made of solid gold. The angels faced one another with their wings touching, covering the Mercy Seat. Their faces looked down toward the golden seat.

After describing it, she said the very presence of God was right there above the Mercy Seat between the cherubim. It wasn't just a symbol of His presence. It wasn't just a picture of His presence. He was there. It is interesting to hear the words of the Lord that Nathan, the prophet, delivered to King David when he wanted to build a temple for the presence of God to dwell in.

> *Go and tell my servant David, "This is what the Lord says: Are you one to build Me a house to dwell in? I have not dwelt in a house from the day I brought the Israelites up out of Egypt to this day. I have been moving from place to place with a tent AS MY DWELLING. Wherever I have moved with all the Israelites did I ever say to any of their rulers whom I commanded to shepherd My people Israel, why have you not built me a house of cedar?*
>
> 2 Samuel 7: 5-6

God made it very clear in this passage that He dwelt in that tent. Whereas the sun provided the light in the outer court, and the lampstand provided the light in the Holy Place; the light in the Holy of Holies came from the presence of God. The Ark of the Covenant, where God dwelt above the Mercy Seat, was first piece of furniture to be built and the last piece to be set in place after the tabernacle was completed.

Before the tabernacle was finished it was placed in a temporary tent called the "tent of meeting" outside the camp. While the Ark of the Covenant was in that temporary tent Moses had many one on one intimate encounters with God. It was the place where God met with Moses and spoke to him.

> *There I will meet with you, from above the mercy seat, from between the two cherubim that are upon the ark of the Testimony, I will SPEAK INTIMATELY with you of all which I will give you in commandment to the Israelites.*
> Exodus 25:2

> *When Moses entered the tent of meeting to speak with the Lord, he HEARD THE VOICE speaking to him from between the two cherubim, above the atonement cover on the ark of the covenant. In this way the Lord spoke to him.*
> Numbers 7:89

> *Whenever Moses entered the tent, a pillar of cloud would descend and stand at the entrance of the tent; all the people would arise and worship, each at the entrance of his tent. Thus the Lord used to SPEAK TO MOSES FACE TO FACE, just as a man speaks to his friend.*
> Exodus 33 9-11

The teacher closed her discussion by saying He wanted to meet with us and speak with us just like He did with Moses. He wanted all of us to hear His voice. She then took us to John 10:27 and read, "*My sheep hear My voice.*" There it was in the New Testament written in red letters, the very words of Jesus. Oh my heart! Everything in me stood at attention. It was my first time to realize that Jesus said it was possible to hear His voice.

She went on to describe what happened in the Holy of Holies after the tabernacle was complete and the Ark of the Covenant was placed in this room. The High Priest would go behind the veil one time every year with the blood of the sacrifice and place it on the Mercy Seat for the forgiveness of his sins and the sins of the people. If God accepted the blood the High Priest was allowed to come out, and the Israelites knew their sins were forgiven for another year.

Just as the High Priest took the blood into the Holy of Holies and put it on the Mercy Seat, he was a picture of the Great High Priest that was to come, Jesus, who went into the true Holy of Holies in heaven on our behalf, once and for all, not with the blood of an animal, but with His own sinless blood. As she described Jesus going into the true Holy of Holies in heaven, I could just imagine Him placing His blood on the Mercy Seat, and hearing it crying out to God on our behalf, obtaining mercy for all of us who put our faith and trust in the Lord Jesus Christ.

I found the Ark of the Covenant in the Holy of Holies and everything that happened there very interesting, but to tell you the truth, what continued to ring the loudest in my spirit that day was the fact that, above the Mercy Seat was the place of His presence; it was the place where Moses HEARD HIS VOICE.

The teacher then went on to talk about what happened to the curtain that separated the Holy Place from the Holy of Holies. When Jesus walked on the earth, the Temple of Solomon in Jerusalem was set up using the same pattern, and the same furniture that was in the Tabernacle of Moses. The Talmud, which is a sacred Jewish archive, described the curtain that separated the Holy of Holies from the Holy Place in the Temple of Solomon as being sixty feet tall, thirty feet wide, and the width of a man's hand.

When Jesus hung on the cross the most amazing thing happened; not only did the earth turn dark for three hours in the middle of the day, but at the moment He died the earth shook, and the veil in the Temple of Solomon was split, not from the bottom to the top, but from the top all the way to the bottom. Man couldn't have split that veil. It had to have been split by someone from above.

> *And Jesus cried out again with a loud voice, and yielded up His Spirit. And behold, the veil of the temple was torn in two from top to bottom, and the earth shook and the rocks were split into.* Matthew 27:50

When Jesus died on the cross as our sacrificial Lamb, the curtain that separated man from God was torn. Many believe it was torn by the hand of God Himself as a picture to the world that separation from His presence was over. The price had been paid. Now there was nothing between man and God. Now we have total access into His presence. We have the freedom to walk right in, not with our heads hanging down, but with boldness knowing we are covered in the blood of the Lamb. We now have the freedom to meet with Him and speak to Him and listen to Him speak to us.

As the teacher spoke, I could feel my heart beating so hard within me I thought it was going to beat out of my chest. That's what I wanted. I wanted Him to meet with me and speak to me just like He did with Moses. I suddenly knew exactly where I was in my walk with the Lord. I had an outer court experience. I knew about Him, but I didn't have a relationship with Him. I didn't know Him intimately. I knew that whatever it took I had to go to the Holy Place in the realm of the Spirit. I wanted to be filled with the Oil of His Spirit. I wanted the Lord to set me on fire, just like the priest set the wicks in the Golden Lamptand on fire. I wanted it and I wanted it all!

It was also in that moment I knew my spiritual life would never be the same again. I knew that I would never again be satisfied staying in the outer court. I couldn't camp there any longer, but I also knew that I couldn't leave the blood that was shed on my behalf at Calvary or the washing of the water of the Word behind. In order to have the freedom to explore all that took place in the Holy Place and all that happened at the Ark of the Covenant, I would have to carry both the blood and His Word with me.

I knew I would need the reminder with me at all times that nothing I would find could be greater than what the Lamb of God did for me on the cross, and I needed to make sure that everything I was getting ready to go after lined up with the Word of God. My quest that had once been fueled by studying the Word for knowledge about Him, changed into a passion to not just know facts about Him, but to actually know Him in a one-on-one intimate relationship.

I wanted to hear all the things that He had said to the saints that had gone before me, but even more than that, I wanted to hear what He wanted to say to me in the here-and-now.

I had loved getting to know Jesus as my Savior in my outer court experience, but I wanted more. Little did I know that my quest for more was about to take me from the outer court, where I came to know Jesus as my Savior, into the Holy Place where I would come to know Jesus as my Baptizer, and then on to the Holy of Holies where I would come to know Him as my Bridegroom.

I Couldn't Move

After the teaching was over, everyone picked up their Bibles, their notebooks, their purses and filed out the back door, but I couldn't move. I was undone. It was as if time stood still, blocking out the world long enough for me to drink in the amazing truth that it was actually possible for me to hear His voice. Somehow I knew in my inner person, without a shadow of a doubt, that if He met with Moses and spoke to Moses, that the day would come when He would meet with me and speak to me.

Like the Shulamite who said, "draw me," I started saying the same thing, only using different words. Within my spirit I cried out to the Lord, "take me past the outer court into the Holy Place, but don't stop there.

Lord take me all the way into the Holy of Holies. Take me to the place of Your presence. I want You to meet with me and speak to me. Lord, bring me to the place that I can hear Your voice more clearly."

At that time, I had no idea that He had been drawing me long before I started crying out to be drawn. He was drawing me to the deep with His Spirit and His Word. The desire to hear His voice overwhelmed me. In that moment, in the realm of the Spirit, I took off the shoes I had used to run after the world and the things of the world, and I put on my spiritual running shoes. I didn't know it at the time, but I was at the entrance to the path of becoming lovesick. My eyes were fixed on the prize, and like the Shulamite in the Song of Solomon, I was ready to start running after my King, the Lord Jesus Christ.

There is a great old song that Marvin Gaye wrote called, "Ain't No Mountain High Enough" that Fantasia and Luke James sang at the 2013 Trumpet Awards. The words say exactly how I felt when I started running after Him:

> *Don't You know there*
> *Ain't no mountain high enough*
> *Ain't no river wide enough*
> *To keep me from getting to You*

At that moment in time, sitting in that church, I knew something amazing had happened to me. I knew without a shadow of a doubt that nothing in this world would be able to keep me from running after the One who was drawing me to Himself with the power of His Word, the power of His Spirit, and the amazing power of His everlasting love.

Lord, thank You, thank You, thank You for drawing us. If You didn't draw us we would never have the privilege of discovering the wonder of You!

2

The Secret of Receiving

Truly, truly, I say to you, if you ask the Father for anything in My name, He will give it to you. Until now you have asked for nothing in My name; ask and you will receive, so that your joy may be made full.   John 16:23b-24

The Shulamite in the Song of Solomon began her journey with a definite destination in mind. She wanted an encounter with the king. She wanted to take their relationship to the next level. She wanted to reach the place of intimacy.

Desire was the fuel that propelled her along that narrow pathway, but what happened next? The answer is simple: She opened her mouth and voiced her heart's desires. She let him know she wanted his kisses, and instead of keeping her thoughts bottled up in the recesses of her mind, she took action. She asked him to draw her to himself.

At first glance you might think she was an exceptionally forward woman. You might think she was too aggressive, too presumptuous. After all, she lived in a culture where a nice girl would never ask for a kiss. Socially, she was out of order, but spiritually she was a biblically-correct trailblazer who left us with a perfect picture of what to do if we want an intimate spiritual relationship with our King. She stepped up to the plate and asked him for it.

The Lord has made Himself very clear on this subject. He has told us over and over what to do if we want something from Him.

> *Whatever you ask in My name, that will I do, so that the Father may be glorified in the Son. If you ask Me anything in my name, I will do it.*   John 14: 13-14

> *Ask, and it shall be given to you; seek, and you will find; knock, and it will be opened to you. For everyone who asks receives, and he who seeks finds, and to him who knocks it will be opened.*   Matthew 7:7-8

> *This is the confidence which we have before Him, that if we ask anything according to His will, He hears us. And if we know that He hears us in whatever we ask, we know that we have the requests which we have asked from Him.*
> 1 John 5: 14-15

The Tweezers

God has made no secret of the fact that asking is the pathway to receiving our heart's desires. If we want Him to help us during our difficult times, protect us when we are in danger, or heal our sick bodies, we need to do what He has told us to do—just ask Him.

Several years ago I found myself in a place where I needed the healing power of God. Sitting in front of the magnifying mirror in my bathroom putting on my makeup, I noticed several unwanted hairs sitting above, below, and between my eyebrows that needed to be removed. Somehow in the middle of tweezing my eyebrows, my elbow slipped off the counter, and with great force I stuck the tweezers into my right eyeball.

I could feel the flesh as I pulled the tweezers out of my eye and fell to the floor in excruciating pain. I screamed over and over as loud as I could, but there was no one in the house to hear me. I thought about trying to crawl to the phone to call 911, but I couldn't see.

Lying on the floor, I knew the Lord was the only One who could help me, so I began to scream, calling out His name, begging Him to heal my eye. I can still remember the warmth that moved over me. It started on one side and moved across me to the other side of my body, and immediately the pain left. I was amazed, not only that the Lord heard my cry, but also that He had touched me.

When Mark got home from work, I told him what had happened, and he insisted I go to my eye doctor and have her take a look. The next day I made an appointment, and after examining my eye the optometrist said, "I can see the deep incision in your eye, and there is no way this could have happened yesterday. It would have taken days for a wound like this to heal. The Lord had to be the One who healed your eye because there is no other explanation for this."

In the next few days I noticed I couldn't see with my glasses, so I made another eye appointment thinking I needed a new prescription. After the examination, the doctor said, "Mrs. Elder, the Lord not only healed the incision in your eye, but He also healed your vision. You no longer have to wear glasses. You now have 20/20 vision."

Show Me Your Glory

In my early Christian life, I was quick to ask the Lord to meet my physical needs, but when it came to asking the Lord to enhance my spiritual life, I didn't do it. I never took the time to ask Him to give me eyes to see in the realm of the Spirit, or to speak to me through a dream or a vision. I never thought about asking Him to give me spiritual ears to hear His voice with greater clarity, or to give me a fresh revelation of Himself. I limited myself to asking Him only to meet the needs of my flesh, but when I started asking Him to meet my spiritual needs, my spiritual life took a sharp turn toward a deeper, more intimate relationship with the Lord Jesus Christ.

I love the encounter that Moses had with God in the cleft of the rock. The reason Moses was allowed to see His glory is found in Exodus 33:18. Moses said to God, *"I beseech thee, show me your glory."* Moses was at a place in his life where he longed to experience the manifest presence of God. Out of a heart filled with desire, he asked God for what he wanted. He not only asked for it, but he got it. God put him in the cleft of the rock, and as His glory passed by He allowed Moses to see His backside.

Oh, my heart be still. Can you even imagine how fast his heart must have been racing to be so close to his Lord, and his God that he saw His backside? Asking is the key to experiencing the manifest presence of God. I think the Lord is just sitting on the edge of His chair waiting for us to ASK Him for all the things He wants to give us.

You Never Asked

> *Ye have not, because ye ask not.*   James 4:2b

I once heard the story about a man who had a dream. In the dream he died and was caught up into heaven. When he got there Jesus was waiting to greet him and took him on a tour of heaven. As they walked along, he saw rows and rows of storehouses with the names of different saints on each storehouse. He asked the Lord to tell him what was inside the storehouses. The Lord replied, "You don't want to know."

They finally came to a storehouse that had his name on it. He then asked the Lord, to tell him what was in his storehouse. The Lord replied, "You don't want to know." He pressed the Lord for an answer. Finally, the Lord said, "In this storehouse are all the things I longed to give you, but they remained here because you never asked Me for them." We should never underestimate the power of asking.

Why Must We Ask?

Some of us in the body of Christ wonder why we have to ask the Lord for anything since He knows our every thought. We are like little children who have been told to do something by our fathers and are always asking, "Why?" The typical answer many dads give their children to the "why" question is, "Because I said so."

Why do we have to ask the Lord for the desires of our hearts? We have to ask because He said so. I didn't move past an outer court experience with the Lord until I started doing what He told me to do, until I started asking. Asking is one of the keys that He has given us to experience all that He has for us in His kingdom.

Distractions

One of the major problems I faced in my early spiritual life was getting so wrapped up in my own little world that I was missing the wonder of the One who created the world. Over the years I have discovered it is the goal of the enemy to distract us. He wants to lead us away from a relationship with the Lord, and in my life he certainly did a good job of it. Paul wrote to the Corinthians:

> *I am jealous for you with a godly jealousy. I promised*
> *you to one husband, to Christ, so that I might present you*
> *as a pure virgin to him. But I am afraid that just as Eve*
> *was deceived by the serpent's cunning, your minds may*
> *somehow be led astray from your sincere and pure devo-*
> *tion to Christ.*   2 Cor. 11:2-3

We have an enemy who wants the Lord to take a backseat in our lives. He wants to flood our minds with distractions. He wants our days to be so full that we have no time for the Lord Jesus Christ. God used

Jeremiah to describe the people of Israel, which is a great description of many of us today.

> *They went far from Me. They walked after emptiness and*
> *they became empty.* Jeremiah 2:5b

There was a time in my life when those words certainly described me. The problem we face today is the same problem the Israelites faced. We walk after emptiness, and we become empty. We are so busy running after all the things we think will satisfy our soul, only to discover that in the long run, they don't satisfy.

We often get to the place in our lives where the world and the things of the world are constantly pulling on us, competing for our attention, luring us with the promise of being that one thing that will bring us happiness. We all know that material things in life bring pleasure for a season, but after a while, when the newness wears off, we find ourselves running after the next new thing we think will bring lasting happiness.

Yes, we do find temporary joy in the things of the world, but they ultimately leave us empty and unfulfilled. I have heard it said that the Lord created us with an empty place on the inside that only He can fill. He is waiting for all of us to discover the truth in Psalm 16:11b: *"In His presence is fullness of joy."* Nothing can satisfy the deepest longings of our souls but an intimate relationship with Jesus.

We need to follow the example of the Shulamite. We need to ask the Lord to draw us. Sometimes I find myself saying those same words over and over and over to the Lord. "Draw me after You! Draw me after You! Draw me after You!" It doesn't matter how many years He has been drawing us, or how many encounters we have had with Him, He is always ready to reveal Himself on a deeper level, but He is waiting for us to ASK him.

The King's Chambers

> *Draw me; we will run after thee; the king brought me into*
> *his chambers.*　　　　　　　　　　Song of Solomon 1:4

In this verse the Shulamite said, *"Draw me and we will run after thee,"* and in the next breath she said, *"the king brought me into his chambers."* It is important to understand that he didn't force her into his chambers. He didn't take her by the hair of her head and drag her into His chambers. He didn't do anything against her will. He waited until she wanted to be close to Him. He waited until she asked Him, and as a result of asking she got to enter in.

The Hebrew word for chamber is *cheder* which means, "innermost place." He didn't bring her into the family room to meet the family. The focus wasn't on the family. He didn't bring her into the kitchen where he opened the cabinet doors for her to get a good look at all the food he had for her to eat. The focus wasn't on the food. He didn't take her on a tour of the castle and show her the magnitude of his riches. The focus wasn't on the finery. He brought her into his innermost chamber where her focus would be totally on him—just him.

That is the place the Lord brings every one of us when we have our first encounter. He wants us to focus on His body. He wants the image of the scars on His hands, His feet, His head, His back and His side to be etched in our minds forever. He wants us to be thrilled with the knowledge that it was His great love for us that caused Him to step out of heaven and go all the way to Calvary to die in our place for our sins.

The Shulamite asked him to draw her to himself, and the first place he brought her was into his chamber. He did exactly what she wanted him to do. She must have known that she couldn't get to the place of intimacy with him by herself. She must have known that no one could come close to the king unless he drew them, so she did the one thing she needed to do. She let him know she wanted him to draw her.

The same is true with our King. We can't come unless He draws us, but the exciting truth is that He wants to draw us even more than we want to be drawn. How does the Lord draw us? He draws us with His, all-powerful, all-consuming, invisible cords of love.

> *I have loved you with an everlasting love, therefore with*
> *loving kindness have I drawn you.*   Jeremiah 31:3

Because she voiced her heart's desires, the king brought the Shulamite to the place of a one-on-one encounter with himself. This is a great spiritual picture of what the Lord wants to do for every one of us in the realm of the Spirit. He wants to bring us to His chambers.

When we understand that He sacrificed His sinless body for each one of us and ask Him to forgive us for our sins and come into our lives to be our Lord and Savior, two things immediately happen. We are sealed with the Holy Spirit of promise as He places His Spirit inside of us, and we are baptized by the Holy Spirit into the body of Christ as He places us into His body.

> *In Him, you also, after listening to the message of truth,*
> *the gospel of your salvation – having also believed, were*
> *sealed in Him with the Holy Spirit of promise.*
> 　　　　　　　　　　　　　　　　　　Ephesians 1:13

> *For by one Spirit, we were all baptized into one body."*
> 1 Corinthians 12:13a

> *In that day you shall know that I am in My Father, and you*
> *in Me, and I in you.*   John 14:20

Before we can ever go to all the places the King has planned for us, we have to be born again. We have to be willing for His Spirit to be placed in us, and we have to be willing to be brought by our King into

His chambers, His innermost place, His body. Just as the Shulamite got into her king's chambers by asking, we need to remember that asking is the key that opens the door to our King's chambers.

There are no shortcuts. There is no getting around it. We have to be willing to ask, but keep in mind, there is nothing to be afraid of in His chambers. It is a place of safety designed by our King to secure our place in His kingdom. It is wonderful to know that when we get there we all find the same thing—a place of great comfort. It is so comforting to finally know that we are in Him, and His Spirit is alive, living inside of each one of us.

The Revelation of the Power of Asking

When the revelation of the power of asking exploded in my spirit, my spiritual life was changed forever. One day as I was reading the Word, the Lord spoke to me through a verse:

> *Call to Me, and I will answer you, and I will tell you great and mighty things, which you do not know.* Jeremiah 33:3

As I read those words, it was as if the Lord was using His Word and His Spirit to speak directly to me. I knew that He wanted me to ask Him to reveal something that I didn't know. As I began to consider what I wanted to ask, I was aware that there were thousands of things I didn't know. I wanted to be very careful, because somehow, I knew in my spirit that whatever I asked, He was going to show me.

While I was trying to decide what to ask the Lord, I picked up a book that talked about discovering our destinies. As I read the book, I knew that was exactly what I wanted. I wanted to know my destiny. I wanted to know what the Lord had put me on this earth to do. Mark Twain once said, "Other than the day we are born, the next most important day in our life is the day we find out why we were born." I don't totally agree with that statement. I think the next most important day is the day when we are born again, but I do think the third most important thing is to find out why we were born.

I knew from scripture that God had told many of the saints who had gone before me their destinies. He told Abraham, Isaac, Jacob, Joseph, Moses, Joshua, John, Peter, and Paul their destinies long before they ever fulfilled them. When David was just a boy God sent the prophet Samuel to tell him that one day he would be king over Israel.

When Samuel came to anoint him with oil I am sure David wasn't ready to be a king. I am sure he didn't look like a king. I am also sure he didn't act like a king, but God knew he would one day be a king because He knows the end from the beginning.

> *For I am God, and there is no other; I am God and there*
> *is no one like Me, declaring the end from the beginning.*
> Isaiah 46:9-10

We find a great summary of David's life wrapped up in just eight words by the Apostle Paul:

> *David carried out God's purpose while he lived; then he*
> *died*   Acts 13:36a

Wouldn't it be a wonderful privilege to have those words written on our tombstones? "He carried out God's purpose for his life," or simply put, "He fulfilled his destiny." God has a plan, a purpose, and a destiny for all of our lives, and He knows the plan. We just need to find out what it is.

> *For I know the plans that I have for you, declares the Lord,*
> *plans for welfare and not for calamity to give you a future*
> *and a hope.*   Jeremiah 29:11

After having settled in my heart what I wanted and deciding, along with my destiny, I wanted a fresh passion for the Lord, I finally began to pray, "Lord, would You inflame my spirit with a fresh passion for You, and would You give me a vision of my destiny?" As I prayed this prayer the strangest thing happened. It was as if I was on a bucking horse, and I couldn't get off. I repeated that same prayer over and over. "Lord, would You inflame my spirit with passion for You, and would You give me a vision of my destiny?"

I would wake up in the morning praying those same twenty words, and go to bed in the evening reciting that same prayer. It was as if the Holy Spirit had a hold on me, and I didn't even have to consciously think about praying. Those words were continually rolling out of my mouth. I don't know how long I prayed, but I do know after fervently praying, the day finally came when it was finished. I knew in my spirit that I had prayed through, and the time for praying was over.

I didn't know when He would do it, or how He would do it, but I did know that He was going to show me my destiny and inflame my spirit with a passion for Himself. I was so excited, but at the same time I knew I would have to wait for the appointed time. I have often thought how wonderful it would be if the Lord were like those clap-on lamps that turn on when you clap your hands, and He would immediately perform like we want Him to, but we all know that is not the way He operates.

We have to wait on His timing and believe while we are waiting that His timing is perfect. On January 16, 1998, the answer came in a most unexpected way. I had gone to bed that night just like I had every other night. As I drifted off to sleep, I had no idea this was the night that He would answer my prayer through a dream.

When we look through scripture we see that dreams are one of the ways the Lord has chosen to speak to His people. I had always loved to read how He spoke to Joseph and many others in the Word through dreams, but I was surprised that was the way He chose to answer my prayer.

And it shall come to pass in the last days, saith God, I will pour out my Spirit upon all flesh: and your sons and your daughters shall prophesy, and your young men shall see

*visions, and your old men shall dream dreams; And on my
servants and on my handmaidens I will pour out in those
days of my Spirit; and they shall prophecy*   Acts 2:17-18

The Rhino Dream

*Indeed, God speaks once, or twice, yet no one notices it. In
a dream, a vision of the night, when sound sleep falls on
men, while they slumber in their beds, then He opens the
ears of men, and seals their instruction.*   Job 33:14-17

As the dream began, I was standing in my breakfast room which
is part of my family room and kitchen. Suddenly, I heard the sound of a
mighty rushing wind. It was almost like the sound of a tornado. It was
deafening as it blew my front door open, rushing through my house. I
have often wondered if it was similar to the sound the followers of Jesus
heard in the upper room on the day of Pentecost.

The next thing I knew, a gigantic rhinoceros was running through
my family room. It was so large it almost filled the entire room. It had a
massive horn that rose up almost touching my twelve-foot ceiling. As I
looked at the rhino I could see the wind swirling around it at a great speed.
I was also aware of the thick skin surrounding the vital organs of the rhino
like a protective armor. The sight was overwhelming.

It ran through my house and out my back door. In my dream I was
concerned, thinking its massive body might have done some damage to
the inside of my house, but to my surprise, there was no damage. I then
decided to go outside to see if there had been any damage to my yard.
The only thing that had been disturbed was the grass on my front lawn.

In the next part of my dream, my mother, sister and brother came
into my house. My mother said, "Jenny, your father has something he
wants to tell you." Because my family was there, I knew I needed to prepare some food, so I went to the refrigerator and found a whole chicken
that had already been cooked. Since the meat had already been prepared,

I decided to make a King Ranch Casserole. In the dream Tim, my brother, came into the kitchen and was right beside me helping me prepare the food for the family.

As I put the casserole together I realized that I had everything I needed except the chili powder which would add the spice that the casserole needed. I woke up with the knowledge that I had the meat, but in order to make this casserole tasty for my family, I had to have the spice to give it flavor; I needed chili powder, but where was it?

Waking up, I was aware that my heart was racing. I knew without a shadow of a doubt that the dream was from the Lord, but I had no idea what it meant. I wrote down every detail.

A man named James Ryle had come to our church a few years earlier and had taught about interpreting dreams from the Lord. I knew from his teachings that God used symbolism to speak through dreams. He had taught us to look into the symbols in our dreams to discover what the Lord was saying.

He told us of dreams that he had when God used many things including animals to symbolize truths. He told us how he looked into things that were significant about those animals to help him interpret his dreams. I also thought about how God spoke to Peter in the tenth chapter of Acts while he was in a trance through clean and unclean animals to help him understand He was opening the door for the Gentiles to come into His kingdom.

I knew nothing about rhinoceroses, other than the fact that they were huge, ugly, animals. I had seen them at the zoo, and as far as I was concerned, there was certainly nothing appealing about them. What could the Lord possibly be trying to tell me through the picture of a rhinoceros?

A few days later I got a call from my Mother. She had been watching a program about animals in the wild, and she called to tell me what she had learned about rhinoceroses. I was surprised because I had not told her about my dream. She said that rhinos were very valuable because of their horns. The natives would kill them, cut off their horns, and sell them to people, who would grind them into a powder, and sell the powder in the form of a pill. People believed there was an ingredient in their horns that acted as an aphrodisiac to stimulate passion in men. That was news to me.

A few days later I received my National Geographic magazine, and inside was an article about rhinoceroses. The article focused on the fact that rhinoceroses were very valuable now because of their horns. The article discussed the fact that their horns were ground into a powder and sold as an aphrodisiac to stimulate passion in men. It was interesting to me, after all these years of never hearing anything significant about rhinoceroses that suddenly two sources had brought this information to me.

Interpretation of the Dream

I still had no idea the meaning of this dream, so I asked the Lord to tell me. When He gave me the interpretation I was shocked. He said, "I am about to do a new thing in your life. The Wind of My Spirit will usher it in. Just as the rhino had a thick, protective armor around its vital organs, and a powerful wind swirling around it, the life of what I am sending through you will be protected by the Wind of My Spirit, by Me."

"The only thing that was disturbed by the rhino was the grass. In I Peter 1:24, I told you, *"all flesh is as grass."* The only ones who will be disturbed by what I am sending through you are those who walk in the flesh. Even as some people believe that the value of the rhino is in their horns that act like an aphrodisiac to stimulate passion, your destiny is found in what they believe about the horn. Your destiny is to stimulate a spiritual passion in My Bride for Me."

"Just as the meat for your family was ready, the meat that I want you to serve My family is ready. It has been marinating in you for years. In the dream you had the meat, but you didn't have the spice. The only thing that has been missing from the food that you have been serving My family is the spice of spiritual passion for Me. However, because you asked, I am now adding the spice of a greater degree of passion for Me to your life."

"When you serve the meat of My Word, those who partake of this meat will taste the passion, and My Spirit will use you to stimulate passion in their lives for Me. Even as your brother was in the kitchen to help you, your brother will be by your side helping you prepare some of the food you will serve My family."

As I heard the sound of His voice interpreting the dream, it was as if He was infusing a fresh passion for Himself into my soul. I immediately wrote down the interpretation of the dream and told several of my friends.

Tim

After the Lord spoke, I have to confess I was shocked. He had answered my prayer in such a surprising way. I now knew my destiny. I now knew my purpose. When I taught the word, serving spiritual food to His family, He was going to use me to stimulate passion in His Bride for Himself. Wow! What a surprise! I had asked Him to give me a vision of my destiny, and He did it through a dream. I had asked Him to inflame my spirit with a fresh passion for Himself, and amazingly, my destiny was wrapped up in the very thing that I asked Him for, passion.

I had studied and taught His Word for years so I understood that the meat of His Word was in me, but the only thing that I couldn't possibly imagine was the part about my brother, Tim. He was living in Arizona at the time and was as far away from the Lord as he could possibly be. He wasn't interested in anything to do with spiritual things. Anytime I mentioned the Lord, he let me know that he didn't want to hear it. I understood how he felt because there was a time in my own life when I felt the same way. Because I loved Tim, I couldn't bear the thought of him not going to heaven.

One day the Lord gave me 2 Timothy 2:25-26 to pray over Tim. I prayed that portion of scripture, inserting Tim's name. I always said, "God, would You grant Tim repentance, lead him to a knowledge of the truth, and bring him to the place that he would come to his senses and escape from the snare of the devil who has taken him captive to do his will." I knew every time I asked the Lord to save Tim that it was going to take a miracle for that part of the dream to come to pass, but little did I know as I prayed that a miracle was just around the corner.

In June of 2001, as I was about to start teaching a series on the Tabernacle of Moses at my church, Tim moved back to Texas from Arizona. One of the things he always loved to do was help anyone who had a need. He was a skilled carpenter, and I decided to ask him to build each piece of furniture in the Tabernacle of Moses to help us get a better visual of what actually happened there. Tim built everything with perfect accuracy and precision, according to the dimensions and descriptions in the Bible. His willingness to build the furniture gave all of us the privilege of walking through tabernacle as if we were actually there.

The best part about the whole experience is that during that time Tim had a supernatural encounter with the Lord and was changed into a new man. God used many people to draw Tim to Himself, but one of the things He used was what happened at the Brazen Altar in the Tabernacle of Moses. When he was ready to start building that altar, we went together to Home Depot to buy the supplies.

While we were walking down the aisle, surrounded by rows of raw lumber, I casually asked him if he wanted me to tell him why this altar was so important. He stopped right in the middle of the aisle. I was shocked. I couldn't believe it—he wanted to hear what I had to say. For years I had tried to tell him about Jesus, and now there we stood, face to face, and he was finally ready to listen.

Because Tim loved stories, I started by saying, "To help you fully understand what happened at that altar, imagine that you are one of the children of Israel, living in the wilderness with Moses, hundreds of years ago. Because the law mandates that all who sin have to bring an animal to the Brazen Altar to be sacrificed in their place, for their sins, go to your flock and select your best lamb. It has to be a male without spot or defect. Tie a rope around his neck, and lead him to the door of the tabernacle, which is in front of the Brazen Altar.

"Now, in your mind, just imagine yourself getting in line behind all the other sinners and their sacrificial lambs. When you finally reach the front of the line, as you stand in front of the priest, take both hands and lay them on the head of the animal. Symbolically your sins are transferred over to the lamb. Now take the knife provided by the priest and kill the lamb. As you watch the blood flowing from the lamb's body, you are very aware that he did nothing to deserve what was happening. But you also know that without the shedding of that sinless blood there will be no forgiveness for your sins."

"Tim, what happened at the Brazen Altar was a picture that the Lord gave to us through the Israelites of what would happen hundreds of years later at the cross where Jesus, the Lamb of God, died in our place for all of our sins. To receive the free gift of eternal life, all we have to do is ask Him to forgive us of our sins and put our faith and trust in Him as our Lord and Savior."

As we stood in the middle of Home Depot with people passing by all around us, it was as if we were the only two people in the store. I can still remember the look in Tim's eyes as the truth of what Jesus had done for him saturated his soul. He heard it. He really heard it. The Holy Spirit had given him ears to hear. No wonder I had always loved the Brazen Altar so much!

It wasn't what some call the Roman road that the Lord used to draw Tim into the place of receiving eternal life. It wasn't anything conventional that I thought He might have used. In His mercy, one of the things He decided to use was what happened at the Brazen Altar. Tim asked the Lord to forgive him of all his sins and invited Him to come into his heart to be his Lord and Savior, and the transformation that took place in his life after he met Jesus was amazing.

I can still remember the day I stood on the stage to begin teaching Tabernacle of Moses. As I looked at Tim standing in the back of the room and at the furniture he had built, suddenly I realized the dream God had given me had come true. My brother had helped me prepare the spiritual food that I was about to serve the family of God.

The Lord is in the business of performing miracles, and to watch Him with my brother was one of the most beautiful miracles I have ever been privileged to witness. Tim died on October 16, 2010, of pancreatic cancer. It gives me great peace to know that God knows the "end from the beginning." He knew before Tim came to Texas he was coming, and He also knew that here in Texas, the place of his birth, he would be born again.

I am so grateful I asked the Lord for a vision of my destiny. Today, comfort floods my soul because I know where Tim is, and when the Lord speaks to us through His Word or a dream or a vision, He watches over His Word to perform it.

Elisha

T. D. Jakes spoke a wonderful message about the prophet Elisha, and I want to share some of his thoughts as well as some of mine concerning things that took place in Elisha's life that illustrate how to make sure we fulfill our destinies and the power of asking.

> *So he (Elijah) departed from there (Mount Horeb) and found Elisha, the son of Shaphat while he was plowing with twelve pairs of oxen before him, and he with the twelfth, and Elijah passed over to him and threw his mantle.*
> 1 Kings 19: 19

Unlike the farmers of today who plow the ground sitting in the lap of luxury in their air conditioned tractors, the first glimpse we get of Elisha in 1 Kings is of him plowing a field, walking behind twelve pair of oxen. Even though his circumstances were much different from farmers of today, some of the things he went through were a perfect reflection of the things we often experience. Elisha spent his days going down one row, only to turn around and go down another row, and then another and another and another. Essentially Elisha spent his days going around, and around, and around.

Like Elisha, there have also been days where many of us have felt the same way. We have sometimes felt like we are spinning our wheels, going around and around, and around, doing the same exact things over and over. Unlike Elisha, most of us don't deal with hard, nasty things like clumps of dirt every day, but we can all relate to having to deal with one hard thing only to turn around and deal with another hard thing, and then another, and another.

While Elisha was plowing, preparing the ground for planting, there is a possibility that he could have escaped from the path he was traveling down by allowing his mind to wander off in a different direction. The same things could have crossed his mind that cross all of our minds at different times in our lives: "Is this all there is? What on earth am I here for? What is the purpose for my life?"

We all know there is nothing wrong with plowing. In fact, I am sure it was a good way to earn a living. Elisha might have been very satisfied with his life. However, on the other hand, if he had this thing deep down on the inside called potential, knowing in his knower that God had more for him than what he was doing, it might have been difficult to stay in his place day after day until God took him to the place of fulfilling his destiny.

Most of us don't like our places of preparation. We want to move past the day-to-day grind, but we all need our difficult places to prepare us for our destinies. God had plans for Elisha, just like He has plans for every single one of us, but like Elisha, we have to wait on His timing.

Divine Connections

On the day of Elisha's breakthrough, while he was going around and around dealing with hard things, he had no way of knowing his breakthrough was on the way. He had no way of knowing a prophet named Elijah was walking down the mountain with orders from God to anoint him to take his place as a prophet to the nation of Israel. He had no way of knowing God was about to hook him up with a divine connection who would walk through a portion of his life with him, mentoring him, teaching him, training him, helping him to become all he was created to be.

A divine connection isn't something any of us can orchestrate. We can't manipulate others to make it happen. It is something only God can do.

The Sweetness of my Divine Connections

Before I leave the subject of divine connections, I want to stop right here, take a short detour and introduce you to some of the women God has sent into my life — just like He sent Elijah into Elisha's life — whom He has used to mentor me, teach me, mold me, and challenge me to become all He has created me to be. Most of us have three layers of friendships in our lives. There are those who are up close and personal. There are those who are just casual acquaintances, and then there are those who fall right in the middle. We talk to them, and laugh with them, but they never see us cry.

All three layers of these friendships add different degrees of joy to our lives, but divine connections are those friends that have been up close and personal, that God has sent to make a spiritual impact on our lives. As I introduce my divine connections to you, I not only want to share their real names, but I also want to share their nicknames.

Nicknames

There is a tradition in my family, the gift of giving nicknames, that was passed down to me from my mother's father. He gave everyone he loved nicknames according to the things that stood out to him from their lives. He called my mother Chicken, because she loved the story of Chicken Little. He called my sister, Robin, Pencil Butt because she was so tiny. I am sure the gift was passed down to him from his father, who called him Stump because he only grew to be five feet, five inches tall.

With my mother, the gift of giving nicknames skipped a generation, so when it came to me, I am sure both of my sons probably think I got a double or maybe even a triple portion of this gift because I inundated them with nicknames. Some were silly names and others were names that described characteristics I saw in their lives. I called Kevin, my first born son, Nen, Nena, Kevin Wevin, Kek, my Suga Suga, my Tutti Frutti, my Wowzers, and my Swooner, but my favorite name for him has always been my Morning Glory.

The Morning Glory is one of my favorite flowers. Its beauty takes my breath away, as it comes to full bloom early in the morning. As a baby, Kevin, my Morning Glory, always came to full bloom early in the mornings, and the beauty of watching him grow into the fullness of becoming all he was created to be, like that flower, sometimes takes my breath away, even today. From the very first day I held him in my arms, my love for him has always been in full bloom in my heart.

When Chris my youngest son was a teenager, he entertained his cousin and best friend one day, provoking hysterical laughter by going down memory lane, with all the silly names I had given him over the years. Among the more than thirty names he remembered were Mississippi, Popalopagus, which I eventually shortened to Pop, R2D2, C3PO, and Pippy. Most of the names I called him came without rhyme or reason. They were just silly, and I used them to play with him.

We have laughed about all those names many times, but my favorite name for him today is my Heart Whisperer. He knows exactly how to pull on my heartstrings as he caresses my heart with his words, causing a love for him that passes all understanding to flow through every fiber of my being.

Almost everyone in my family knows their nickname, but most of my divine connections have no idea that I have given them another name. Over years of being with each one of them, their nicknames just popped into my mind, and each name is a reflection of the impact and the different layers of sweetness they have added to my life.

My Sweet Strawberry Delight

My first divine connection was my mother, Jacqueline Hope Giles. She was the Sweet Strawberry Delight in my life. She loved eating big, red, fresh, delicious, juicy, sweet strawberries. I still remember the day I told her that studies had shown there were seven hundred and fifty micro nutrients in each average-sized strawberry. The look on her face was price-less. She was thrilled that something so wonderful to eat could also be so good for her body.

She was not only my Sweet Strawberry Delight because she ate strawberries, but also because, like each strawberry that contained hun-dreds of nutrients, she loved to read, spending her free time filling her mind with the nutrients she found in the hundreds of books on her book-shelves. She not only filled her mind with delightful stories, but like most mothers, she deposited many of those wonderful stories into me. From her, I received the joy of telling stories, and the joy of reading, which enhanced my ability to enjoy reading the many stories in the Word of God.

My Sweet Sugar and Spice

My second divine connection was my grandmother, Ruth Frye. She always took me to church when I was a young girl, which allowed me to have a taste of the Word of God. There was a sweetness about her that was greater than the sweetness of all others, but combined with that sweetness was the spice of being feisty. She didn't mince words. She said exactly what she thought. When a friend of hers at the age of 70 "pranced around on the beach in her bathing suit" as my grandmother would say, telling everyone she looked just like she did when she was a teenager, my grand-mother said, "Well, at least MY mirror doesn't lie."

My Sweet Sapphire Rooster

The third divine connection in my life was my sister, Robin O'Connell. I have a new name for her today, but when we were girls I called her Sapphire Rooster. The reason I gave her the name Sapphire is because one of my favorite shows was Amos and Andy. It was my favorite not only because it was one of only a handful of shows on television, but because of the loveliness of the characters, Amos, Andy, Kingfish, his wife Sapphire, Mama, Calhoun, and Lightnin'.

As I watched them on that old black and white, ten by ten-inch television screen, I fell deeply, madly, passionately in love with these amazing, precious characters. What first captivated my attention was the fact that they were funny. I would laugh so hard tears would run down my face. I rolled on the floor with laughter until my sides ached. I not only loved them for their sense of humor, but I thought the color of their skin was so beautiful.

I loved Sapphire with all my heart, so because I loved Robin too, I decided to give her what I thought was that very special name. I added Rooster to the name Sapphire because I thought the combination of those two names were hysterically funny, and being a big sister, it gave me great pleasure to tease my baby sister by calling her a silly name. I called Robin Sapphire Rooster when we were young, but after we grew up and stepped into the Kingdom of God, I gave Robin a new name. I removed the word Rooster, and just thought of her as My Sweet Sapphire.

Let me tell you why. In the Old Testament in Exodus 28:6-21, 29, and 30, I read that the high priest wore a breastplate which was called the breastplate of decision. There were twelve stones on his breastplate set in four rows, and each stone represented one of the twelve tribes of Israel which were made up of Israel's twelve sons and their descendants. The second stone on the second row of stones was a sapphire, representing Israel's son, Simeon. Jacob gave all his sons a name that described their character, and the name Simeon, represented by the sapphire, meant hearer.

In the kingdom of God, Robin is a like a beautiful sapphire. She is a hearer who has been given by God the ability to hear the cries of the needy. When she hears their cries, I have watched her run to them over and over, meeting their needs, standing by them with her time and her money, no matter what the cost. From Robin O'Connell, my Sweet Sapphire, the hearer, I have learned about the beauty of having ears to hear the cries of the needy, and a heart of mercy that responds to those in need.

My Sweet Peppermint Twist

When I was fifteen years old I met my next divine connection, Judy Neely. She has been the Sweet Peppermint Twist in my life for fifty-four years. From her I have learned about the beauty of the gifts of the Spirit operating in our lives and about being a friend that sticks closer than a brother. Like a Peppermint Twist candy cane, she has sweetened my life with her presence all the way back to the time we were just girls learning to do the twist.

My Sweet Home Alabama

Next on my list of divine connections is my Sweet Home Alabama, Betsy Hall, who was born in Alabama. From her I have learned about the beauty of living my life with such integrity that it is possible to look at another person and see Jesus. When I am with Betsy, I always feel like I am at home. I can just relax, let down my hair, and say anything I want to say, any way I want to say it. She has added a sweetness to my life that is beyond measure.

My Sweet Apple Pie

From Jane Jarrett who is a lover of God, I have learned about the beauty of hearing God and doing whatever He tells me to do. She is the Sweet Apple Pie in my life, because she has a gift of making those with whom she walks know that they are the "apple of His eye."

My Sweet Doublemint Gum

The Lord sent my next divine connection, Beverly Sheasby, all the way from South Africa to teach me about life in the Spirit. She is the Sweet Doublemint Gum in my life, which is one of my favorite flavors. The sweetness she poured into me can only be explained by the sweetness

I experience when I put a piece of Doublemint Gum in my mouth. Her presence in my life has allowed me to "double the pleasure and double the fun," not only in my life with her as a person, but also in my life in the Spirit with the One I love.

My Sweet Pop Rock

When I was a girl, I loved Pop Rocks. They were unlike any other candy I had ever experienced. They were not only sweet, but they added another dimension of excitement with their fizziness that felt like explosions as they dissolved in my mouth. That is why I named my next divine connection, Cindy Langley, my Sweet Pop Rock. From this mighty woman of God, I have learned about the beauty of enjoying the life God has given me to the fullest. Watching His life flow through her has been like experiencing an explosion of Pop Rocks in my mouth. She is a blast to be with in the kingdom of God.

My Sweet Honey Delight

From my divine connection Nancy Frank who is a deep well, I have learned about the beauty of giving a word of wisdom in due season. She has graced my life over and over with wisdom from above. She is my Sweet Honey Delight. Being with Nancy is like experiencing the sweetness of delicious honey dipping into my life. Her words are always sweet to my taste.

My Sweet Ding Dong

Another awesome gift God sent into my life is Larie White. From her I have learned about the beauty of unconditional love. When she walks into a room, everyone knows love has walked in. She is the Sweet Ding Dong, in my life who knows exactly how to ring my chimes.

My Sweet Pumpkin Pie

From Helen Bavousett, I have learned about the beauty of being steadfast, surrounding those we love with unwavering support, not just in the bad times but also in the good times. Being with her is like eating a delicious slice of Sweet Pumpkin Pie. She always brings me to the place of thanksgiving.

My Sweet Lollipop Swirl

From Kaye Moreno I have learned about the beauty of standing in the world, standing for the things for which our Lord Jesus Christ stands. She is the Lollypop Swirl of sweetness to whom has the God given ability to turn others around to Christ's way of thinking.

My Sweet Sugar Queen

From Nancy Briggs, who has gone home to be with the Lord, I have learned the beauty of not spending my life looking only after my own interests but also looking after the interests of others. She is the Sweet Sugar Queen in the kingdom of God that spread sweetness across our lives with every step she took.

My Sweet Iced Tea

From Leslie Detamore, I have learned about the beauty of being a refreshment to the weary, of refreshing them with the sweetness of a word. Being with her is always like drinking a large delicious glass of Sweet Iced Tea that refreshes my soul.

My Sweet Rock Candy

From Betty Godwin, who has also gone home to be with the Lord, I learned about the beauty of embracing intimacy with Jesus in such a way that He has become my favorite dwelling place. She is my Sweet Rock Candy who taught me how to build my life on the Rock.

My Sweet Starburst

From Carolyn Weisinger, I have experienced the delight of watching someone allow the love of God to flow through them in such a beautiful way that the one being ministered to knows it was God, not man, who touched them. She is like a Sweet Starburst—she has blessed my life with a burst of sweetness at the times when I have needed it the most.

My Sweet Honeysuckle Vine

From Theresa Phillips, I have learned about the beauty of humility and transparency. Just like the fragrance of a soft breeze that flows through a honeysuckle vine and floods our lives with sweetness, the sweet breeze of the Lord's presence flows so sweetly through Theresa that there are times when she takes my breath away.

My Sweet Bit-O-Honey

From my divine connection Shelly Burkett, I have learned about the beauty of lifting others up into heavenly realms with our words. She is the chewy Sweet Bit-O-Honey in my life who always leaves me with heavenly words to chew on.

My Sweet Hubba Bubba

From Nancy Norris who is a woman of the Word, I have learned the beauty of laughter that is medicine for my soul. Nancy is my Sweet Hubba Bubba. Being with her is like chewing a delicious piece of Hubba Bubba Bubble Gum. Her presence is full of juicy, sweet flavor that is addictive, always tempting me to come back for more.

My Sweet Firecracker Bar

From Sherrice Copeland, I have experienced the beauty of hearing God through the mouth of another person and the impact being a mouthpiece for God has on those who walk in His kingdom. She is a mouthwatering Firecracker Bar to the body of Christ. When she gives words they are so hot off of God's heavenly grill they are still sizzling.

My Sweet Potato Pie

From Janie Harp, I have experienced the beauty of being a servant, of ministering and supporting others in their time of need. She is my Sweet Potato Pie that is sweet and nourishing all at the same time.

My Sweet-Smelling Rose

From Mary Shelton, I have learned about the beauty of being a witness in such a winsome, loving way that others are born into the kingdom of God. She is like a beautiful Sweet-Smelling Rose because she carries the sweet aroma of Christ wherever she goes.

My Sweet Almond Joy

From Wendy Elder, Chris's wife, I have learned about the mind blowing beauty of allowing the fruit of the Spirit to flow through our lives, lifting others up in such a way that it encourages them to be all they were created to be. She is my Sweet Almond Joy who has filled my life with unspeakable, indescribable joy.

My Sweet Hershey's Kiss

From Brandi Elder, Kevin's wife, I have learned about the overwhelming beauty of not just being a hearer of the Word, but also being a doer of the Word. She doesn't just talk the talk—she walks the walk. The thrill of watching her live her life is like eating my favorite candy, a delicious Sweet Hershey's Kiss. The Lord definitely gave me a special kiss when He sent her into my life. She brings great delight to my soul.

My Sweet Cup of Hot Chocolate

From Pat Fry, a precious gift the Lord brought into my life, I have learned about the beauty of kindness and the impact that being kind has on the lives of others. Being with her is like drinking a Sweet Cup of Delicious Hot Chocolate. Her presence warms my soul.

My Sweet Popsicle Delight

From Janey Braudrick, one of my newest friends, I have learned about the beauty of being a runner in the kingdom of God, of not being satisfied with business as usual but running in the Spirit after all the Lord has for us. She is like a delicious, beautiful, colorful, runny popsicle that gets all over you with its sweetness. She is my Sweet Popsicle Delight.

My Sweet Blueberry Surprise

I eat blueberries almost every day. Studies have shown they not only protect the brain but also add much needed nutrients the brain needs to help our thought processes. From my new friend, Elena Cook, my Sweet Blueberry Delight, I have learned about the beauty of thought-fulness. She always remembers me with a card, or a call, or a gift. I am blessed to have her as a one of the divine connections in my life.

How to Make Sure We Fulfill our Destinies

Now, back to the subjects of asking and fulfilling our destinies. When Elijah, Elisha's divine connection, reached him, the Word of God tells us he threw his mantle on him, and the anointing of God fell on Elisha giving him the ability to step into his destiny. All of us long for the time in our lives when just like Elisha, destiny kicks in and we have a life-changing encounter. But before Elisha embraced his destiny, he did the one thing all of us need to do in order to insure that we fulfill our destinies.

> *So Elisha returned from following him, and took the pair*
> *of oxen and sacrificed them and boiled their flesh with the*
> *implements of the oxen, and gave it to the people and they*
> *ate. Then he arose and followed Elijah and ministered to*
> *him.*   1 Kings 19:21

We know oxen are very strong animals, but the dictionary tells us they are also known for being stupid animals. Basically, that means Elisha spent his days following after dumb things. However, after tasting the supernatural, anointing power of God and discovering his God-given purpose, he had no intention of ever going back and following after those dumb things ever again. He had no intention of allowing those dumb things to stand in the way of fulfilling his destiny.

What Elisha did before he fulfilled his destiny is a picture of what all of us need to do in order to make sure we fulfill our own destinies. We need to get rid of the dumb things in our lives. Dumb things are the things in our lives that are of no eternal value that distract us. They are stumbling blocks that lead us in the wrong direction, keeping us from doing what God has created us to do.

Are there any dumb things in your life? There have been many dumb things in mine, and the spiritual picture of what Elisha did by getting rid of the dumb things in his life challenges me to the core of my being.

Asking: A Double Portion

> *When they had crossed over, Elijah said to Elisha, "Ask*
> *what I shall do for you before I am taken from you." And*

> *Elisha said, "Please, let a double portion of your spirit*
> *be upon me." He said, "You have asked a hard thing,*
> *Nevertheless, if you see me when I am taken from you, it*
> *shall be so for you; but if not, it shall not be so."*
>
> 2 Kings 2:9

Elisha did something else that challenges me. He asked Elijah for a double portion, and under the inspiration of God, Elijah said he would grant the request if Elisha saw him when he was taken away, which Elisha did. Amazingly, in Elijah's lifetime the Bible records in I and 2 Kings exactly fourteen miracles that God performed through him, and before Elisha died the Bible records exactly twenty-seven miracles that God performed through his life. He died having missed the double portion by one miracle, but after he died something happened.

> *Elisha died, and they buried him. Now the bands of the*
> *Moabites would invade the land in the spring of the year.*
> *As they were burying a man behold, they saw a marauding*
> *band, and they cast the man into the grave of Elisha. And*
> *when the man touched the bones of Elisha he revived and*
> *stood up on his feet.*
>
> 2 Kings 13:20-21

Holy moly! There was still so much anointing in Elisha's dead bones that a dead man was revived and stood up on his feet, miracle number twenty-eight, a double portion. He asked for it and he got it. Elisha is just another example to all of us of the power of ASKING.

Far from The Maddening Crowd

The movie, "Far from the Madding Crowd," released in 2015, portrayed a scene of exactly what the Lord has done when it comes to the subject of asking. At the end of the movie, the leading man and woman stood face-to-face. She knew he was in love with her and wanted her to marry him, but he wouldn't ask her for what he wanted. In the movie she stood before him and said, "We will never marry because you will never ask." She then looked into his eyes and without blinking said, "Ask me." Then saying the same words with an even stronger and sweeter tone, she said, "Ask me." Then finally, once again, with an even more desperate tone in her voice she said, "Ask me."

The Lord hasn't just said those two words three times like the woman in the movie. He has said them over and over and over in His Word, hoping we would get the message. He knows what we want. He is just waiting on us to ask Him. I wonder if He added the phrase, "I double-dog dare you to ask Me," if that would encourage us to do what He wants us to do?

Asking! Asking! Asking!

Asking! Asking! Asking! Thank You for giving us the example from the Schulamite and Elisha of what can happen if we will just do what You told us to do. Keep on reminding us to ask, Lord, because it is so easy for us to forget!

3

The Secret of the Banqueting House

He brought me to the Banqueting House and his banner over me was love. Sustain me with raisins, refresh me with apples; for I am lovesick. His left hand is under my head. His right hand embraces me. Song of Solomon 2:4

One of the greatest secrets revealed in Song of Solomon—how we can begin to love the Lord with all of our heart, all of our soul, all of our mind, and all our strength—is tucked away in this seemingly unimportant verse. The first few times I read it, I skimmed over the words, giving no thought to the fact that they contained a life-changing secret. Because of the Shulamite's strong desire for a closer relationship with her king and voicing her heart's desire by asking for what she wanted, the king brought her into his chambers but he didn't stop there. She was so fervent in her quest for him, so diligently spending her time running after him, he brought her into his Banqueting House.

It is important to notice that she didn't just wonder in all by herself. He was her escort. He took her there. Even though she had already been to the king's chambers, we know that it wasn't until she got to the Banqueting House that she became lovesick. Thus, the question we have to ask is, what happened in the Banqueting House that changed the way she loved him? From this verse, we quickly see four things that took place in the Banqueting House that didn't happen in the king's chambers.

In the Banqueting House we know she saw a banner. It wasn't just an ordinary banner. It was a banner of love. She was also sustained and refreshed in the Banqueting House—and finally we know she was embraced by the King. I am sure all these experiences added to the thrill of the Banqueting House, but to say that any one of them or the combination of all four had the power to make her or anyone else lovesick doesn't make sense.

To find the answer put on your spiritual ears and listen very carefully. It is not only the secret of her journey to the Banqueting House, but what actually happened there that unfolds the mystery of how many of us become lovesick today.

I found the key that unlocks the door to what happened in the Banqueting House by looking at the Hebrew word for "banqueting," which is *yayin. Yayin* means "WINE." The Banqueting House was actually the House of Wine. Wine was flowing in that house. In the House of Wine, the Shulamite had the ability to become filled with the abundance of that free-flowing, royal wine. Before we can become truly lovesick, most of us have to be willing to go to the House of Wine in the realm of the Spirit.

What is the spiritual meaning of the word wine in the Bible? We know from Jesus' encounter with the disciples in the upper room that wine is symbolic of the blood of Jesus, but what else does it symbolize? Where else in the word do we find information about wine? Before Jesus ascended into heaven He told the disciples in Acts 1:4, *"John baptized with water, but in a few days you will be baptized with the Holy Spirit."* We read in Acts 2:2-4 that while they were waiting for the promised Baptism of the Holy Spirit:

> *Suddenly there came the sound from heaven as of a rushing mighty wind and it filled the whole house where they were sitting. There appeared to them divided tongues of fire, and one set on each of them. They were all filled with the Holy*

> *Spirit and began to speak with other tongues, as the Spirit*
> *gave them utterance*   Acts 2:2-4

The crowd of people who were watching the disciples responded by saying in Acts 2:13, "they are drunk on NEW WINE". In response to the crowd Peter got up and said:

> *For these are not drunken, as ye suppose, seeing it is but*
> *the third hour of the day. But this is that which was spoken*
> *by the prophet Joel; "And it shall come to pass in the last*
> *days that I will POUR OUT my Spirit on all flesh. Your*
> *sons and your daughters shall prophesy. Your young men*
> *shall see visions. Your old men shall dream dreams. On my*
> *menservants and my maidservants, I will POUR OUT my*
> *Spirit, and they will prophesy."*   Acts 2:15

They were drunk, but not like the people supposed. They were not drunk on the wine that comes from the vines of the world. They were drunk on the New Wine that comes from the True Vine, the Lord Jesus Christ. Bible scholars recognize New Wine as well as the Wind, Rivers of Living Water, Oil, Fire, and the Dove, as well-known symbols of the Holy Spirit.

Is The Baptism of the Holy Spirit for Today?

As a new Christian in a wonderful Baptist church, I knew nothing about the baptism of the Holy Spirit until one day I ran into a woman I had known as a teenager who asked me if I had been baptized in the Spirit. That was my very first time to even hear that term. I told her I didn't know anything about it, but I tucked that thought away in the back of my mind, thinking I needed to do some studying to find out what she was talking about.

I started my quest in the book of Acts reading about Pentecost and soon discovered there was much debate in religious circles about whether or not the baptism of the Holy Spirit still happened today. There was one group that said it was over, it only happened in the early church, but there was another group who said it was still happening. They said it was a second encounter with Jesus, the first being conversion where Christians receive some kind of supernatural power to be His witnesses.

> *You shall receive power when the Holy Spirit has come upon you, and you shall be My witnesses, both in Jerusalem, and in all Judea, and Samaria and to the end of the earth.*   Acts 1:8

As a new Christian I listened to both sides of the discussion and wondered how two groups of well-meaning Christians, who both loved the Lord Jesus Christ, could read the scriptures and interpret them so completely differently. Both groups believed exactly what had been passed down to them from the generations in their denominations that had gone before them.

As I listened to the different opinions I wondered which group was right. I had heard about what some called the "holy roller churches" where some of the people who had been baptized in the Spirit were doing strange things. My mom had visited one when she was a girl and told me they were dancing and shouting and falling on the floor. Her account of what she saw left me with an uncomfortable image in my mind of what might happen to me if I ever experienced this thing called being baptized in the Spirit; however, as I continued to read the Word about this baptism I became curious. I was intrigued by the words of John the Baptist

> *John answered them all, "I baptize you with water. But One who is more powerful than I will come, the straps of whose sandals I am not worthy to untie. He will baptize you with the Holy Ghost and with fire"*   Luke 3:16

What did John mean? What was this baptism BY Jesus with the Holy Ghost and fire? I had read about the baptism BY the Spirit into the body of Christ and being baptized BY the body of Christ into the baptismal waters.

For by one Spirit we were all baptized into one body...

1 Corinthians 12:13a

I indeed baptize you with water unto repentance...

Matthew 3:11a

He that believeth and is baptized shall be saved...

Mark 16:16

Both experiences had happened to me. I had been baptized BY the Spirit into the body of Christ, and I had been baptized BY my pastor into the baptismal waters, but being baptized BY Jesus with the Holy Ghost and fire sounded like a different baptism. Every time I read about the baptism of the disciples in the upper room I wondered if it could be possible that the same thing could ever happen to me. One day as I was reading in 1 Corinthians, I ran across the words of Paul.

I thank God that I speak in tongues more than you all.

1 Corinthians: 14:18

I was surprised to learn that Paul, who had not been in the upper room with the disciples on the day of Pentecost, spoke in tongues just like they did. I couldn't help but wonder why Paul thought this gift that accompanied the baptism of the Holy Spirit in the early church was so wonderful that he thanked God for it. What was the value of this gift that made him want to speak in tongues more than anyone else?

I thought about these questions, but the real question I wanted answered was, "Is the Lord still baptizing His people with the Holy Ghost and fire today?" As I searched the scriptures for truth, a Bible-study leader supporting the fact that speaking in tongues was not for today quoted:

> *Love never fails; but if there are gifts of prophecy they will*
> *be done away; if there are tongues, they will cease; if there*
> *is knowledge, it will be done away.*   1 Corinthians 13:8

She assured all of us that tongues had ceased; however, the thought kept rolling around in my mind that knowledge was still alive and well. It had not ceased. If knowledge had not vanished, maybe it was possible that the gifts of prophecy and speaking in tongues had not vanished.

Public and Private Use

I was interested in looking in the Word to see what it said about this gift of speaking in tongues that happened in the early church. I read 1 Corinthians 14 over and over, only to discover that there was a public use of speaking in tongues in the church that always required an interpretation, and there was also a private use of speaking in tongues where they spoke directly to God which was called "praying in the Spirit." Obviously there was a problem with the public use of speaking in tongues and Paul was addressing the abuses that were taking place.

He made it clear that without love, speaking in tongues was just a sounding brass or a clanging cymbal. Love had to be the basis through which this gift must flow. We don't know for sure what the problems were, but like most new gifts, they obviously needed instruction about the proper way to use it. Paul was correcting them, but he also said, "*Forbid not to speak in tongues*" (1 Cor. 14:39). Just because there were problems, he wasn't saying not to do it. He was teaching them the correct way to use the gift. The public use of speaking in tongues was interesting, but what intrigued me was the private use, praying in the Spirit, speaking directly to God.

Jesus Came Up with the Idea

One day as I was reading the Word, I came across the words of Jesus in Mark 16:17, *"And these signs shall follow them that believe, in My name shall they cast out devils; they shall speak with new tongues."* There it was, written in red, the very words of Jesus. His disciples would not only have the capacity to cast out demons, but they would also speak with new tongues. Really?

I began to realize that this gift came from Jesus. It was His idea, but what was the purpose of this gift? I was definitely curious about this baptism, wondering if it was something that would enhance my relationship with Jesus, but what did the Word have to say about this thing called tongues. What would ever make me want this gift? I saw that the public use of this gift was for edifying the body of Christ, but what about the private use of praying in the Spirit. What was the benefit?

Benefits of the Private Use of Praying in the Spirit

1. I discovered one benefit of praying in the Spirit was the ability to speak directly to God in a language given to me by Him. Paul wrote:

> *For he that speaks in an unknown tongue speaks not unto men, but unto God, for no man understands him, but, in the Spirit he speaks mysteries.* 1 Cor. 14:2

> *For if I pray in an unknown tongue, my spirit prays, but my understanding is unfruitful. What is it then? I will pray with the spirit and I will pray with the understanding also. I will sing with the Spirit and I will sing with the understanding also.* 1 Cor. 14:14-15

When I read these verses I immediately liked the idea of speaking directly to God in a private language that had been designed by Him. If this language came from Him, there must be a good reason for it. Why would He give his disciples a gift that was of no value? I also thought that if Paul thought it was a good idea to pray with words he understood and also pray in the Spirit, it must be a good idea.

2. The one who speaks in tongues edifies himself.

> *He that speaks in an unknown tongue edifies himself, but*
> *he that prophesies edifies the church.*   1 Cor. 14:4

As I read this verse I understood exactly what it was saying. It was more important to edify the church rather than edify myself, but I also knew without a shadow of a doubt that I needed to be edified.

3. Praying in the Spirit builds up our most holy faith.

> *But you, beloved, build yourselves up on your most holy*
> *faith, praying in the Holy Ghost.*   Jude 1:20

How could I build myself up in my most holy faith? The Word said I could build myself up in my most holy faith by praying in the Spirit. The desire to experience more, sparked by the truth of God's Word, began to slowly but surely rise up in my spirit. The question I found myself continually asking was: Could there be more to the Christian life than I was experiencing? Could this experience bring me into a closer walk with the Lord Jesus Christ?

4. When we pray in the Spirit, He prays according to the will of God.

> *Likewise, the Spirit also helps in our weaknesses, for we*
> *do not know what we should pray for as we ought, but the*
> *Spirit Himself makes intercession for us with groanings*
> *which cannot be uttered. Now He who searches the hearts,*

knows what the mind of the Spirit is, because He makes
intercession for the saints according to the will of God.

Romans 8:26-27

I knew there were many times in my life when I had no idea what the will of God was, but if I could pray in the Spirit, He could pray through me, not according to my will but according to the will of God.

Shocked by Her Answer

In the meantime, as I studied I continued to talk to people, and everyone I talked with seemed to be in agreement that the baptism of the Holy Spirit was not for today until one night I ran across a person in my church who had a different story to tell. She was a woman I didn't know very well. Her name was Lonna Tweedy. She asked me if I wanted to ride with her to a Sunday school class social. I still remember getting into her car not even realizing that I was about to make one of the greatest discoveries of my life.

She was so kind, so loving, so full of peace, so full of joy, and so full of humility. I was intrigued by the fragrant aroma of Jesus that was coming forth as she spoke. I finally decided to ask her the question I had been asking everyone, expecting of course to get the same answer. Did she know anything about the baptism of the Holy Spirit? I was shocked by her answer. She told me that the same thing happened to her that had happened to the disciples in the upper room at Pentecost. She had been baptized by Jesus with the Holy Ghost and fire and she spoke with other tongues. Oh, my heart!

I suddenly realized that everything that I had suspected was true. It was real. It was for today, and I was face to face with someone who was alive, walking, talking, breathing, living on planet earth that had experienced this baptism. I knew, in that moment, that if Jesus would baptize her with the Holy Ghost and fire, He would surely baptize me with the

Holy Ghost and fire. Little did I know that that encounter would be the catalyst that would seal my spiritual fate forever.

I had a million questions. How did it happen? What did she do to get it? She told me that she became so hungry to experience more of Jesus she ASKED HIM to baptize her with His Spirit, and He did. She told me that the baptism of the Holy Spirit was a free gift given to those who wanted it and were willing to ASK FOR IT, and all we had to do was RECEIVE it by faith.

I had read about it for a long time. Now I knew someone who was oozing with Christ-like qualities who had experienced this baptism. Suddenly DESIRE began to consume me, and before I knew it desire grew until it turned into full-blown desperation. I wasn't satisfied anymore with where I was in my relationship with Jesus. I suddenly realized there was more, and I wanted it.

Embraced by His Presence

The memory of that day is etched in my mind and heart forever. I was totally unaware when I got out of bed on that beautiful Saturday morning in October of 1973, that I was about to have what I now call a close encounter of the third kind—the Holy Ghost kind.

The day started out like any other Saturday. Mark was sitting on the sofa reading the paper. I had just fed Kevin, my oldest son, who was a baby and was doing what I loved to do most, holding him in my arms, rocking him to sleep in the old rocking chair we had stripped and repainted a bright yellow. As I rocked him I can still remember thinking I didn't know until he was born a love like that existed in the universe. After he fell asleep, I carefully laid him down in his crib, and instead of leaving the room, I stood over him for the longest time watching him breathing in and out, so slowly, so peacefully.

On the outside life seemed calm, normal, but on the inside the desire for a deeper relationship with Jesus started spinning around in my spirit like a whirlwind. The time for waiting was over. The time had come. I was ready. I made up my mind. I was going into His presence, and I was going to ask for what I so desperately wanted. I walked into the family room and asked Mark to listen for Kevin in case he woke up.

As I went into our guest room, closing the door behind me, I realized I was at a place in my spiritual life that there was no turning back. I walked over to the bed, placing my hands together on the green bedspread as my knees touched the gold shag carpet. I remember feeling nervous. I was going into the presence of the Lord, and I wasn't certain about what was getting ready to happen to me. I guess it is normal to fear the unknown, to fear what we don't completely understand, but I remembered the words of Jesus,

> *And I say to you, ask and it shall be given to you. Seek and you shall find. Knock and it shall be opened to you. For everyone who asks receives, and he who seeks finds, and to him who knocks, it shall be opened. And which of you that is a father shall his son ask a loaf, and he give him a stone? Or a fish, and he for a fish give him a serpent? Or if he shall ask an egg, will he give him a scorpion? If you then being evil know how to give good gifts to your children, how much more shall your heavenly father give the HOLY SPIRIT to them that ASK Him.*   Luke 11:9-13

Was that really all there was to it? Was He just waiting for me to ASK Him? Did He want me to ask Him to fill me with His Spirit just like I had asked Him for the gift of salvation? The truth that what I was about to experience was coming from Jesus immediately took away all fear, because I knew He would never give me anything that wasn't good.

Not knowing exactly what to say, I just said what was in my heart: "Lord, I don't really understand this thing called being baptized by You with the Holy Ghost and fire, and I don't understand this thing called speaking in tongues, but I know from Your Word that it comes from You, and because it comes from You it must be good, and I want it. So, now I am asking You, 'Would You baptize me with Your Spirit?'"

I waited for His response in total silence. My heart was filled with anticipation. I don't know how long I waited, but I do know that I had made up my mind when I got down on my knees that I wasn't getting up until I had received what I was ASKING for. Nothing could have pried me from that carpet. I had set my face like flint. I was going into His presence to get what the disciple of long ago had received; however, nothing could have ever prepared me for what happened next.

Suddenly I realized I was being caught up into a realm I had never been before. It felt like I was lifted out of time, into another dimension where time no longer existed. I began to hear something that sounded like angelic music. As I listened it felt like the Lord was filling every fiber, every cell, every atom of my being with the New Wine of His Spirit. I was on holy ground being embraced by His presence. I was conscious of the fact that waves of His love were washing over me like the waves of the ocean washing over the sands on the seashore, while a tsunami of liquid love was flooding my soul.

I don't know why I should have been so surprised because the Word says that *"God is love"* (I John 4:16), so since I was being filled with His Spirit, it was only logical that His love would consume me. His Word was true and His Spirit was alive, escaping from the confines of my spirit, flooding my soul, my mind, my will and my emotions. Oh, the joy!

Then it happened. The beginnings of a new language that I had never heard before began to flow out of me. I had majored in French in college and had spent hours and hours learning French, but now a language I had never heard before, a language my mother and father hadn't taught me, was coming out of my mouth. I was reminded of the words of Jesus, "They will speak with new tongues." All I could do was laugh and cry all at the same time. I ask for it and I got it.

After it was over I told the Lord that if that moment in time was the only glimpse I would ever get of Him this side of Heaven, it was enough, but little did I know that was not the last encounter I would ever have. It was only the beginning of many more to come, and like a baby who first says just one word, and then a few words, and then goes on the speak a fluent language, the first few words of the new language grew, blossoming into a full-blown, spiritual language.

Lovesick

I had gone into the Banqueting House, the House of Wine in the realm of the Spirit and was intoxicated by the revelation of the way He loved me. After being baptized in the Spirit, I never again doubted that His banner over me was love. It was there I discovered that His banner over me was not worthless. His banner over me was not failure. His banner over me was not useless. His banner over me was not sinner. His banner over me was not full of condemnation. His banner over me was not a banner of rejection.

All the things that I had suspected in the past were not true. There was only one banner flying over me in the Wind of His Spirit, and His banner over me was a banner of LOVE. It was a love I had never known before. It was love without legalism. It was love without boundaries. It was love without fear.

When I got into the House of Wine just like the Shulamite, He sustained me in a way I had never been sustained before, refreshed me in a way I had never been refreshed before, and I was embraced by His presence, in a way He had never embraced me before, but the greatest change that took place when I got up off my knees, was an overwhelming, powerful awareness of the presence of Jesus, and without a doubt, I was LOVESICK.

It wasn't the foolish, infatuated, surface kind of love that we experience when we simply have a crush on someone. It was a tender, deep, devoted, thrilling kind of love that grows stronger and stronger over the years and stays forever.

What was it that caused me to be lovesick? It was the divine revelation of the abundance of His love. It was being aware of the extravagance of the way He loved me that moved me from the place of passivity into an all-consuming love affair with the Lover of my soul. The dictionary describes being lovesick as "in love, so much that one is unable to act in a normal way." If you have ever been love sick you know exactly how it feels. You act in a way you have never acted before because you are consumed with that "loving feeling."

When you are lovesick you think about the one you love all the time, and that is exactly what happened to me. I devoured His love letter to me. I just couldn't get enough. His words thrilled my soul. Just to hear someone mention His name made my heart beat faster. I talked about Him all the time. I just couldn't stop talking about Him. I was madly, crazy, out of my mind in love. I not only talked about Him, but I also talked to Him all the time, and amazingly, I began to hear His voice with greater clarity than I had ever heard Him before.

Out of the abundance of my time in the Banqueting House, a divine romance began to blossom, and over time that romance ultimately bore fruit. It was in the Banqueting House I discovered why He made me, not just as a fact in my head but as a reality in my heart. I was made for Him. He created me for His pleasure.

> *Thou art worthy, O Lord, to receive glory and honour and power: For thou hast created all things, and for "THY PLEASURE" they are and were created.* Revelation 4:11

Like the Shulamite, desire caused me to start asking, which took me past the king's chambers into the House of Wine where I became lovesick, and my relationship with my King, the Lord Jesus Christ, was never the same again. The beginnings of loving Him "with all my heart, all my soul, all my mind, and all my strength" started to become a reality in my life. I began to understand what it meant to love Him the way He wanted to be loved. I am still aware that the words "all" my heart, "all" my soul, "all" my mind and "all" my strength are not a complete reality, but the way I love Him now is deeper, and stronger, and sweeter after my encounter in the House of Wine than it had ever been before.

Oliver Wendell Holmes once said, "a mind stretched by a new experience can never go back to its old dimensions." When it came to my experience in the Banqueting House, he was right. I knew I would never be going back. I discovered many things in the House of Wine, but the most thrilling of all was the fact that I was not the only one who was lovesick. He was lovesick too.

Emily

One of the best examples of how to receive the baptism of the Holy Spirit is an encounter that took place between me and my niece's daughter Emily. When she was just three years old my mother kept her a couple of days a week while her mother worked. I had my own business and worked just a few blocks away, so I went by to see her all the time. She loved it, and so did I.

She loved playing imaginary games. I often pretended to be her mother, and she pretended to be my baby. She would pretend to be sick, and I would tell her that I would have to take her to the doctor. We would get in the imaginary car, and I would be the driver while she would moan and groan in the imaginary backseat. When we got to the doctor, of course, I had to be the doctor and deliver the bad news that she was going to have to have a shot, which caused her to break down with imaginary sobs.

One day as I was leaving, I told her if she wanted me to come back to call me on the telephone, and if she would just ASK me, I would come. Several days later I got the call. She had asked my mother to dial the number for her, and I heard her sweet little voice on the other end of the line say, "Gigi, would you come?"

The minute I heard her voice I dropped everything, got in the car and started driving. In the meantime, she put on her shoes and went outside to sit on the front porch because she BELIEVED I would do what

I told her I would do. My Mom said she looked up and down the street expecting me to pull up any minute.

When I was a few houses away where I could see her, I started blowing the horn. She immediately stood up with the biggest grin on her beautiful face. As I got almost to the porch, she opened her arms wide getting into position to RECEIVE me. As I ran to the porch, grabbing her, twirling her around and around, I knew she was thrilled, but not as much as I was.

What Emily did is a picture of how we receive the baptism of the Holy Spirit today. We ASK, BELIEVING He will do what He said He would do. We get in the position to RECEIVE Him when He comes, and just like Emily enjoyed my presence, we get to enjoy His presence.

Negative Reactions

After my experience in the Banqueting House with Jesus, I learned it was not a good idea to tell anyone in my precious Baptist church what had happened. After telling one of the teachers who was one of my best friends who taught in the same department with me at church, she assured me that what had happened to me was from the devil. I knew her intentions were good, and because she loved me she didn't want me to take a wrong turn in my spiritual life.

I was surprised when she called me the next day and apologized. I was anxious to find out what had happened in such a short time to change her mind. She told me she had called our Baptist pastor letting him know what was going on in my life. She said he told her not to worry because what had happened to me was from Jesus. I had never heard him teach on that particular subject, and I had never discussed it with him, but I was totally surprised by his response. I just assumed he felt the same way as everyone else I had talked to.

I guess it is a good idea never to assume. I will forever be grateful to him for writing me a letter that I have kept to this day, giving me some wonderful advice. He wrote, "Never allow the enemy to rob you of what has been given to you from the Lord Jesus Christ."

Judy Neely

The second person I told was one of my best friends, Judy Neely. We met at the age of fifteen and have been forever friends since that day. When we were in high school, we would double date together all the time. She would spend the night at my house, or I would spend the night at her house. We were so close that we told each other everything, even our deepest darkest secrets. Nothing, and I mean nothing, was off limits.

After I was baptized in the Spirit, of course I wanted to tell her what had happened. When I did she promptly told me to never mention that experience to her again. I was saddened by her response, but I quickly began to realize that telling others in the Baptist church that I had been baptized in the Spirit, like the disciples were on the day of Pentecost, offended them. It offended what they had been taught, what they believed, so I quit mentioning it.

It was almost ten years later when I heard a knock at the back door of my bedroom. In hindsight the scene was funny, but at the time it was very serious. It was in the days when we ratted our hair. I had just ratted my hair, getting ready to comb it down. It looked like I had stuck my finger in a light socket. It was sticking out in every direction.

When I opened the door, there she stood. She told me that she wanted me to lay hands on her and pray for her to receive the baptism of the Holy Spirit. I could see by the look in her eyes she was ready. The time had come. She laid down on my bedroom carpet. I can still remember backing up and sitting down, not even taking the time to remove my house shoes from underneath me because there was no time.

It was such a blessing to watch her go into the House of Wine and receive the baptism of the Holy Spirit and hear her speak the first word of her new heavenly language which ultimately became a full language.

That was in 1983. It has been fun running together after Him in the Spirit for the last thirty-two years of our spiritual life.

God Doesn't Give All of us the Same Gifts

After praying for many to be baptized in the Spirit, I have discovered that everyone who goes into the House of Wine to be filled with the Holy Spirit has their own story to tell. Some express the emotion of laughing or crying and some don't. Some hear things and some don't, some feel things and some don't, some speak in tongues and some don't, but no matter what our experience, it doesn't mean it is any less valid or any more valid than everyone else who has gone before us into the House of Wine to receive the precious baptism of the Holy Spirit.

Even those who do speak in tongues have their own story to tell. Some speak in tongues both publicly and privately. Some use this gift only in a public setting, with the interpretation following, edifying the church with their heavenly language, but most of us, like me, use this gift only in their private lives, praying in the Spirit, speaking directly to God.

For a long time, I believed the baptism of the Holy Spirit would always be followed by the evidence of speaking in tongues, not only because that is what happened in the early church, but also because that is what happened in my life. Have you ever noticed how easy it is to make doctrines out of our experiences? I believed those who had been filled with the Holy Spirit and didn't speak in tongues had received that gift but just hadn't released it.

I once heard Pastor Jack Hayford, one of my favorite preachers, say when he was filled with the Holy Spirit he heard some foreign words in his head but didn't release those words for three years. As I have prayed for different ones to be baptized in the Spirit, some spoke in tongues immediately, some didn't pray in the Spirit until the next day or the next month, and some have never spoken in tongues.

I have watched many Christians who are my very close friends who have never spoken in tongues and been overwhelmed with how passionately in love they are with Jesus. I have seen the fruit of the Spirit flow just as strongly in their lives as those who speak in tongues and have been bowled over with the powerful witness they are in the kingdom of God. Over the years I have come to the realization that those who are filled with the Holy Spirit and never speak in tongues are just as filled as those who speak in tongues the minute they are baptized in the Spirit.

We read in 1 Corinthians 12:27-32: *"Now you are the body of Christ, and members individually. And God has appointed these in the church: first apostles, second prophets, third teachers, after that miracles, then gifts of healing, helps, administrations, and tongues. Are all apostles? Are all prophets? Are all teachers? Are all workers of miracles? Do all have gifts of healings? Do all speak with tongues? Do all interpret?"* The answer to all of those questions is NO.

We see a list of all the gifts God gives to His bride in 1 Corinthians 12, Romans 12, and Ephesians 4. God doesn't give all of us the same gifts, but distributes each one of His gifts as He pleases for His glory and for the building up of His body. He knows which gifts each one of us need in our lives to accomplish His purposes.

Are Tongues Real Languages?

Before I leave the subject of tongues, I want to explore one last question. We know when the one hundred and twenty disciples were baptized in the Spirit in the upper room, the tongues they spoke that day were recognizable languages. The question I want us to look at is, are those who speak in tongues today speaking recognizable languages?

> *And when this sound occurred, the multitude came together, and were confused, because everyone heard them speak in his own language. Then they were all amazed and marveled, saying to one another, Look, are not all these who speak Galileans? And how is it that we hear, each in our own languages in which we were born. Parthians and Medes*

*and Elamites, those dwelling in Mesopotamia, Judea and
Cappadocia, Pontus and Asia, Phrygia and Pamphylia,
Egypt and other parts of Libya adjoining Cyrene, visitors
from Rome, both Jews and proselytes, Cretans and Arabs
we hear them speaking in our own tongues the wonderful
works of God.* Acts 2:6-11

There are approximately 6,500 languages spoken in the world today. If there are that many languages, it's possible that some who speak in tongues today could still be speaking real languages. There are documented reports of those who speak in tongues today that have discovered that their heavenly language is a real language.

Jack Hayford shared one of my favorite stories about the fact that some spiritual languages are real languages. He said he was getting on an airplane one day after speaking at a meeting, hoping for a nice quiet two-hour flight home when a man in a business suit sat next to him. After exchanging greetings, they began a casual conversation.

When Jack asked the man what he did for a living the man said he was a civil engineer. In the course of the conversation, Jack told him he was a preacher, and the man explained to Jack that he didn't believe in Jesus or the Bible. Jack very graciously continued the conversation. Because he detected a Southwestern accent, he asked the man if he were from the south.

The man told him he always felt a little awkward about his speech because he had not learned to speak English until he was almost five years old. He told Jack that he was from Oklahoma and had been raised by his mother who was a full-blood Indian from the Kiowa tribe.

During the conversation, Jack heard the Lord say, "Speak to him in tongues." The thought made Jack feel very uncomfortable. He didn't like the idea. He hated the thought of looking like a "religious kook" to this stranger, but he had heard from God and he knew he had to obey no matter how he looked.

He finally got up the courage to ask his flying companion if he would mind if he spoke some words out loud in another language in the off chance he might recognize them. The man agreed, and Jack obeyed the Lord speaking out loud in tongues. When he finished, the man was astonished and said, "That is a pre-Kiowan language from which our Kiowa Indian tongue came from. Jack said he was stunned, asking what the words meant.

He translated Jack's words by telling him, "you spoke about the light that came down from above." Jack went on to witness to the man about the light, Jesus, who came down from above. I have heard reports, just like Jack's, where the tongues other people received were discovered to be real languages.

Jack also tells his sister Luanne's experience with speaking in tongues. As she prayed in her God-given tongue, some people around her recognized the language. She was speaking Chinese. She ultimately went to China as a missionary to the people in that country.

Don Basham, a pastor who has ministered in many places around the country, told the story of a friend in Oregon who was also a pastor. He had a young Japanese woman who was married to an American in his congregation. She had never accepted Christ, but would come to the altar with her husband to pray to her god, Buddha!

One morning, as the couple knelt at the altar she heard a woman close to her praying in Japanese. The woman who was praying had no idea the language she was speaking was Japanese. As she prayed the woman heard her speak her full name which no one in this country knew. She then heard in her native language, "God says you have tried Buddha and he has not helped you; why don't you try Me, Jesus Christ?"

I guess when we get to heaven we will find out if all spiritual languages given by the Lord today are real earthly languages or if some could simply be heavenly languages understood only by our heavenly father.

Awakened

> *The Lord God has given me the tongue of disciples, that I*
> *may know how to sustain the weary one with a word. He*
> *awakens me morning by morning, He AWAKENS MY EAR*
> *to listen as a disciple.*   Isaiah 40:4, NASB

After my time in the Banqueting House, I realized that something amazing had happened. The New Wine of His Spirit had affected my spiritual senses. They had been awakened. I realized the Holy Spirit had saturated my mind with that royal wine and as a result, I began to think about Jesus all the time. He had saturated my ears, and I began to hear His voice with greater clarity and greater frequency.

He had saturated my spiritual eyes, and I began to see things I had never seen before. He had also saturated my heart. It was no longer luke-warm; it was on fire, burning with love for my Bridegroom. A perfect example of what had happened to me is the wino who has been drinking the wine that comes from the vines of the world. Some say they are UNDER THE INFLUENCE of the wine.

The same thing was true about me. I realized I was under the influence of the Holy Spirit. I was also aware that just as wine connoisseurs had always said that wine was alive in the bottle, I was now more aware than ever that the New Wine of the Holy Spirit was alive, living inside of me. I also became conscious of the fact there was a Ghost in my life, and His first name was Holy. I couldn't see Him but I could feel His presence, and He had filled up my spiritual senses, all of them, with a fresh revelation of the Lord Jesus Christ.

John Denver wrote and sang, a song he entitled "Annie's Song." The first few lines of that song reveal a glimpse of how I felt after the baptism of the Holy Spirit:

> You fill up my senses like a night in the forest
> Like a mountain in springtime, like a walk in the rain

Like a storm in the desert, like a sleepy blue ocean
You fill up my senses, come fill me again

El Rancho Grande

*And don't be drunk with wine, wherein is excess; but be
filled with the Spirit.*   Ephesians 5:18

I Am the True Vine and my Father is the Vinedresser.
                                                        John 1:15

I was also surprised to find out after being spiritually awakened that getting drunk on the alcohol in the wine that come from the vines of the world and getting drunk on the New Wine that comes from the True Vine, the Lord Jesus Christ, affected the same areas of my body. They both affected my speech. They both affected my thought processes. They both affected my vision, and they both affected the way I walked; however, there was one big difference. The alcohol in the wine that comes from the vines of the world had a negative effect on my body, whereas the wine that comes from the True Vine, the Lord Jesus Christ, had a positive effect on my spiritual body.

You may be wondering how I know so much about getting drunk. I have another confession to make. I am not proud of what happened, but I want to tell you about it because I know what it is like to be intoxicated, and I want to use what I learned to illustrate a powerful point about the New Wine of the Holy Spirit.

One time, years ago, Mark and I went to El Rancho Grande, one of my favorite Mexican restaurants in Fort Worth, Texas, for dinner. I had been working all day and had been so busy I failed to take the time to eat. It was in the very hottest part of summer, and when we got to the restaurant we had to wait for a table. We were told that we could wait in the bar area.

When we sat down I saw some lime green drinks that looked like delicious snow cones in beautifully shaped glasses with long stems at the bottoms. I was so thirsty that my mouth started watering. Now the truth be told I knew what they were. They were margaritas. I knew that like wine they had alcohol in them. I didn't see any problem whatsoever with having one until later when I discovered what drinking too much, too fast, did to me.

When they brought my drink to the table, I just downed it. It took me about two minutes to empty the glass. I know now it is never a good idea to drink on an empty stomach. I also discovered that when you are not accustomed to drinking, just a little bit of alcohol can have a huge impact on your body. I also know that it is not a good idea to just drink alcohol like you are drinking a glass of water.

While we were sitting there waiting to be seated, Mark smiled at me and said, "I have good news and bad news—which would you like to hear first?" I asked him to give me the good news first. Mark said, "Well the good news is that I am the designated driver." I laughed and said, "What is the bad news?" Mark then informed me that some people that we had visited and been instrumental in encouraging them to join our church had just come into the restaurant.

My heart sank. Not only was I drunk, but I now realized I was going to get caught. It is bad enough to do something you don't want other people to find out about, but becomes even worse when they catch you doing it. About that time, they called our name. It was time to be seated.

In hindsight I wish I had turned around and walked out the door. When I stood up, I realized that I couldn't walk straight. Mark had to hold on to me. My vision was blurred. My speech was slurred. I was horrified. I realized that what Mark implied was true—I was intoxicated. I was drunk. Then, of course, the sweet family we had encouraged to visit our church was seated right next to us. I was mortified.

That was the one of the worst moments in my life. Even though it was a terrible experience, after I was baptized in the Spirit it helped me to understand the similarities in being drunk on the New Wine of the Holy

Spirit compared to being drunk on anything that contains alcohol, like margaritas or the wine that comes from the vines of the world.

Benefits of the New Wine

1. My mind was affected.

When a person gets drunk, one of the first things that happens is the wine penetrates the brain, changing normal thinking patterns. To the earthly drunk this is a bad thing, but to the spiritual man who has been drinking wine from the TRUE VINE this is a good thing.

The Lord tells us in His Word that *"our thoughts are not His thoughts"* (Isaiah 55:8). He wants us intoxicated on the New Wine of His Spirit so that His thoughts can more easily become our thoughts. It is when we are baptized in the Spirit that we begin to think like He thinks. His wisdom, His words, and His revelation begin to flow through our minds.

Set your mind on things that are above… Colossians 3:2a

Before I was baptized in the Spirit I would occasionally think about Jesus, and the thought of Him always brought great joy, but after I was baptized in the Spirit, I realized my mind had been affected because my thoughts were suddenly consumed with Him. He was always on my mind. I thought about Him when I woke up in the morning. I thought about Him all day long and every night before I went to sleep, my thoughts were filled with Him.

Something had changed. I was now able to set my mind on things above. One evening, after my encounter in the House of Wine, I went to a PTA meeting at my son's school. When the meeting was over, as I was walking down the hall, the Lord spoke to me saying, "I am going to give you some elementary teachings about how you can spend more time thinking about Me." I walked into one of the empty class rooms and saw numbers written on pieces of card board all around the room.

A new secret!

As I focused on the number one, He said, "When you see the number one, always remember I am the One. I am the Alpha and the Omega, the First and the Last. I am your One and only. When you see the number two, always remember you are never alone. I am always with you. I will never leave you or forsake you. When you see the number three, think of the three of Us, Father, Son, and Holy Ghost." He went on through the numbers telling me when I looked at a number, it could trigger my mind to think about Him.

I loved that insight because everywhere I looked I was always surrounded by numbers. He then took me through the colors. He said, "When you see the color red think about My blood. When you see the color white, remember that I have removed your sins away from you as far as the east is from the west and colored you as white as the wind-driven snow. When you see the color green, remember I am growing you." He continued taking me through different colors.

I now knew a new secret. I could look at the natural and see the spiritual. I could look at numbers and colors and they could be triggers the Holy Spirit could use to help me set my mind on Him.

2. My speech was affected.

When you listen to someone that is intoxicated from the wine that comes from the vines of the world, you know they have been drinking because their speech is affected. The same thing is true when you listen to someone who has been drinking the New Wine that comes from the True Vine, the Lord Jesus Christ. Their speech is affected, but not in a negative way. Their speech is affected in a positive way.

Before I was baptized in the Spirit, I had a terrible fear of speaking in front of more than two or three people. In high school I had to take a speech class where I was forced to get up in front of the room and speak. The teacher liked for us to speak extemporaneously. When it was my turn to speak, my mouth always seemed to be as dry as a bone, and paralyzed with fear.

I don't know if you know it or not, but fear can be a cruel companion—at least it was for me. The teacher had a box that she would pass around each day, and we would all put a topic in the box. She would then ask each one of us to come up, take a topic out of the box, and speak for two minutes. I knew there was no way I could think of something to say while standing on my scared to death feet in front of my peers for two minutes.

As a result, I devised a plan of deception. Every night I would go home, make up a speech on a topic of my choice and memorize it. The only reason I did it was just in case there might be the slightest chance that if I could open my mouth I would have something to say. The next day when my time came, I would go to the front of the class and take a topic out of the box. I would look at the paper, crumble it up in my hand and throw it in the trash. I would then proceed to try to speak on the topic I had written the night before.

I thought my plan would help me, but because fear was always lurking in the corners of my mind, I would stumble my way through the disastrous speech. When I was born again and joined a Sunday school class, the first thing I did was tell the teacher not to call on me for anything because I couldn't speak in front of a group.

Later Mark and I joined a couples' class together. One Sunday at the end of the class, the teacher asked me if I would mind making the announcements the following Sunday. I have no idea why in the world I agreed, but I did. When I stood in front of the class the next Sunday, not only my knees were shaking, but also my voice and the hand that held my notes.

When I was finished I sat down next to Mark. After a sufficient amount of time had passed, I tried to inconspicuously lean my head over close to Mark's ear. I then whispered, "How did I do?" Mark, being the comedian that he is said, "Well, you sounded like a professional speaker that doesn't get to speak very often." We both looked at each other and started laughing.

After I was baptized in the New Wine of the Spirit an amazing thing happened. A paradigm shift took place in my life. The fear that had plagued me for years was totally gone. Not even a drop of it was left. There was something in that wine that took my fear away. I had always wondered what happened to Peter who was so full of fear he denied Jesus three times, only to get up in front of thousands and speak fearlessly after he was baptized in the Spirit.

Now I knew. The same thing had happened to me that had happened to him. Peter and I had gone into the land of promise in the realm of the Spirit and consumed some of that royal wine produced from those large, delicious Holy Ghost grapes, and we were never afraid of the giants in the land again. Years after being baptized in the Spirit, I stood on a stage to speak in front of several hundred people and there was no fear what-soever. It was gone.

Before getting up to speak, I thought about Moses' conversation with God when he was arguing with Him about having to tell Pharaoh to let His people go:

> *Moses said to the Lord, O Lord, I have never been eloquent, neither in the past nor since you have spoken to your ser-vant. I am slow of speech and tongue." The Lord said to him, "Who gave man his mouth? Is it not I the Lord? Now go; I will help you speak and teach you what to say.*
> Exodus 4:10-12

Like Moses, I had never been able to speak well. I couldn't even open my mouth without shaking, but now the Lord was with my mouth. He was helping me speak and teaching me what to say.

3. My vision was affected

When I got drunk in that Mexican restaurant, my vision was affected. It was blurred. I couldn't see the world the way I had always seen it. My vision was affected in a negative way. After I was baptized in the Spirit, my vision was also affected but in a positive way. I didn't see things the way I saw them before. It was as if I were looking at things and seeing them in a brand new, different way.

I started seeing things from a new perspective. I started looking at others and seeing them the way He saw them. I started feeling a love well up within me for others I had never had before. I think He was just giving me a glimpse of the way He felt about them.

After I was baptized in the Spirit I also started seeing visions. I have experienced two types of visions. One is seeing a vision with my eyes open. It is like watching a movie screen open up in front of you and seeing a display of what God wants to show you. The other is an inner vision where you see a picture of what God wants to show you in your mind.

I still remember the first vision I ever saw. It was an open vision. My eyes were wide open, and what I saw was just as real as anything I have ever seen with my physical eyes. I had spent the day cleaning my bedroom. It was spotless. I went on to other parts of the house, but when I came back into my bedroom there were three bags of trash in the chair that sat in the corner of my room. I knew in my mind that what I was seeing was impossible. No one had been at home but me, and I had not left anything in that chair.

Suddenly the three bags of trash were gone. There was nothing in the chair. I began to realize that I was in the process of seeing a vision from God. Instead of the trash all I could see was a huge tree full of pure white blossoms. I was overwhelmed. What in the world was the Lord trying to say to me?

Then I heard Him speak. He said, "In your life there has been what looked like garbage, but I want you to know that it is gone. I have removed it from you as far as the east is from the west. Everything is clean. Now what comes forth from your life, will be clean and white, a thing of beauty, because it will come forth from Me." As I heard His voice I fell to my knees. His Word was true. We really do see visions.

The next vision I saw was with my eyes closed. I was praying, and as I prayed I saw a vision in my mind. In the vision the Lord was walking toward me. When He reached me, He turned around facing the opposite direction and stepped up on my feet. As He did, I realized when I walked, wherever I went, I was carrying Him. He then spoke to my spirit and said, "Jenny, from this day forward I want you to always remember that you carry Me."

I had known that truth in my mind, but on that day the truth was sealed in the deepest recesses of my soul in a way that surpassed knowledge. I carry Him. Wow! All of us who have been born again carry Him.

Date Night

> *The spiritual did not come first, but the natural and after that the spiritual.*   1 Corinthians 15:46

Another way my vision was affected after I had been filled with the Holy Spirit is I suddenly had the ability to look at the natural things that were taking place around me and see spiritual pictures. Friday night has always been date night for Mark and me. Mark gets all dressed up in his best clothes and puts on his best-smelling cologne.

We go to different restaurants in the area, but one of our favorites is Romano's Macaroni Grill. If you have ever been there, you know they use white tablecloths, and over the cloths they put white paper. When the waiters come to the table, they take crayons and write their names on the paper. One night when we sat down at the table at Romano's, the Lord spoke to me and said, "Watch Mark." After the waiter wrote his name, Mark ordered the same thing we always order, chicken scaloppini with lemon butter sauce, Caesar salad, bread, accompanied by a dish mixed with olive oil, balsamic vinegar, and spices, a glass of their blush wine, and iced tea, unsweet with a lot of ice for me.

After the waiter left, Mark took the crayons and started writing all over the paper, "I love you! You are beautiful! I love you! You are beautiful. He then looked at me and told me he loved me and that I was beautiful. Of course, we all love for our husbands to tell us they like the way we look and that they love us.

We ate the delicious meat and the bread, sopping the bread in the oil. Mark likes blush wine with his food. That night, like always, he offered me some of his wine from his glass and like always, I drank from his glass. At the end of the evening Mark paid the check, so for me the meal was free, the bread was free, the oil was free, and even the wine was free.

When we got home, because Mark and I both love to dance, he turned on the music. We like the oldies but goodies. Some of you remember those oldies like, "Heard It Through the Grapevine," by Marvin Gaye. We like to do an old dance called The Push. That night he held my hands and pushed me backward and then forward, twirling me around and around. After a few twirls, he let me go and we just danced in front of each other any way we wanted to.

After the fast dancing was over, Mark put on the slow music. He took me in his arms, holding me securely in his embrace and moved to the right. He didn't tell me that was the way he was going to move— I just felt him moving and moved with him. He then moved to the left and at the same time he moved to the left, I moved to the left. I just followed his lead. While we were dancing he whispered sweet nothings in my ears. We had a wonderful night and I realized when the night was over, I smelled like him because I had been with him.

Later, as I thought about the evening I realized it was indeed a huge spiritual picture. Just like Mark the Lord wrote it all down, not on a paper tablecloth, but in His Word. He told me in His written Word how much He loves me and exactly how He sees me. He not only wrote it all down, but there have been times when just like I heard Mark, I have heard His voice tell me exactly how He feels about me. I realized that like Mark, He had not only given me the meat of His Word but also the bread of His Word which had been sopped in the Oil of His Spirit, and when He offered me the New Wine of His Spirit, which was flowing from His cup of grace, I just had to have it. It was too delicious to resist.

Just like Mark paid, the Lord has also paid for everything. The meat of His Word is free. The bread of His Word is free. The oil is free and even the New Wine of His Spirit is free. Just like I followed Mark's lead, the Lord likes for me to follow His lead. There are times when I don't hear Him say which way to go, but I just feel Him moving, and I move with Him. Sometimes we even move together as one. Like I have heard Mark whisper sweet nothings in my ears, I have heard Him whisper sweet nothings in my spiritual ears, caressing my soul with His words of love, and amazingly, there are times when I smell like Him in the realm of the Spirit because I have been with Him.

> *For we are to God the pleasing aroma of Christ among those who are being saved and those who are perishing. To the one we are an aroma that brings death, to the other, an aroma that brings life.* 2 Corinthians 2:15-16

4. My walk was affected.

> *I say then: Walk in the Spirit, and you shall not fulfill the lust of the flesh. For the flesh lusts against the Spirit, and the Spirit against the flesh; and these are contrary to one another, so that you do not do the things you wish.*
> Galatians 5:16-17

The baptism of the Spirit not only affected my vision, my ability to speak, and my mind, but it also affected my walk. People who are drunk on the wine that comes from the vines of the world can testify that alcohol affects the way they walk. They don't walk like the world walks. Their balance is affected. They can't walk a straight line. We can all agree that the sight of them trying to walk without stumbling is not a pretty picture.

Those who drink the wine that comes from the True Vine have the same thing in common with the earthly wino. They no longer walk like the world walks, but there is a big difference in their walk and the walk of the worldly wino. When we walk in the Spirit we walk under the influence of the Holy Spirit. It doesn't mean those who have been baptized in the Spirit never sin again. We all sin. The temptation to sin is still there. Even Jesus faced temptation.

After Jesus was baptized and the Spirit of God descended on Him like a dove, Matthew 4:1 tells us, *"Jesus was led up of the spirit into the wilderness to be tempted of the devil."* If Jesus was tempted by the devil, we know that all of us are tempted, but after the baptism of the Holy Spirit I noticed I had a new weapon in my arsenal against sin. In Ephesians 6, included in the list of the weapons of our warfare against the schemes of the devil, we are told to pray in the Spirit.

> *Put on the whole armour of God, that ye may be able to stand against the wiles of the devil. For we wrestle not against flesh and blood, but against principalities, against power, against the rulers of darkness of this world, against spiritual wickedness in high places. Wherefore take unto you the whole armour of God, that ye may be able to withstand in the evil day, and having done all, stand...And take the helmet of salvation, and the sword of the Spirit, which is the word of god; praying always with all prayer and supplication IN THE SPIRIT.*   Ephesians 6:11-18

During some of the greatest temptations in my life, I have cried out to the Lord, praying in the spirit until the temptation to sin was lifted from me. There was a time in my early Christian life when I was teaching a Sunday school class of high school girls. My brother who lived in Arizona had hitchhiked with a friend to my home. When he got there he and his friend, who were teenagers at that time, were a mess. They were dirty, unshaven with long hair and their clothes were sprinkled with holes. I adored my brother, and I was thrilled to see him.

He told me at the end of the evening that he and his friend were going to come to my Sunday school class the next morning. Instead of being happy that he would come and hear about Jesus, sin took over. Pride rose its ugly head. What would the girls in my class think? I am so ashamed to even confess how I felt. I didn't see any other clothes in their possession, so I was sure they would come just like they were. I hated what was in my heart.

After they left to spend the night with my sister, I went into my bedroom and laid flat on my face on the floor. The fact that I cared so much about what other people thought made me sick. How could I be so shallow? I didn't know how to pray, so I just prayed in the Spirit. As I released the language the Lord had given me, every word was accompanied by my tears. I don't know what I prayed that night, but I do know that horrible heaviness was lifted off of me. When I got up, the sin of pride was gone. The thought of them coming to my class just like they were made me happy.

I don't know how praying in the Spirit works, but I do know that it helps in my battle against the enemy. There are many times in my life when I don't know how to pray, but when I pray in the Spirit I know the Holy Spirit is praying the perfect prayer on my behalf. Even though I didn't know how to pray that night when Tim and his friend left my home, the Spirit of the Lord did.

The next morning, I went on to Sunday school fully expecting them to show up just like they had left me the night before. To my amazement and surprise, when they came in it was like two different people walked through the door. They had showered, shaved, and changed their clothes. After the class they came for lunch, and Tim's friend sat with me at the kitchen table the entire afternoon asking me questions about the Lord. He was hungry. The Holy Spirit was drawing him.

As a result of his visit he prayed and received Christ as his Savior! Believe it or not, when he was married and had a daughter he named her after me, Jennifer. Wow! I will never know all that I prayed in the Spirit that night, but I do know my burden was lifted and someone was born again into the kingdom of God.

He Didn't Stop Pouring

The Banqueting House or the House of Wine has wonderful benefits. It is an amazing place to go. There is nothing like a fresh, Holy Ghost-powered baptism. All it took was one sip of the New Wine of His Spirit and I was addicted for life. The Holy Spirit gives a spiritual high unlike any high the wines of this world can ever give. There is nothing better than getting saturated with the New Wine and finding ourselves under the influence of His Spirit. Over 2000 years ago, Jesus started POURING the New Wine of His Spirit, and He is still serving that same wine today.

> *In the last days I will "POUR OUT" My Spirit upon all flesh...* Acts 2:17a

There were just one hundred and twenty people in that room when He started pouring. He poured it out on all of them, including His very own earthly mother. He started serving that New Wine in the upper room, but HE DIDN'T STOP POURING. We read in the Word where Peter saw the Lord pour out that same new Holy Ghost wine on the Gentiles:

> *While Peter was still speaking these words, the Holy Spirit fell upon all those who were listening to the message. And all the circumcised believers who had come with Peter were amazed, because the gift of the Holy Spirit had been POURED OUT upon the Gentiles also, for they were hearing them speaking with tongues and exalting God.* Acts 10:44-46

He poured it out on the Gentiles, but He didn't stop pouring. We read in Acts 9 where Paul, who was on his way to persecute Christians, had an encounter with the Lord. A light from heaven blinded him. He went to Damascus to Straight Street where Ananias laid hands on him, and Jesus poured that same New Wine of the Holy Spirit on Paul. He poured it out on Paul, but He didn't stop pouring. When Paul was at Ephesus, we have a first-hand account that the Lord was still pouring.

> *And when Paul had laid his hands upon them, the Holy*
> *Spirit came on them, and they began speaking with tongues*
> *and prophesying.* Acts 19:6

Throughout the Centuries

We have documented accounts throughout the ages of many who have received the New Wine of the Holy Spirit after Pentecost. It would be impossible to write all their names in this book, but I want to share a list of some of the saints from each century who received the baptism of the Holy Spirit and were used by God to pour out His Spirit on the nations.

In the first century, around 96 A.D., He poured out His Spirit on Clement, bishop of Rome. He was still pouring. In the Second Century A. D., He poured out His Spirit on Irenaeus of Lyon who was used by God to pour out His Spirit in his Gallic church. He was still pouring. In the third century, He poured out His Spirit on Origen of Alexandria. He was still pouring. In the fourth, fifth, sixth, seventh and eighth centuries A. D., the Messalians, practiced the laying on of hands for the baptism of the Holy Spirit. He was still pouring.

In the tenth and eleventh Centuries A. D. (949-1022) the famous eastern charismatic Christian Symeon, received the baptism of the Holy Spirit, and many received the baptism of the Holy Spirit under his ministry. He was still pouring. In the twelfth, thirteenth, fourteenth, and fifteenth centuries, A. D., Hildegard of Bingen, Gregory Palamas, Francis of Assisi, and Vincent Ferrer along with others were reported to have been baptized by the Holy Spirit and experienced the gifts of the Spirit. They had a significant impact on the medieval church. He was still pouring.

In the sixteenth century A. D., Catholic reformer Thomas Muntzer experienced and preached the necessity of the baptism of the Holy Spirit. He was still pouring. In the seventeenth century among many others, He poured out His Spirit on a French group known as the Camisards, as well as a group in the Roman Catholic Church who became known as the Jansenists. He was still pouring. In the eighteenth century He poured out His Spirit on Seraphim of Sarov, a Russian Orthodox leader. He was still pouring.

In the nineteenth century among many others He poured out His Spirit on A. B. Simpson, D. L. Moody, and Charles Finney. Charles was used by God in what was called the Second Awakening. Charles said he experienced "a mighty baptism of the Holy Ghost which was like a wave of electricity going through and through me...seemed to come in waves of liquid love."

When D. L. Moody described the day He was filled with the Holy Spirit in 1872, he said, "One day, in the city of New York, oh what a day. I cannot describe it. I seldom refer to it. It is almost too sacred an experience to name. I can only say that God revealed Himself to me, and I had such an experience of His love that I had to ask Him to stay His hand." He was still pouring. In 1901, Charles Parham received the baptism of the Holy Spirit in Topeka, Kansas. In 1906 in Los Angeles, California the Holy Ghost was poured out on William Seymore. He was still pouring.

In the twentieth century He also poured out His Spirit on Smith Wigglesworth, A.W. Tozer and John G. Lake. They were all saturated with the New Wine of the Holy Spirit. He was still pouring. In 1960, Father Dennis Bennett, rector of the Episcopal Church of Van Nuys, California, was baptized in the Spirit. He was still pouring. The good news is He doesn't just pour out His Spirit on famous preachers. He will pour out His Spirit on any Christian who wants to be filled.

In 1973 I got on my knees and found out He was still pouring. Since 1973, I have seen thousands who can testify that He is still pouring. In the twenty-first century, 2012, my eighty-six-year-old mother was baptized in the Spirit and spoke in tongues. He was still pouring. It has been reported that there are more than five hundred million Christians today who have been baptized by Jesus with the Holy Ghost and fire, and the exciting news is He hasn't stopped pouring. He is still pouring this very day.

Belly Up to the Bar

Are you thirsty? If you are, it may be time to belly up to the bar and ask the Lord to baptize you with the New Wine of His Spirit. The Lord wants to pour out His Spirit on you. He wants to saturate your eyes so you can see Him in the realm of the Spirit like you have never seen Him before. He wants to saturate your mind so you can spend more time thinking about Him. He wants to saturate your ears so you can hear His voice with greater clarity through the many ways He speaks. He wants to saturate your heart, intoxicate you with fresh revelations of His love, and bring you to the place of being "lovesick."

The first leg of the journey to the place of becoming lovesick always begins with DESIRE. Without desire we will never get there. If we allow desire to have its way, He may take us to a turn in the road called DESPERATION. We come to the place of desperation when we realize we are empty, and nothing else but Jesus will satisfy our souls.

Desperation will not allow us to sit back in a place of passivity but will lead to the place of taking action. It will lead us to the place of running after Him. It will lead us to the place of asking.

Asking will allow Him to take us into His chambers. It is easy to get into His chambers, but even though the next leg of the journey is easy, too, you may need to do a little pressing. You may have to press past those who will tell you that there is nothing more. You may have to press past the established way of doing things; you may even have to press past friends or family, but don't give up. Don't let anyone talk you out of it. The pressing will be worth it.

You see, the King's Banqueting House is waiting for you. The New Wine of the Holy Spirit is waiting for you, and as it was for the Shulamite of old, finding yourself in the wonderful, thrilling place of being forever lovesick is waiting for you!

We Love Being Saturated by You

Lord, we know You have been very busy pouring out Your Spirit on Your bride. Thank you for showering us, not only with Your love, but with the fruit of Your Spirit and the power to be Your witnesses, but also with Your precious gifts. Don't stop pouring, Lord. We love being saturated by You.

Your Love
Your Spirit
Your Power
Your Gifts

4

Beauty Secrets

*How beautiful you are my darling, how beautiful you
are!*   SOS 4:1

*Then your fame went forth among the nations on account
of your BEAUTY, for it was perfect, because of MY GLORY
AND MY SPLENDOR which I bestowed on you!*
                                                    Ezekiel 16:14

In Song of Solomon, the king didn't tell his bride that she was beautiful just one time. He told her that she was beautiful ten times. He told her over, and over, and over. The exciting reality is—that is exactly how the Lord sees us. When He looks at all of us who have been born again He sees beauty. That is so hard for many of us to believe because most of us don't see ourselves the way the Lord sees us. In fact, most of us see ourselves the same way the Shulamite saw herself.

> *I am black, but lovely...*   Song of Songs 1:5

Like the Shulamite, many Christians believe there is a part of us that is lovely because the lovely One lives inside of us, but we live our lives always conscious of the fact that there is a part of us that is black. There is a part of us that believes the lie that says when Jesus looks at us all He can see is our sins, our failures, and our shortcomings. There is a part of us that feels like we never live up to all we think the Lord expects us to do.

Many of us have fallen into this trap and tend to hide from the presence of the Lord, thinking He is always disappointed in us. I have discovered from the Word that nothing could be further from the truth. When He looks at all of us who have been born again, He sees the blood. His blood is the heavenly beauty product that has erased all our sins. It is the divine liquid cleanser that wipes away all the sins that we have ever committed in the past, all the sins that we will commit today, and all the sins that we will ever commit in the future.

His blood is all we will ever need to make us beautiful in His eyes. There is not a sin that has ever been committed that the blood of Jesus can't wipe away from us as far as the east is from the west. We don't need anything except the blood of Jesus that He shed on Calvary to make us beautiful in His eyes.

Many people think how the Lord sees us is based on what we do or what we don't do, but our beauty isn't based on our performance—it is based on His performance on the cross when He willingly allowed His precious blood to flow from His sinless veins. We don't need His blood plus good works to be more beautiful in His eyes. We don't need His blood plus reading our Bible every day to be more beautiful to the Lord. We don't need His blood plus witnessing every day to be more beautiful to the Lord. We don't need His blood plus praying every day to make us more beautiful in the eyes of the Lord. We don't even need His blood plus giving all our money to the Lord to be more beautiful in His eyes. We only need one thing to be beautiful in the eyes of the Lord, the wonder-working power of His blood.

The most exciting news about His blood is that it is free to all who will receive it. It is a gift. How do we receive the blood? The Word is very clear. To receive all the benefits of His blood all we have to do is repent, ask the Lord to forgive us of our sins, and come into our lives to be our Lord and Savior, believing all the while in the power of His death on the cross when He chose to shed His blood in our place for our sins.

The moment we ask, He applies the blood, and all we need is one application. It lasts for a lifetime. I know — it sounds too good to be true, but it is! When He looks at us, He sees the beauty of His blood. If you are a believer, He has applied the blood and there is nothing more you can ever do to make yourself more beautiful in the eyes of the Lord than you are this very minute.

The Atmosphere was Pregnant with His Presence

Several years ago, I got a call early one morning from a friend telling me she was at the home of another friend of mine who was crying inconsolably because in her mind there were sins she had committed in the past for which God couldn't possibly forgive her. She was sure those sins were standing between her and her ability to have a close relationship with the Lord.

I got my boys off to school and drove directly to her home only to find her in a very bad way. She was curled up in a ball on her dining room floor. She was not just crying — she was wailing. She was an awesome Christian, but somehow the devil had filled her head with lies that day. She was crying so loud we couldn't even talk to her. She couldn't stop. We didn't have any idea what to do, but we did know that if the Lord didn't show up, she was in big trouble.

As I anguished over her situation, calling out to the Lord, I heard Him say, "She doesn't understand the power of My blood." I had no idea how to get that across to her, because she was in no condition to listen and to tell you the truth, I didn't fully understand the power of His blood either.

Again I heard the voice of the Lord say, "Go to her closet." When I got to the closet that she and her husband shared, my eyes were riveted by a red robe. He said, "Cover her in that red robe." I grabbed it and ran into the dining room where she was lying on the floor screaming. When I threw the robe on her, I made sure that it covered her completely, that nothing was sticking out; nothing was exposed. Every part of her body was covered by that red robe, but I also knew there was no power in that cotton robe that could help her. The Lord was the only One who could do it.

At the same time the robe fell over her, the most amazing thing happened. The atmosphere was suddenly pregnant with the presence of the Lord. As I walked a few feet to the entry way, the glory of the presence of the Lord was so strong that I fell on my knees. As I fell, I saw my other friend falling over by the staircase. She was engulfed by His presence, too.

I was reminded of the priests of old who couldn't stand when the glory of the Lord was filling the temple in 1 Kings 8: 10-11, *"And it came to pass, when the priests were come out of the holy place, that the cloud filled the house of the Lord, so that the priests could not stand to minister because of the cloud: for the glory of the Lord had filled the house of the Lord."* The only thing I was conscious of was the presence of the Lord in that room.

I laid down on the floor and began to just bask in His presence. He was not only there for my friend who was distraught, He was there for us, too. I remember coming to the realization I was being consumed with the revelation of His presence. I don't know how long we all laid on that floor, but after what seemed to be quite a while, I heard a sound coming from beneath the robe.

I listened intently only to hear my friend singing on old familiar hymn in a soft, calm, beautiful voice:

What can wash away my sins
Nothing but the blood of Jesus

What can make me whole again?
Nothing, but the blood of Jesus

Oh, precious is the flow
That makes me white as snow

No other fount I know
Nothing but the blood of Jesus

As she began to sing, I knew from the sound of her voice that the Lord had used the robe as a spiritual picture to show her the truth that she was covered in His blood, and she not only saw it, but the truth had exploded in her spirit. After she sang it once, she began to sing it again, only this time it sounded even sweeter; and then again, even sweeter.

After singing that song several times she got up, walked over to me and covered me with the same red robe. The sensation was overwhelming. As I laid under that robe I could feel the Lord ministering to me. I realized when He looked at me all He saw was His blood. I began to sing with my friend and the words to that song took on a greater meaning than they ever had before. We then took the robe and covered our other friend by the stairs.

The red robe that covered all us was such a huge spiritual picture. If you looked at all of us when we were under that robe, you couldn't see any flesh—all you could see was the color of the blood.

Blessed are they whose transgressions are forgiven, whose sins are COVERED. Blessed is the one whose sin the Lord will never count against them. Romans 4:7-8

I have heard it said, "A picture is worth a thousand words," and on that day we discovered those words to be true. The revelation that our sins were covered by His blood bypassed our brains and saturated our souls. The Holy Spirit took us to a deeper level of revelation about the blood than we had ever been before. Oh, the power of His blood.

Later, my friend told me that the robe belonged to her husband and had been given to him by her father. Wow. I thought about our spiritual husband, the Lord Jesus Christ, and how His father had sent Him to the earth to shed His blood so our sins could be covered with it. I will treasure that day forever, because on that day we were all overwhelmed with the divine revelation of His blood.

Today we all know an amazing beauty secret, not just in our heads but with every fiber of our being. We know from a divine encounter that there is an amazing wonder-working power in the blood that removes the darkness in us and makes us "beautiful" in the eyes of the Lord.

We Will Dream Dreams

There was a time in my life when I didn't see myself the way the Lord saw me. Like so many in the body of Christ, I had a poor self-image. Somewhere on the inside of me was an undercurrent that ran deep telling me that I wasn't as good as other people. I never felt like I measured up.

An adult who was a distant member of my family didn't help the way I saw myself. She enjoyed making fun of me. I always dreaded to see her coming because I hated to hear what she was going to say. I can still hear her voice in my head criticizing my hair, or my clothes, or laughing at something she didn't like about me.

I can also remember standing in a line at a store as a young girl, and when someone would stand behind me, I went to the back the line. I didn't think I was good enough to stand in line in front of anyone else. I know that sounds ridiculous, but it is true.

I also remember a time in the ninth grade when my self-image was sealed. I lived in Fort Worth for the first fourteen years of my life, but when I was fifteen my father built a new house in Euless, Texas, where I entered into Hurst Junior High School. I can still remember the feelings of loneliness that accompanied me as I walked down the halls and sat in the classrooms surrounded by my new classmates. I didn't have one friend.

Just like in my previous school, the kids in my new school were very comfortable in the groups they had formed over years of being together. The worst time for me was lunchtime. Everyone sat with their friends, laughing and talking, and I didn't have anyone to sit with.

I realize now my lack of friends was my fault because I was shy and didn't know how to make friends. Day after day for nine months I would agonize over the approaching noon hour. I would go through the line to get my lunch and scan the lunchroom to see where I would sit. In hindsight, I am sure I could have sat down by someone and started a conversation, but the truth is I didn't think anyone would want to talk to me so I sat by myself, longing for that thirty minutes of agony to be over.

In high school I made some wonderful friends, but always in my heart of hearts I felt I didn't measure up. Even though I never felt like I was important as I walked through life, it never occurred to me to examine why I felt that way. After I was grown and had been baptized in the Spirit, the Lord spoke to me one night through a dream.

We see throughout the bible that God has spoken to many of His saints through dreams. In the book of Daniel, Nebuchadnezzar had a dream from the Lord, and God used Daniel to interpret the dream.

> *The king answered and said to Daniel, whose name was Belteshazzar, "Are you able to make known to me the dream which I have seen and its interpretation?" Daniel answered before the king and said, "As for the mystery about which the king has inquired, neither wise men, conjurers, magicians, nor diviners are able to declare it to the king. However, there is a God in heaven who reveals secrets...*
> Daniel 2: 26-28

In the first part of my dream from the Lord, I was driving down the road in a car but I wasn't alone. In the back seat of the car was a gigantic big blob of green slimy substance that looked like (I hope you are not eating) snot. It completely filled the back seat. As I drove down the road the green slime fell out of the car. When it fell out, I stopped the car, got out, and with every ounce of strength I had, picked it up and put it back in the car with me.

In the second part of the dream, I was outside the home of one of the girls that had been in junior high and high school with me. She invited me into her home, and when I came in she asked me to sit down at her kitchen table, which was rectangular in shape just like the tables I had sat at in Junior High School. I was excited to visit with her until I realized she wasn't going to sit with me. I had an overwhelming feeling of sadness because she left me sitting there all alone just like when we were in school. She didn't look at me or talk to me, but ignored me as if I weren't even in the room.

For some reason, in the dream I pulled out a checkbook to write a check. I wrote the tiniest "v" that I could write, followed by the tiniest "a." In the dream I could barely see the letters because they were so small. That is how I felt, very small. After I wrote those two letters I ripped the check out of the checkbook, and on a new check I wrote the same two tiny letters again, the little "v" and the little "a."

I would write and rip, write and rip, only to find myself repeating this same process over, and over, and over. You know how dreams are. It seemed like what I was experiencing would never end. I had no idea what word I was trying to write, but I did know whatever it was, I couldn't write it.

In the last part of the dream, I walked into a different room where a woman was seated at a different rectangular table. She faced me, and sitting across from her was a man whose back was turned toward me; I couldn't see his face. I am sure you have seen men and women who have their hair in braids all over their heads. Some people call them corn rows, and this woman's head was covered with them.

As I looked at her I was aware of an atmosphere of royalty that surrounded her. I could see she knew she was a person of worth. It wasn't a haughty thing as if she thought she was so much better than me, but in my dream I knew she was confident because she knew who she was. As I looked into her eyes, I could see she was staring into the eyes of the man that sat across from her. Her eyes were fixed. She never took her eyes off of Him.

I walked around the table and stood behind her, and I instantly realized that the man she was staring at was Jesus. He was looking into her eyes just as intently as she was looking into His eyes. There was so much love in His eyes. As I looked into His eyes more closely, I could see what she saw. She was looking at a reflection of herself in His eyes. She was seeing herself through His eyes.

In my dream, I saw the reason she knew she was important. It was because she could see herself the way He saw her. Suddenly, as I looked into His eyes, it was as if the blinders were taken off and I realized that the woman He was looking at, the one seated at the table, was me. When I woke up from my dream, I knew it was a dream from the Lord but I had no idea what it meant.

Later, the Lord spoke to me and gave me the interpretation of the dream. He started talking to me about the second scene in the dream, where I was sitting at the table being ignored. He said, "Jenny, in the dream, when were you sitting at the first table, you were ignored just like you were ignored in the ninth grade. The word that you were trying to write was 'valuable,' but you couldn't write it. No matter how many times you tried, you couldn't write it. The reason you couldn't write it was because you don't feel valuable. That is how you have always felt, but you are wrong."

He added that the woman seated at the second table was a picture of how He saw me. He then asked me a question, "Jenny, what is a braid?" I answered by saying "Lord, you make a braid by taking three groups of hair and wind them around each other until they become one. The Lord then asked, "Who is the Three in One?" I answered, "Lord, it is You. You are the three in One."

He continued, "I want you to know that I have anointed you with My presence. My roots go down deep in you, and I don't want you to ever again doubt the fact that you are valuable. In the past, you have looked at yourself through your own eyes and the eyes of others, and as a result, you didn't feel valuable. Never do that again. If you want to know how valuable you are, you have to look at yourself through My eyes. I want you to see yourself the way I see you, and when you do you will never again doubt the fact that you are valuable."

He then interpreted the first scene of the dream, saying, "The huge green ball of slime is a picture of the man-pleasing spirit you have carried around with you for years. The reason you have never wanted to get rid of it is because you wanted to please the men and women of the world so they would accept you. If you will get into My Word and read what I have written about you, you will see yourself the way I see you, and when you see yourself the way I see you, you will gladly let that man-pleasing spirit go. You will realize you don't need it anymore. When you see yourself through My eyes the opinions of the world won't matter to you."

Wow! He wanted me to see myself the way He saw me. I decided to go to the Word and write down every verse that described how He saw me on three-by-five cards. I then took those cards with me everywhere I went. When I was putting on my make-up I would memorize the verses. When I was driving down the road I would memorize verses, reciting them out loud. When I cleaned my house I kept them in my pocket, rehearsing each verse over and over. I memorized every verse I could find in the Bible that told me how He saw me. What actually happened is I ate what He said about me.

Your words were found and I ate them.   Jeremiah 15:16a

I not only chewed on each verse but I swallowed them, allowing my spiritual body to absorb truth into my system. In the middle of my adventure through the Word I began to realize that the power of His Word was doing a great work. Each verse was changing the way I saw myself.

After a few months, I decided that the easiest way to remember some of the things He said about me was to take the main word in each verse and alphabetize them. The words could then trigger the verse, and I could just pull the truth up in my mind and recite what He said about me wherever I happened to be without anyone being aware of what I was doing. Sometimes I would even recite the truth of the verses, by saying them back to the Lord in my prayers.

I always started with the As:

Thank You, Lord, that I am so valuable that I am the Apple of Your eye.

Thank You, Lord, that I have not been rejected, but I have been Accepted.

Thank You, Lord, that I am so valuable that You made me Your Ambassador.

Thank You I am so valuable that You have assigned Your Angels to watch over me.

Thank You, Lord, I am so valuable You have given me Authority over all the power of the enemy.

Then I would go through the Bs:

Thank You, Lord, that You made me Your Bride.

Thank You that I am so valuable You Bought me, paying a great price.

Thank You, Lord, that Your Beauty and Your splendor lives inside me.

Thank You, Lord, for taking my life and turning it around, giving me Beauty for ashes.

Then the Cs:

Thank You, Lord, that I am so valuable that You Called me to be Yours.

Thank You for Choosing me.

Thank You for Changing me.

Thank You, Lord, that I am Complete in You.

Thank You, Lord, for Creating me for Your pleasure and taking great pleasure in me.

Next, the Ds.

Thank You, Lord, for Delighting in me.

Thank You that I am Your heart's Desire.

Thank You for Delivering me.

And on through the alphabet:

Thank You, Lord, for Enduing me with power from on high.

Thank You, Lord, that I am so valuable that You allowed me to Escape the corruption that is in the world.

Thank You that I am so valuable You have Edified me.

Thank You for Enlightening me.

Thank You for Forgiving me.

Thank You, Lord, that I am so valuable to You that You set me Free.

Thank You that I am so valuable that You, the Great One, the One who is greater than he that is in the world, have chosen to live in me.

Thank You, Lord, that I am so valuable You have given me Gifts.

Thank You, Lord, that I am the Head and not the tail.

Thank You that I don't have to stand at the back of the line anymore.

Thank You that by Your stripes I have been Healed.

Thank You that I am so valuable that You sent Your Spirit to live In me, and You placed me in You.

Thank You for letting me know that I am so valuable that Your Father, the creator of the universe, chose to give me to You for Your Inheritance.

Thank You for telling me I am so valuable I am a Jewel in Your crown.

Thank You for Justifying me.

Thank You that I am so valuable that I am Kept by Your power.

Thank You, Lord, for letting me know that I am Loved by You.

Thank You for Lifting me out of the miry clay and setting my feet on the Rock.

Wow, Lord, Thank You, that I am not just a conqueror—I am More than a conqueror.

Thank You that I have the Mind of Christ.

Thank You that I am so valuable You have given me a New Name.

Thank You, Lord, that I am a New creature.

Thank You, Lord, for making me an Overcomer.

Thank You that I am so valuable that You made me a Partaker of Your divine nature.

Thank You, Lord, for making me a Priest in Your kingdom.

Thank You that I am so valuable You have made Plans for my life.

Thank You, Lord, for being so wild about me that You Rejoice over me with singing.

Thank You for bringing me to the place of Royalty by making me part of Your royal family.

Thank You that I am so valuable that You chose to Redeem me.

Thank You for Strengthening me by Your Spirit in my inner man.

Thank You for telling me that I am a Saint.

Thank You that I am so valuable You Sealed me with Your Spirit.

Thank You for giving me a Sound mind.

Thank You that I am so valuable that You are taking the time to Transform me into Your image.

Thank You that I am so valuable that You Think about me all the time.

Thank You for letting me know that I am not useless but I am Useful to You.

Thank You for making me a Vessel of honor.

Thank You for making me Your Wife.

Thank You for letting me know that I am not a piece of junk, but I am Your Workmanship, the workmanship of the One who created the universe.

I was always sad that I couldn't find anything about the letter "x" until one day He told me that there was no "x" because I was not His "x," and I would never be His "x." He was never going to leave me or forsake me.

Since that day when I thank the Lord I always say:

Thank You, Lord, that I am not an X, and I will never be an X.

Thank You, Lord, that I am Yours and You are mine.

Thank You, Lord, for making me Zealous for You, even as You are Zealous for me.

Every time I rehearsed what the Lord said about me by reciting the verses from the word, the fact that I was valuable became stronger and stronger in my mind. Paul writes in Romans:

> *Do not conform to the pattern of this world, but be transformed by the renewing of your mind…"*   Romans 12:2a

That is exactly what happened to me. The way I saw myself was transformed by the Word. I replaced the lies that had flooded my life with the truth, and it not only changed me, but it dealt a death blow to that huge, green blob of slime that the Lord called a man-pleasing spirit.

I now see myself the way He sees me. It thrills me to know when He looks at me I don't have to worry anymore. I know without a shadow of a doubt that I am beautiful in His eyes. I know now that I am valuable. I can not only write the word "valuable" now—I can write it as many times as I want to. I can even say it out loud.

The truth that I am beautiful in His eyes has always made my heart skip a beat. Instead of running away from Him, I now run into Him every time I think about how much He loves me. If for any reason you need to see yourself the way He sees you, I have included some of the verses the Lord used to change me at the end of this chapter. If you choose to eat them, I pray you will enjoy the rich meat that He has so eloquently provided on the banqueting table of His Word.

We are His Inheritance

Of all the scriptures I memorized, the one that surprised me the most, the one that melted my heart was in the first chapter of Ephesians:

I pray that the eyes of your heart may be enlightened, so
that you will know what is the hope of His calling, what are
the riches of the glory of His inheritance in the saints, and
what is the surpassing greatness of His power toward us
who believe.   Ephesians 1: 18-19

Wow! When I read that verse, I did a double take. Oh, my heart. I realized that the saints, which include every one of us who have put our faith and trust in Jesus, are His inheritance. It blew my mind to see I was so valuable to the Lord that I was part of His inheritance.

I once heard Mike Bickle preach a sermon about the fact that we are the Lord's inheritance. He told us to use our imaginations and go back through the portals of time and think of the Father and the Son sitting together side-by-side, with the Son sitting at the Father's right hand. He told us to imagine they were just having a talk, communing with One another.

He said the conversation could have gone something like this: The Father says, "Son, I have something I want to give You. I want to give You a special inheritance." The Son (remember we are just imagining) might have wondered, "What is it that My Father who created the sun, the moon, the stars, and over one hundred billion galaxies in the universe wants to give Me for an inheritance? Earthly fathers give their sons money, houses, cars, and mansions, but what does He want to give Me?"

We all know the answer to that question. His Father gave Him the one thing He truly wanted. He gave Him our hearts. From the very beginning, God had a plan. He knew when we found out that it was His love for us that caused Jesus to willingly go to the cross to shed His sinless blood that He would win our love. He left His Father's side for one reason—He was coming after us. He was coming after His bride. He was coming after His inheritance.

On His last trip from Galilee to Jerusalem, Jesus knew His time had come. He knew what was waiting for Him, yet the Word tells us He set His face to go to Jerusalem. There was no turning back. He was coming after His inheritance. He was coming after you. He was coming after me, and nothing could have stopped Him. He could have called ten thousand angels, and they would have rescued Him from the cross, but He didn't do that. He was on a mission to rescue us. He wanted to rescue His bride from the penalty of sin so we could live with Him forever. He was on a mission to capture our hearts. Hebrews 12 says:

> *Looking unto Jesus, the author and finisher of our faith;*
> *who for the joy that was set before Him endured the cross,*
> *despising the shame, and is set down at the right hand of*
> *the throne of God.* Hebrews 12:2

What was the joy that was set before Him? I think it was you. I think it was me. As they slashed His back open with a whip thirty-nine times, put the crown of thorns on His head, mocked him, spit in His face, drove the nails through His hands and feet, nailing Him to the cross, took a sword and ran it into His side, we were on His mind. We were the joy set before Him.

I know it must have been more than any man has ever suffered as God placed on Him the sins of the world, but I also wonder as His body pulsated with pain, if the pain He endured might have paled in comparison to His great love for you and His great love for me. We are the inheritance that the Lord Jesus Christ longed for. We are His heart's desire, and it was at Calvary that He won our hearts.

> *I am my beloved's, and his desire is toward me.*
> Song of Solomon 7:10

The Alphabet Song

One day after going through the alphabet for years reciting how the Lord saw me, I heard a tune in my mind to a song that I had learned when I was a young girl. I loved that old song and decided to sing it to the Lord using the same tune but changing the words to make them say what I wanted to say to Him. The song is called the "Alphabet Song." It was written in 1948. I began with the letter "a," singing each letter and then the corresponding words:

A   I Adore You,

B   You are Beautiful,

C   You're the Captain of the Host.

D   You're my Darling, and

E   You're Exciting, and

F   You're the Friend I love the most.

G   You're so Good to me.

H   You are Heavenly.

I   You're the One I Idolize,

J   We're like Jack and Jill,

K   You're so Kind to me.

L   You're the One I love the Most.

MNOP   I could go on all day,

QRST   Alphabetically speaking, You're the WAY.

U   Make my life complete,

V   You make life Very sweet,

WXYZ   I love to wander through the alphabet with You and tell You what You mean to me.

When I finished singing to Him, I heard the Lord repeat the same last seventeen words back to me that I had just sung to Him. He said, "I love to wander through the alphabet with you and tell you what you mean to Me." There was silence as I felt a lump rise up in my throat.

I suddenly knew what He was talking about. I remembered all the years I had used the alphabet to rehearse the things He said about me. At that moment I realized that, as I had been wandering through the alphabet over and over, I had not been wandering alone. He had been wandering through it with me. I am so grateful that I not only found His words, but I ate them and the power of those words changed the way I saw myself.

Later, I wandered through the alphabet one last time, taking time to share with Him how I saw Him through a poem. As I came to the end of my words I realized His beauty is beyond description. There is a German word, *grenzbegriff*, that describes exactly how I felt. It means "that which is real but beyond analysis and description." That is a great word to use when I try to describe Jesus. He is real, but there are no words to adequately describe Him. He is too marvelous for words.

Beyond Description

You're the Amazing One, The Awesome One, and, yes,
You are Astounding
You're the Author and finisher of my faith, oh such love Abounding

You're the Beautiful One, my Bridegroom,
You're Brilliance Beyond Belief
You're the Beloved One, the Breathtaking One, The One I do Beseech

You're my Captivating Conqueror, The Captain of the host
You're my Champion, My Creator, the One I love the most

You're the Delightful One, Delectable, oh so Deep, Divine
You Are my Dazzling Dwelling place, Desire oh so sublime

You're Everlasting to Everlasting, Exciting Ecstasy Elevates
You are my Exhilarating *El Shaddai*, my all-Consuming Consummate

You're the Fabulous One, the Fantastic One,
Your presence oh so Freeing
You're my Faithful Friend Forever, Fathomless
Fragrance never Fleeting

You're the Glorious One, the Glistening One,
Grand in all Your Grandeur
You're the Holy Ghost, the Great I Am, Garnished with
heaven's splendor

You're my Heart's desire, my Hiding place, my Happiness supreme
You're Heaven's Hound, I honor You, my Husband, we're a team

You're Intoxicating, Invigorating, and yes, my King Indwelling
You're Infinite, Indescribable, oh such joy, I'm telling

You're *Jehovah Jireh*, my Provider, *Jehovah Nissi* and *Shammah* too
You're *Jehovah Shalom*, my Prince of Peace, *Jehovah*, I Love You

You're the all-Knowing One, so Knowable, I want to Know You more
You're my King of Kings, Keeper of my soul,
You make my Knower soar

You're the Lovely One, so Limitless, such Love, so Large, so Lavish
You're the Liberating Lord of Lords, came Lowly, became Lambish

You're the Marvelous One, the Magnificent One, Melchizedek so grand,
You're the Majestic One, Messiah, I love Your nail-scarred hands

You have the Name above all Names, oh That Name so thrilling

You made something out of Nothing, oh such power, it's chilling

You're Omnipresent, Omnipotent, Omniscient three in One
You are Overwhelming love divine, the Father's only Son

You're the Perfect One, all Powerful, and my Prince of Peace
You're my Patient One, my Portion, Protection will never cease

You're my Radiant Reason for living, Refresher of my soul
You're my River of Revelation, my Redeemer who makes me whole

You're my Stimulating Strong tower, You're all my Streams of joy
You are Splendidly, Spectacular, Your Word You do deploy

You're my Treasure, You are Timeless, I pay Tribute to my King
You're my Teacher, You are Thrilling, Your presence makes me sing

You're Unforgettable, Unfathomable, Unequaled, that's what You are
You're Unlimited, Unimaginable, my Unspeakable daystar

You're So Vibrant in Your beauty, Vigilant, Vigorous in Your love
You're Vital, so Victorious, Your Voice resonates from above

You're my Wise all-Wonderful Warm place, my Well-being You insure
You're my living Water Wetting me, Washing over What needs cure

I am Yours, and You are mine, Yesterday, today, and forever
We meet together all the time, rendezvousing in the river

You are Zealous for my Love, as I am Zealous for Yours
I am Zealous for love divine, Your Zealous love does lure

The Thrill of the Rainbow

It is a wonderful thing to consume the Word of God because it has the power to change us, but let's be honest, all of us have gone through periods in our lives where we just don't want to be in the Word. We don't want to read it, let alone eat it because it sometimes seems so dry, so hard to swallow.

That was exactly how I felt during the months leading up to May 17, 1995. On that date something amazing happened that changed the way I looked at the Word forever. I was in my car driving east on I-30 heading from the DFW area to a revival meeting in Tyler, Texas. Beverly Sheasby and Margo Mills were riding with me. They can both testify that what I am about to tell you is true.

As I drove, I noticed some people pulling off to the side of the road while some were stopping under overpasses. I was so focused on all the fun we were having inside the car I didn't pay much attention to what was going on outside. Suddenly I saw the most shocking sight. The end of a rainbow was in the lane to the left of my car directly in front of me. I couldn't believe it. For a moment I thought I was seeing things, but everyone in the car was seeing it too.

I am sure you can guess what I did. I immediately changed lanes. If my window had been down, I could have reached out and put my hand right through it. Finding ourselves inside the end of the rainbow, we all began to shout and laugh and scream as the full spectrum of colors—red, yellow, blue, green—engulfed us. You can Google, "end of the rainbow picture Jason Erdkamp" to see an actual picture of a car inside the end of a rainbow just like we were. He took the photo while traveling down the highway in southern California.

The picture shows exactly what happened to us. It was a once-in-a-lifetime experience, one that we will never forget. After our time in the rainbow, we drove on to the revival only to find out that some of the people who knew we were coming were worried about us because tornadoes had been touching down all around the road we had been traveling on. We had been in danger and didn't even know it.

Later that night the Lord spoke to me. He said, "If you had stayed in the lane you were in and had not changed lanes, you would have reached your destination, but you would have missed the thrill of a lifetime. I want you to know you can stay in the lane you are in and you will reach Me. You will still make it to heaven, but if you will change lanes and get back into My Word like you got into that rainbow there will be times when you are so overcome with revelation you will scream out loud at the beauty of My Word just like you did in that rainbow."

Guess what I did. I changed lanes and got back into His Word only to discover over the years that He was right. There are times when He speaks to me through His Word that I just can't contain myself. I sometimes scream and laugh out loud just like I did in that rainbow because of the thrill of the revelation of His Word. I also discovered on that stormy day in May that there wasn't a pot of gold at the end of the rainbow, but even better than a pot of gold was a Word from the Lord to me.

Today, when I see the beauty of a rainbow it always reminds me of the beauty of His promises to me in His Word. If you are at a place in your life where the Word seems dry and hard to swallow, let me encourage you to change lanes and get back into the Word with a secret from Song of Songs 5:1. In this verse, the King says,

> *Eat oh friends and drink deeply oh lovers.*
> Song of Solomon 5:1

I have learned to never eat the Word of God without drinking deeply from the streams of His Spirit. In other words, when I open the Word I ask the Holy Spirit to anoint my eyes giving me eyes to see and saturate my ears, anointing them with the ability to hear from Him as I read. Once I started eating and drinking, both at the same time, the Living Waters of His Spirit saw to it that the Word of the Lord was never dry again. Over the years I have learned, you can eat all day long, every day, and end up

being His friend, but if you will eat and drink deeply from the streams
of the Spirit you will end up being His lover.

The World Says You Are What You Eat

The world says we are what we eat. Nutritionists also tell us that in
order to be beautiful and look our best, it is very important to eat healthy
food instead of junk food. Just like the food we eat that comes from the
world nourishes and strengthens our physical man, the spiritual food we
eat goes to work to nourish and strengthen our spiritual man. When we
fail to eat properly our physical bodies don't function like they should.
We are left looking and feeling tired and lifeless.

We are told in order to look and feel our best we need to eat foods
like fresh fruits and vegetables because they are full of antioxidants that
not only nourish us but help our bodies fight cancer-causing free radicals.
Certain foods rich in vitamin C, like oranges, help maintain the collagen
in our skin which helps prevent wrinkles.

Bananas are a great food that contributes to the health of our bodies.
They are rich in potassium which helps prevent heart disease and bone
loss. We have all seen one of the most obvious results of bone loss, osteo-
porosis. Bananas also lower the risk of vision loss as we get older, helping
us to have better eyesight. When we eat good food like a banana, all the
nutrients that are in it become part of us, nourishing and strengthening
us, helping us be the best that we can be.

It is so important not to underestimate the power of what we eat
both physically and spiritually. The Word of God is powerful. As we
renew our minds by eating the Word of God we are allowing the nutrients
in the Word to get into us and do their work, fighting against the lies of
the enemy and transforming us into the image of the Lord Jesus Christ.
There is power in His Word, and when His words get into us, they have
the power to change our world as we know it. They have the power to
change our eyesight, allowing us to see things the way He sees them;
allowing us to see that in His eyes we are beautiful.

Variety is the Spice of Life

Several years ago, I heard a sermon from a CD that made a huge impact on my life. I can't remember the name of the preacher, but I want to share the exciting truths I learned from him. He talked about the three different diets the Children of Israel ate that were all spiritual pictures of the kinds of foods we absorb into our spiritual bodies today.

While the children of Israel were in slavery in Egypt, they ate the foods the Egyptians provided for them. While they were in the wilderness, they ate manna that came down from heaven, and when they entered into the promised land they ate the food that came from that land. I have eaten all three diets in my spiritual lifetime, and I can testify that two of the diets are a picture of what we need to eat for our spiritual wellbeing, but the diet they ate while in Egypt is a picture of the spiritual diet we need to avoid at all cost.

Junk Food, The Food of Bondage

When it comes to seeing ourselves the way the Lord sees us, we need to quit wasting our time eating anything that isn't good for us. Junk food harms our physical bodies, but spiritual junk food harms our spiritual bodies. Eating it robs us of time we could be spending eating the healthy food of God's Word.

What is spiritual junk food? It is the food of bondage. The children of Israel could tell us all about the place of bondage. When Joseph was a ruler in Egypt, he brought them to Egypt to survive the famine, but after he died a new leadership took over, and the children of Israel became slaves to the Egyptians. The food they ate during those years was the food of bondage. It did the same thing to them that eating the food of bondage does to us today.

The Bible tells us their diet consisted of lentils, garlic, and onions. Of course, we all know another word for lentils is beans, and we also know that beans, garlic, and onions all have one thing in common—when people eat them they stink. The Israelites in Egypt ate food that made them stink, and when we eat the spiritual food of bondage today, it makes us stink.

We all know some people we can be around for just a few minutes and tell by the aroma in the air what they have been eating because their spirit stinks. Their attitude stinks. The air around them is not pleasing. Why? They are feeding on the food of bondage. Christians who eat the food of bondage are the ones who are always eating offenses. They are always eating old, negative memories. They are eating the stuff that holds them in the place of captivity.

The Word of the Lord is very clear. If we don't forgive, if we keep eating offenses over and over, we give Satan an advantage, a foothold in our lives, and just like the Egyptians we end up in a place of bondage.

> *But one whom you forgive, I forgive also, for indeed what I have forgiven, if I have forgiven anything, I did it for your sakes in the presence of Christ, so that no advantage would be taken of us by Satan, for we are not ignorant of his schemes.*　　　　　2 Corinthians 2:11

> *Then Peter came up to Jesus and said, Lord, how many times may my brother sin against me and I forgive him and let it go? As many as up to seven times? Jesus answered him, I tell you, not up to seven times, but seventy times seven!*　　　　　Matt 18: 21-35

Jesus then went on to tell the parable about a man who owed a king 10,000 talents, but the king chose to forgive him his debt. Then that same man turned around and demanded a man who owed him 100 talents pay him. When the man couldn't pay, he refused to forgive him. He had him thrown into jail, the place of bondage where the torturers were turned loose on him. When the king found out what happened, he said:

*You contemptible and wicked attendant! I forgave and can-
celled all that debt of yours because you begged me to. And
should you not have had pity and mercy on your fellow
attendant, as I had pity and mercy on you? And in wrath
his master turned him over to the torturers (the jailers), till
he should pay all that he owed. So also shall My Heavenly
Father deal with every one of you if you do not freely forgive your brother from your heart his offences.*

Matt 18:32-35

Just as our King, the Lord Jesus Christ has forgiven us for all of our sins against Him, He expects us to forgive others for their sins against us. If we want to give Satan an advantage over us, we know what to do—refuse to forgive. If we refuse to forgive just as the attendant who was placed in jail, we end up in the same place, the place of bondage.

When we refuse to forgive we give Satan the right to torture us, and we all know what that feels like. Have you ever noticed when someone offends us and we refuse to forgive them, we eat that offence repeatedly rehearsing it in our minds over and over? Sometimes we even spit it out, telling ourselves we are going to quit eating it, only to scoop it up and start chewing on it again. We allow that offence to consume us.

When we are chewing on offences, the devil has us right where he wants us. When we are so busy eating things that are harmful to us, we don't take the time to eat the things that we should be eating. We don't usually realize it, but refusing to forgive has the same result on our spiritual bodies that drinking a bottle of poison has on our physical bodies. There are some things that make our spirits stink that we have to stop feeding on. We have to start doing what God has told us to do, which is forgive and stop eating the food of bondage.

In the natural lentils, onions, and garlic are three of my favorite foods, but I have tasted the food of bondage in the spiritual realm and I can tell you from firsthand experience, I don't like the bad taste that bitterness, anger, and unforgiveness leave in my mouth. I don't like the way they make me feel when I think about them, and I don't like how I smell when I am carrying them around. It is a stench in the nostrils of everyone who gets close to me. We need to quit wasting our time eating the junk food of unforgiveness.

Manna

On the other hand, there is a food all of us must eat on our way to our spiritual promised land that is good for us. When the children of Israel were wandering around in the wilderness they ate the food that God sent down from heaven. When they first saw it they didn't know what it was, so they called it *manna*, which in Hebrew means, "What is it?" They were uncertain about what it was, but they ate it anyway because they knew that it was from God.

There are times on our way to the promised land, for our own well-being we have to eat the bread of uncertainty. When we first get saved, we have to swallow a lot of things we are uncertain about. People tell us what we need to do, and if it is in the Word, we just do it even though we may not fully understand it. They tell us, "Now that you are saved, you need to get baptized in the baptismal waters." "What is it?" We are uncertain about it. We don't have a full understanding of it, but because we know God said to do it, we go ahead and do it anyway.

We go into the church services where everyone is singing their songs to the Lord. The Word tells us some of the songs they are singing are songs of praise and some of the songs are songs of worship. We have no idea what the difference is. We don't have a full understanding of what is going on. What is it?

We have no idea how much the Lord loves it when we praise Him. We have no idea that He leans in and inhabits our praise. In the beginning we usually have no idea that as we sing, we are ministering to Him with our songs. We don't understand everything. We are uncertain, but uncertain or not we jump in with everyone else and start singing, because the Word of the Lord tells us to do it. God will allow us to eat the bread of uncertainty while we are not yet convinced. We may not be sure about what we are doing, but if God said it that is good enough for us.

We can all look back over our lives and see how God kept us alive while He was leading us to the place of revelation. We need to thank Him for not letting us die in the wilderness. We need to thank Him for feeding us when we didn't even understand what we were eating. We need to thank Him that He fed us while He was walking us to a place that we didn't even know how to get to. If we will eat what God says is good for us, even when we don't understand it, it will keep us alive until we can make it to the place of revelation in the land of promise.

Food from the Promised Land

Another food that strengthens our spiritual bodies is the food of promise. We know when the children of Israel finally crossed over the Jordon into the promised land, the manna that fell down from heaven every day stopped. Room service was over, and they started eating the "food of promise." After being in the desert for forty years eating manna, the food in the promised land must have tasted amazingly wonderful. They had heard about it for years. They had thought about it for years, and when they finally got there I am sure no one had to coax them to start eating it. They ate the food in the promised land, and it strengthened them, enabling them to walk in the land, overcome their enemies, and claim their inheritance.

The best thing about the food in the promised land was that everything was fresh. They ate the fresh fruit. They drank the fresh wine. They feasted on the fresh honey. They drank the delicious fresh milk. They consumed the fresh oil from the olives. As they ate the fresh food, they ate their inheritance. They ate what God had promised them. They consumed it. They possessed it.

There comes a time in all of our lives when just like the Israelites, our breakthrough comes. Our time in the wilderness is over, and we enter into the realm of revelation. We arrive at that place when we step over into the land of promise and start feasting on the fresh revelation of all the promises that God has given us. Nothing can compare with fresh food from the promised land.

I want to share a secret that I learned years ago about the power of eating everything in the Word of God that is fresh. There is a difference in the truth of God and the revelation of God. Even though they are both full of power and truth, the written word, *logos*, is where God has been, but revelation, *rhema*, is where God is. Revelation is the divine food that is fresh, that speaks directly to us right where we are at a moment in time.

When I am reading a portion of the Word and it starts speaking to my spirit, I don't just read it. If it is fresh and alive in my spirit and God is speaking to me through it, I always eat it. I memorize it. When I get it into me, it strengthens my inner man. When I eat His words that are fresh and alive, they give me strength to start walking in everything God has promised me. The fresh food of promise gives me the strength to walk in my inheritance.

The food from the promised land gives me the strength to walk in the Spirit and walk in the place of hearing His voice with greater clarity. It gives me the strength to walk in the place where the gifts of His Spirit flow. The food of promise gives me the strength to walk in the place where fresh dreams and visions flow. When I stepped over into the promised land I was empowered by the food and finally came to the place where I stopped wandering around in the wilderness of my life. It gave me the strength to step over into the place of entering into His rest.

Just as the Israelites consumed the fresh oil, when the fresh Oil of His Spirit starts to surge through our spiritual veins, amazing transformations take place. New things happen. Just as the Israelites consumed the fresh fruit in the promise land, when we are filled with the fruit of the Spirit we begin to realize we aren't the same person we used to be, but best of all, after eating the promises of the Lord Jesus Christ, we begin to see ourselves the way He sees us.

You Are Beautiful

One night, as I was reading the Word, a passage, Ezekiel 16:8-14, jumped off the page and did high kicks. In the first sentence I read, *"I passed by you and saw that you were at a time for love."* I knew the background. I knew He spoke those words through Ezekiel to the nation of Israel, but that night as I read those words they came alive, and the Lord was speaking to me. He knew my heart. He knew what I needed. I was at a time for a fresh revelation of His love.

I was so overwhelmed, it honestly felt as though my heart would stop beating. He went on through all the verses talking directly to me, but when He came to verse 14, I was undone. *"And your fame went forth among the nations, on account of your beauty, for it was perfect because of My beauty and My splendor which I bestowed on you."* He then said, "Jenny, you are beautiful because I have bestowed My beauty on you."

Oh, my heart! It was in that very moment I understood one of the main reasons He saw me as beautiful. I saw one of the reasons He sees all of us as beautiful. Wow! We are beautiful because the "Beautiful One," the Lord Jesus Christ, has placed His beauty inside of each one of us!

> *Then your fame went forth among the nations on account of your BEAUTY, for it was perfect, because of MY GLORY AND MY SPLENDOR which I bestowed on you!*
> Ezekiel 16:14, NASB

How Our Bridegroom Sees Us

As the apple of His eye	Zechariah 2:8
As accepted in the beloved	Ephesians 1:6
As ambassadors for Christ	2 Corinthians 5:20
With angels in charge over us	Psalms 91:11
With authority over the enemy	Luke 10:19
As the bride of Christ	Revelations 21:9

As bought with a price	1 Corinthians 6:20
As beautiful in His eyes	Ezekiel 16:14
Covered with a banner of love	Song of Solomon 2:4
Receiving beauty for ashes	Isaiah 61:3
As created for His pleasure	Revelations 4:11
As called	2 Timothy 1:9
As chosen	Acts 9:15
As complete	Colossians 2:10
As changed by His Spirit	2 Corinthians 3:18
As a delight to Him	Isaiah 62:4
As desire by Him	Song of Solomon 7:10
As delivered	Colossians 1:13
As endued with power from Him	Luke 24:49
As enlightened	Ephesians 1:18
As escaped from corruption	2 Peter 1:4
As forgiven	1 John 2:12
As free	Galatians 5:1
With the great One living in us	1 John 4:4
As heirs	Titus 3:7
As the head and not the tail	Deuteronomy 28:13
As healed	1 Peter 2:24
As indwelt by His Spirit	2 Timothy 1:14
As His inheritance	Ephesians 1:18
As justified	Titus 3:7
As jewels	Malachi 3:17
As kept by the power of God	1 Peter 1:3-5
As loved by God	Romans 8:38-39

As lifted out of miry clay	Psalms 40:2
As more than a conqueror	Romans 8:37
With the mind of Christ	1 Corinthians 2:16
With new names	Revelations 2:17
A new creature	2 Corinthians 5:17
As overcomers	Revelations 12:11
As partakers of His divine nature	2 Peter 1:4
As priest	2 Peter 2:9
As having a plan for our lives	Jeremiah 29:11, NIV
With rejoicing and singing	Zephaniah 3:17, NIV
As royalty	1 Peter 2:9
As redeemed	Galatians 3:13-14
As strengthened	Ephesians 3:16
As saints	1 Corinthians 1:2
With sound minds	2 Timothy 1:7
As sealed	Ephesians 1:13
As transformed	Romans 12:2
As in His thoughts	Psalms 139:17-18
As useful to the Master	2 Timothy 2: 20-21
As vessels of honor	2 Timothy 2:20-21
As a wife of the Lamb	Revelations 21: 9
As His workmanship	Ephesians 2:10
As never an X	Hebrews 13:5
As Yours	Song of Solomon 6:3
As zealous for Him	Acts 22:3

(All NASB unless otherwise noted.)

5

Secrets from the Seasons

My lover spoke, and said to me. Arise, my darling, my
beautiful one, and come with me. See the winter is past;
the rains are over and gone. Flowers appear on the earth.
The season of singing has come. The cooing of the doves
is heard in our land. The fig tree forms its early fruit. The
blossoming vines spread their fragrance. Arise, my darling,
my beautiful one, come with me.

Song of Songs 2:10-13, NIV

As we read this passage, we realize the beautiful one, the darling of the king, the Shulamite, has just come through a winter season in her life, and she is now entering a new season, the season of spring. Winter has passed, and it is now the time for the season of singing.

We get the feeling from this passage that the king, wanted the one he loved to fill up her senses with the sights, sounds, and smells of spring. He called her attention to the fresh fragrances from the blossoming vines carried throughout the land in the crisp, clean air of springtime. He wanted her to listen to the calming sound of the cooing doves whose voices were created to soothe even the weariest of souls.

He must have known that the sight of flowers rising up from their long winter nap, coloring the earth with splendor and majesty would thrill her, making her heart glad. We can only imagine how the fruit from the fig tree refreshed her taste buds with their sweetness.

After the long, cold winds of winter, she must have welcomed the spring winds as they blew against her, caressing every fiber of her being with their warmth. I am sure her eyes, ears, sense of smell, taste, and touch were all awakened by the wonders ushered in by the coming of spring.

Springtime is exhilarating. Some of us wish we could stay in this season all of our lives, but that is not the way God created nature to work. He created the earth to go through the four seasons of winter, spring, summer, and fall, only to repeat that same cycle over and over, year after year.

The king reminds his bride, "Winter is past." If the Shulamite was like most of us, she probably breathed a sigh of relief, glad that the hardships of the winter season were over. We are never sad to watch winter's cold winds wave their final, farewell goodbyes because winter is the difficult season, the season of adversity.

Spring

When we look at the effects that different seasons have on trees with our spiritual eyes, we can see an amazing picture of the effects that the different seasons we go through have in our own lives.

Springtime is one of our favorite seasons. After looking at the barren, lifeless-looking trees of winter, we love to wrap our senses around the exciting process of the trees changing from the place of what looks like deadness to the place of shouting to the world with their buds, blossoms, and beauty that they are still very much alive. Spring ignites the process of growing, causing trees to spread their limbs reaching higher and higher toward the heavens.

Just like the trees, all of us have gone through times when we have felt barren in the winter seasons of our spiritual lives, only to suddenly begin to experience the thrill of new growth coming forth in our spiritual spring times. When we finally begin to reach into the heavenly realms once again, we are always excited to enjoy the process of becoming all we were created to be. Spring is life-changing, but during our spring times, we need to keep in mind that the year has more in store for us than just the joys that spring has to offer.

Summer

There are also times in our lives that resemble the trees of summer. In the summertime when the living is easy, we watch the trees get all dressed up in their garments of green. We are amazed at how the trees that are watered properly can bear so much fruit. Some trees are so full with the sweetness of fruit that their limbs hang down.

In the summer season, trees that were created to bring forth peaches bring forth peaches; trees that were created to bring forth apples bring forth apples. They do what they were created to do, fulfilling their destinies. The exciting thing to remember is that the trees don't have to grunt or strain or go through great turmoil to push out the fruit. All they have to do is just receive the sap that is alive inside their innermost being and allow the sap to do the work that needs to be done to bring forth fruit.

The Lord has created all of us to bear fruit. He tells us that some will bear thirty-fold, some sixty-fold, and some one-hundred fold. In order to bear much fruit, all we have to do is exactly what the trees do, relax and receive the fullness of the sap of the Holy Spirit. The Lord has a plan, a purpose, and a destiny for all of our lives. I can't fulfill your destiny and you can't fulfill mine, but in order to fulfill our destinies, we all have to do the same thing—be continually filled with the sap of the Holy Spirit. He is the One who will bring us to our full potential. There are gifts inside all of us, and if we stay full of the sap of the Holy Spirit, in the fullness of time the Lord will bring them forth for His glory.

Another interesting thing about the trees in the summertime is they provide shade for those who are weary from the summer heat. Just as the tree provides shade, there are seasons in our lives when He allows the Comforter who lives within us to comfort those in our lives who have been scorched by the heat of life.

Fall

Just like clockwork, when summer comes to an end the trees know that a significant change is in the air. The hot winds of summer that have been blowing against their bark are ushered off the horizon by the cool refreshing winds of fall. Fall gives trees the opportunity to exchange their dresses of green for beautiful multi-colored garments of glorious golds, brilliant yellows, deep reds, and vibrant oranges. In some parts of the world the trees are so magnificent that their beauty takes our breath away.

Just like trees, there are those in the kingdom of God who are so full of the Holy Spirit that we can see a rare beauty that comes forth from the beautiful One who lives within. We look at them and see His character, His love, His kindness, His goodness, His mercy, His grace. It would be wonderful if we could enjoy the beauty of fall three hundred and sixty-five days a year, but with the coming of the winter winds we are reminded that fall is just a season. It shows up every year, but at the appointed time it fades away.

Winter

Without fail, winter always follows fall. We watch the trees that were once brimming with beauty as they are stripped by the winds of winter, leaving them colorless, unproductive, with no visible signs of life. At times the winter winds blow so hard against the trees that they bend over, some even to the breaking point.

No matter how much the trees long to escape the hardships of winter, escaping is impossible. Winter is part of God's plan, and He allows it to show up right on schedule. He knows that the trees need the difficulties of their winters just as much as they need all of the other seasons in their lives. When the winter winds of adversity blow against our lives, we often feel just like the trees, unproductive, void of spiritual life. Sometimes, we even feel like we are at the breaking point. There are times when we all experience a winter season of our souls, when it seems to be frozen over with the trials and pressures of life, when it feels like the chill has even frozen the windows of heaven.

If you are in a winter season in your life, you can testify that winter can be a miserable place. People describe their seasons of winter in different ways. Some say it is a painful place. Others say it is a shameful place, a shaking place, a desolate place, a hopeless place, a lonely place, an empty place—and for almost everyone it is a tearful, uncomfortable place. Many times when we are in the middle of our winters, we feel like we are sitting on the side of the road and life is just passing us by.

It is in our seasons of struggle that we are most vulnerable to the attacks of the enemy. He comes against us with fear, discouragement, depression, and the agony of defeat. Sometimes the winter seasons of life bring us to the place of even feeling half-dead. Some feel both spiritually and emotionally like they have one foot in the grave.

This literally happened to a friend of mine. After expressing condolences to a grieving family at the graveside, she took a step backward and discovered to her horror that there was Astroturf over the grave but nothing solid. One foot went down into the grave, while her other foot was perched precariously in the approximate location of her ear. Without firm footing, there was almost no way to extricate herself. After inching along toward the end of the grave, she was vastly relieved to look up and find a helpful funeral attendant who lifted her out of that place of death.

When we are going through our spiritual winters, we often find ourselves in places, just like my friend, that feel like death. We long for the Lord to reach down and pull us out. Sometimes, we cry out to Him from our places of deadness, and when He doesn't respond as quickly as we think He should, we feel like He has forgotten about us.

During those times we need to remember His words to us. *"I will never leave you or forsake you"* (Hebrews 13:5). We need to keep in mind that, *"His thoughts toward us outnumber the sands of the sea"* (Psalms 139:17-18). We are always on His mind. He also tells us that, *"Our times are in His hands"* (Psalms 31:15). No matter how bad it looks, He knows where we are and exactly what we are going through. We may not understand why He allows us to stay so long in those places from which we long to escape, but He has a purpose for everything He allows us to go through.

Why Lord?

We all love the fragrances of spring. We love the fruit that comes forth in the summer. We love the fiery beauty of fall, but the deadness of our winter seasons are the seasons that we could do without. Winters, oh winters, why do you come? Lord, we know that You don't cause bad things to happen to us, but why do You allow the winter winds of adversity to intrude upon our lives? We don't like them. We don't even want them, but whether we want them or not, we know they will come.

You tell us in Ecclesiastes 3:1, *"To everything there is a season, a time for every purpose under the sun,"* but Lord, it is hard for us to see the purposes for our hard times, especially when we are in the middle of going through them. Thank You for not leaving us without answers. Thank You for not only giving us the reasons for our difficult seasons from Your Word, but for giving us clear answers from the trees. Lord, give us eyes to see that the reasons You allow trees to go through their winters are some of the same reasons You allow us to go through the winter seasons in our lives today.

The Trees of Winter

1. Dead things fall off, exposing flaws and defects.
With the coming of winter, we see the leaves on the trees that were once full of vivid, vibrant beauty slowly die, turning to the dull, drabness of various shades of brown. The dead leaves then fall off the trees exposing the flaws and defects of the trees.

Just like the trees, we need our winters so that those things that have been hidden can be brought to the light. We all want our flaws hidden from the view of others. None of us like for our sins to be exposed, but there are times when just like the trees, the Lord allows our deepest darkest sins to be uncovered.

Why? Why would He allow such a terrible thing to happen to us? It is usually when our sins are exposed that we are forced to deal with them. The Lord knows we need our seasons of struggle to destroy pride, to destroy our sins of failing to forgive others, to destroy the works of darkness in our lives. It is the Holy Spirit's job to convict us of sin and change us into the image of Jesus, and sometimes He uses our seasons of adversity to bring us to the place where we are ready to "lay aside every weight and the sins that so easily beset us." Just like the dead leaves, He wants the dead things that are hanging on us to fall off.

Strongholds in My Life Fell Off

I clearly remember a winter season of my life when I was dealing with strongholds, areas where I had given ground to the enemy. The Holy Spirit had convicted me of my sins, and I was miserable. You may know how that feels. I loved the Lord, and I wanted to please Him, but just like Paul, I did the things that I didn't want to do. I wanted to be free of these sins, but the devil would continually come to me saying, "You will never be free. You will deal with these sins for the rest of your life."

Right in the middle of my misery the Lord gave me a word that I held on to until freedom finally came:

> *Be sober, be on the alert. Your adversary, the devil, prowls around like a roaring lion, seeking someone to devour, but resist him, firm in your faith, knowing that the same experiences of suffering are being accomplished by your brethren who are in the world. After you have suffered a little while, the God of all grace who called you to His eternal glory*

in Christ, will Himself perfect, confirm, strengthen, and
establish you.   1 Peter 5:8-10

When I read that verse, it was so strong in my spirit it was as if God were speaking directly to my heart with an invisible microphone. I was definitely suffering. I wanted Him to perfect me. I wanted Him to strengthen me. I wanted freedom, but there was no freedom in sight.

I also read, "He came to set the captives free." I knew that I was definitely held captive by sins; they controlled me. I couldn't seem to say no to them. I begged the Lord for deliverance. I still remember the day when deliverance came, and the Lord set me free. Just like the dead leaves on the trees, those dead things fell off of me. What joy! I was beside myself. It really was true. The Lord was my Deliverer and the devil was a liar. He told me that I would never be free, but I was free.

Several months later I was reading 2 Peter 1:4, *"For by these He has granted to us His precious and magnificent promises, so that by them you may become partakers of the Divine nature, having escaped the corruption that is in the world by lust."* When I read the words "having escaped the corruption that is in the world," something on the inside of me did high kicks. It dawned on me that I had truly escaped from the captivity of the sins that had so easily beset me.

I put my Bible down that day and ran to the back yard. With a loud voice, I shouted to the world, "I have escaped." I ran to the front yard and shouted, "I have escaped." I ran and got into my car. While driving up and down the highway with the windows down, I shouted, "I have escaped."

I have no idea if anyone heard me. If they did, I am sure they probably wondered where I had escaped from, but I didn't care. It was true—I had escaped from the strongholds where I had been held captive by the devil. I was free! Do I still sin? Yes, but do I have strongholds in my life? Absolutely not. *"It was for freedom that Christ set me free"* (Galatians 5:1).

A Stronghold in Mark's Life Fell Off

I was not the only one with strongholds. Mark was addicted to nicotine. He hated smoking, but he couldn't quit no matter how badly he wanted to, and believe me, he wanted to. A stronghold is something that you have given permission to have control in an area of your life.

One day a precious friend of ours, Dudley Hall, who has had an amazing impact on both of our lives, invited Mark to go on a hunting trip. While he was gone, I went into my son Kevin's room to pray with him like I had every other night of his young life, only to find him with his head pressed down in his pillow crying. I put my arms around him and asked what was wrong.

He had heard someone on television talking about the fact that cigarettes could kill you, and he was worried about Mark dying. I remember saying to Kevin, "Why don't we ask God for a miracle? Why don't we just ask Him to help Dad quit smoking?" We knelt down together by the side of his bed, and Kevin began to pray. He said, "Lord, would you help daddy quit smoking, and I want to thank you God for doing it."

I was startled that he thanked God for doing it before he even saw Mark. He really believed when He prayed that prayer that God was going to do it. I knew that he was going to be devastated if Mark came home with a cigarette in his mouth. The night that Mark returned from the hunt, he sat all of us down and told us he had something to tell us. He said, "I want you to know that I met with God on a mountaintop in Colorado. Dudley and some of the men there laid hands on me and prayed for me to be delivered from nicotine, and I haven't wanted a cigarette since.

When I looked over at Kevin I saw a big smile on his face, and I knew his heart was thrilled because God had answered his prayer. Mark told us that day he was taking over as the spiritual leader of our home. He told the boys it wouldn't be just Mom on her knees with them anymore. He was going to be there too. I learned a great lesson from Kevin through that experience. It is always a great idea to thank God for moving before we ever see the evidence that He is going to send the answer.

Faith is the substance of things hoped for, the evidence of things not seen.   Hebrews 11:1

Mark came back from that trip a changed man. Just like the leaves on the tree, his addiction to nicotine had fallen off. He had seen firsthand the power of what God could do. Not only did he take over as the spiritual leader praying with our boys, but he has never smoked even one cigarette since that day.

The other amazing thing that happened is Mark started praying with me, just the two of us. I can still remember that first morning after Mark came home from the hunt like it was yesterday. After getting the boys off to school, I laid back down on the bed to talk to him while he was getting dressed for work. When he was fully dressed in his suit and tie, he came over to kiss me goodbye. As he sat down on the side of the bed, to my surprise he laid his body over the top half of my body and started praying for me out loud. I couldn't believe it. Tears started streaming down my face. Mark not only took over as a spiritual leader for the boys, but He had taken over and he was covering me.

2. They may look dead, but there is still life in those trees.

When we look at the trees of winter we often see no visible signs of life. Many trees that were once productive appear to be dead, but no matter how dead they look there is still life in them. God is not finished with them yet. God is planning to use them to bring forth fruit again in another season.

The situations we go through may look dead, but like the trees they might not be dead at all. You may be going through what appears to be the death of a marriage, the death of a relationship, the death of a ministry, the death of your health, the death of a job, the death of your finances, the death of a situation with your child, or even the death of your dreams.

Joseph can surely tell us about things that look dead but in actuality are still very much alive. He went through a difficult winter season that took him through what looked like the death of his dreams. When he was just a young boy, God gave him two dreams. He first dreamed that he and his brothers were binding sheaves of grain out in a field, and his sheaf stood up while their sheaves bowed down to him. He also had another dream that the sun, moon, and eleven stars were bowing down to him.

From his dreams, the Lord was telling Joseph his destiny; one day, others would bow down to him. The Lord allowed Joseph to go through a heartbreaking journey to bring him to the place where his dreams would come to pass. Why would the Lord allow that to happen? The answer is simple. He knew that Joseph needed every situation he went through to prepare him for his destiny, just as we need everything we go through to prepare us for our destinies.

Most of us know the story. Joseph was betrayed by his brothers and thrown into a pit. These were the same brothers who were supposed to bow down to him. From the pit he was taken to the foreign land of Egypt where he became a servant in Potiphar's house. He didn't become someone to whom people would bow down. He became someone who would learn how to bow down to others.

After Potiphar's wife lied about him, he was thrown into a prison for a crime he didn't commit. He then spent years in prison seemingly forgotten and overlooked. I am sure that there were times as he sat in that prison when he thought that the dreams that he had weren't from God. I am sure as he looked at those prison bars day after day, year after year, there were times when he thought that his dreams would never come to pass. He may have had times when he felt like it was over; that there was no hope. There were probably times when he wanted to give up.

You may be in a situation just like Joseph where your circumstances are taking you through the death of your dreams. You may feel like the dreams that God has given you will never come to pass. You may have even allowed your God-given dreams to die. When we are in the middle of what looks like the death of our dreams, we need to remember that there is always a death before there can be a resurrection.

Joseph's circumstances took him in what looked like the opposite direction from his dreams. In his eyes it may have looked like the situation in which he found himself was impossible. He had to travel down a long road that took him from the pit to Potiphar's house to a prison before he finally reached a prominent place in the palace. Every step he took in the natural appeared to take him further and further away from his dreams, but in the fullness of time God brought him to the place where his God-given dreams came true, and he fulfilled his destiny. *"God watches over His Word to perform it"* (Jeremiah 1:12).

With God All Things Are Possible

> *But Jesus beheld them, and said unto them, With men this is impossible; but with God all things are possible.*
> Matthew 19:26

I have gone through many experiences that looked in my flesh like there were no solutions; it looked like there was no way out and the situations would be impossible to overcome, but I have learned through my many winters of adversity that, *"With God all things are possible."* That is my forever, go-to, verse. When difficult times come it is the first thing I say. If faith isn't rising up, I say it again; *"With God all things are possible."* I say it until I hear it, really hear it. I say it over and over until faith rises up and comes alive in my spirit.

There are times when we may need to say, "I know the enemy wants me to think my child is too far gone and there is nothing more that can be done, but it's not over. With God all things are possible. I know that I lost my job and it looks like my financial situation is going down the drain, but it's not over. With God all things are possible. I know that I am still in pain and it looks like I will be in pain for the rest of my life, but it is not over. With God all things are possible. I know that I am struggling with this sin issue right now, but it is not over. With God all things are possible. I know that it may look like I don't have a future, but it is not over. With God all things are possible."

No matter what we are going through, God is bigger than any problem we will ever face. It is during our days of winter that we need to remember that no matter how dead a situation may look, it may not be dead at all. Even if it is dead, remember that God is in the business of getting involved with dead things. Remember Lazarus? He died and was in the tomb for three days. He was so dead his flesh was stinking, but Jesus just spoke the word, and he came back to life again. Your situation may be as dead as a doornail and stinking to high heaven but if it is God's will, He can turn that situation around and bring it back to life in a heartbeat.

Do you remember Aaron's rod that budded? If that rod could be here and speak to us, I am sure that it would testify that God is in the business of getting involved with dead things. It was just a dead stick. There was no life in it but God got involved with it, and overnight that dead stick budded, blossomed, and bore almonds. It was in a "suddenly" situation. One day it was a dead stick. The next day it brought forth almonds.

You may have witnessed the death of a situation, but God could get involved and turn that dead thing around overnight. Sometimes God allows us to go through a process before resurrecting dead things, but if it is according to His will He can show up with a "suddenly." In the midst of our winters, no matter how dead or impossible our situations appear to be we need to repeat those six faith-building words over and over and over. With God all things are possible.

Joseph's Words Echo Through the Corridors of Time

Joseph was one of God's old-testament heroes who found himself in a situation that looked impossible. Just think about what God did to turn his situation around. While he was sitting in prison in a foreign land Pharaoh had a dream and couldn't find anyone that could tell him the meaning of his dream. After hearing that there was a man in his prison that could interpret dreams, he summoned Joseph.

Joseph interpreted Pharaoh's dreams, telling him about the famine that was coming upon the land. He also told him how to get ready for the famine. Because of Joseph's God-given gift of interpreting dreams and his God-given wisdom, Pharaoh put Joseph in charge of Egypt, second in command. When Joseph's brothers came to Egypt to buy food, they discovered that Joseph was not only alive but was now a ruler in Egypt.

It is so thrilling to read how Joseph's dreams came true as his brothers finally bowed down before him just like their sheaves had bowed down before his sheaf in the dream that God gave him as a boy. It wasn't the fact that they bowed down that was so thrilling, but it was thrilling to know that God knew what was going to happen before it ever happened. God had a plan for Joseph's life, a destiny. He knew even when Joseph was a young boy that the day would come when he would be a ruler, and his brothers would bow down before him.

God knew the end from the beginning in Joseph's life, just like He knows the end from the beginning in our lives (Isaiah 46:10). After his brothers bowed down before him, Joseph told them why he had to go through all that he had to endure. His words echo down through the corridors of time to give us hope for today in our seasons of adversity. He spoke to his brothers saying, *"As for you, you meant it for evil, but God meant it for GOOD to bring about that many people should be kept alive, as they are this day"* (Genesis 50:20).

Wow, God meant it for GOOD. After all he went through, Joseph understood why it happened. God had a plan and all that Joseph went through was to prepare him to fulfill his destiny to keep many people alive. God has a plan for all of our lives, and He sometimes allows us to go through difficult circumstances to bring us to the place where we fulfill our own destinies.

Joseph is not the only one for whom God works everything in their lives together for good. He made the same promise to another group of people.

*And we know that God causes all things to work together
for good to those who love God, to those who are called
according to His purpose.* Romans 8:28

God didn't say He causes SOME things to work together for good.
He said that He causes ALL things to work together for good to those who
love God and to those who are called according to His purpose. The things
that we go through may not feel good. They may not sound good and they
may not look good, but God promised that no matter what we go through,
if we love Him and are called according to His purpose, He is going to see
to it that it works together for good.

When we are going through our spiritual winters and we feel like we
are not going to make it, we need to hold on to Romans 8:28 with all of our
might. We need to keep Romans 8:28 running across our computer screens
to constantly remind us that no matter how bad it looks, in the end He is
going to cause it to work together for good. If we have Romans 8:28 tucked
securely under our spiritual belts we can run through troops and leap over
walls. With this magnificent promise, we can make it through anything.

Thank You, Lord, for using the story of Joseph to help us through the
winter seasons of our lives. Thank You for reminding us by giving Joseph
those dreams as a young boy that You know the end from the beginning.
Thank You, Lord, that You had a plan for Joseph's life and You have a plan
for our lives today. Thank You for the promise of Romans 8:28. I am sure
You knew we were going to need it.

A Season of Adversity in the Wilderness

Why did God allow the children of Israel to go through their difficult season of adversity in the wilderness? Why did God allow them to
wander in the desert for forty years? Did He lead them around in circles
just for the fun of it? Were those forty years wasted years?

The Lord is very clear about His purposes for allowing the wilderness wanderings. We know from Numbers 13 and 14 that God's

original plan was not for the Children of Israel to wander in the wilderness for forty years. He wanted them to go in and possess the land, but when the spies went in to explore Canaan all but Caleb and Joshua came back with a bad report. They focused on the fact that there were giants in the land, filling the hearts of the Israelites with fear. They told the people, "We seemed like grasshoppers in our own eyes, and we looked the same to them."

Because of fear, the children of Israel rebelled against God. They grumbled, raising their voices, weeping out loud. They wanted to go back to Egypt. Moses, Aaron, Joshua, and Caleb all fell on their faces, tearing their clothes, begging them to obey the Lord, assuring them that God was with them, but they didn't believe God would give them the land. They didn't believe He would do what He said He would do, and because of their unbelief God allowed them to wander around in the desert for forty years. In Deuteronomy 8:2, the word of the Lord says, *"The Lord your God led you these forty years in the wilderness to humble you, to test you, to know what was in your heart."* In Deuteronomy 8:15-16, He says, *"Who led you through the great and terrible wilderness, with its fiery serpents and scorpions and thirsty ground where there was no water. Who brought you forth water out of the flinty rock? Who fed you in the wilderness with manna, which your fathers did not know, that He might humble you and test you, to do you good in the end."*

God had a definite purpose for the Children of Israel to go through their wilderness. It was to humble them and test them in order to show them what was in their hearts. It was also during those forty years that He taught them that they could rely on Him for all of their needs. Where there was no water, He supplied water from the rock. Where there was no food He sent manna from above. He taught them during their wilderness wanderings that He would supply all of their needs.

IF THEY HAD NOT GONE THROUGH THEIR WILDERNESS EXPERIENCE, THEY WOULD HAVE NEVER KNOWN HIM LIKE THEY CAME TO KNOW HIM. He states His final purpose in verse sixteen, *"to do you good in the end."* There it is again, to do them GOOD.

The Lord has the same four purposes for us in our wildernesses experiences. Sometimes He needs to humble us. Sometimes He allows us to go through a testing time to show us what is in our hearts. Sometimes He knows we need to discover, not just by memorizing a verse but with a life experience, that He is going to supply all of our needs according to His riches in glory. We need to always remember His ultimate goal. No matter what we go through He is going *to* do us GOOD in the end.

The Secret for Passing Our Test

One of God's goals in allowing difficult seasons to come into our lives today is to test us just like He did the children of Israel. We can never know the strength of our faith until it is tested. I don't know of anyone who enjoys taking tests. For most of us there is an undercurrent of anxiety running through our minds during a test that taunts us with the fear of failure. The Lord sometimes allows us to go through testing times to show us our hearts.

During a testing time, have you ever noticed that the Lord is often silent? Why does He choose testing times to be silent? THE TEACHER IS ALWAYS SILENT DURING A TEST.

Three of my grandchildren, Parker, Nate, and Luke just took a special test at school called the TAKS test. Their teachers spent the entire year talking to them, teaching them, getting them ready, but when it was time to take the test their teachers didn't say a word. They were silent. Why? They knew they didn't need to speak because they had already taught the students everything they needed to know to pass the test.

The same thing is true with our Teacher. Before we ever started through the difficult seasons of our lives, He knew everything we would have to go through. He knew we would need answers to our questions; so He wrote them down in His Word. He doesn't need to always speak during our testing times. He has already spoken. He has already answered our questions. Now, all we have to do is reach into His Word to find the answers we are looking for.

3. *Looks can be deceiving.*

When we look at the trees in the bareness of their winters, it often appears that nothing is going on in the life of the trees but nothing could be farther from the truth. In their seasons of winter, if we had eyes to see beneath the surface of the trees, we would discover that the sap that was once used to produce the fruit has gone down into the root system to nourish the most important part of the tree. It flows through the roots, pushing out new roots and forcing the old roots deeper and deeper into the soil. It is in their winters that the sap does its greatest work in the trees, strengthening the very foundation of the tree.

In our winters the exact same thing happens to us. In our difficult times we often look at our lives, and because of our circumstances we are left feeling barren, like nothing is happening. We often feel like God has abandoned us but if we only had eyes to see, we would know nothing could be farther from the truth.

It is during our winter seasons that God does His greatest work in us. It is in our times of adversity that we are forced by our difficult circumstances to press into the very presence of God. It is in our times of adversity that He strengthens our spiritual foundation by taking us deeper and deeper into the soil of His Word. It is in our winters that He strengthens the very roots of our spiritual being.

Philippians 1:6, tells us that, *"He who began a good work in you will perform it until the day of Jesus Christ."* There may be times when it doesn't look like God is at work in us but no matter how things may look, He is working. He wants us to be rooted and grounded in Him, and it is in during our times of adversities that we are rooted and grounded in ways that could never happen without our seasons of winter. It is during our difficult times, that we find ourselves in positions to see His power in ways we could have never known without our need.

Someone once said, ADVERSITY IS THE ATMOSPHERE THAT ACTIVATES OUR FAITH, AND FAITH IS THE ATMOSPHERE THAT ACTIVATES MIRACLES. We don't need faith during the good times. It is in our seasons of winter that we come to know our Lord and our

God in ways that we could have never come to know Him without our adversities.

The Power of His Name

Several years ago the Lord allowed me to go through a very difficult season. It was very short season. It lasted only five hours, but I learned more about the Lord in those five hours than I learned in years from just studying the Word. I was teaching a Bible study to the women in our church when one of the women who was not a member asked to meet with me.

The offices were upstairs, but she wanted me to meet with her in the chapel which was downstairs at the opposite end of the building. Because I knew she was going through a difficult time, I agreed to meet with her. I got to the chapel early and waited, not expecting what was about to happen.

When she arrived, I saw her reach up and turn off the lights. Because there were no windows, the room was suddenly very dark, almost pitch black. There was only one small stream of light coming through the doors which were in the back of the room. When I ask her to turn the lights back on, she spoke, telling me the time for sitting in the light was over.

I realized as she spoke she didn't sound like herself. Her voice sounded strange, evil, and deep like a man's voice. I couldn't see her after she turned out the lights, but I could hear her footsteps as she came closer and closer. I was shocked when I suddenly felt the first sharp, stabbing pain as she kicked me hard right in my stomach. When I fell, she continued to kick me over and over. I didn't understand what was happening until she told me I was going to have to die. She came to kill me.

As I anticipated the next blow, not knowing which direction it would come from, I knew she had the advantage. If I stayed in the dark, I wouldn't have a chance. I knew I was facing the back of the chapel, so by reaching for the edge of the first pew which was right in front of me, I felt my way to the back of the room pew by pew finally reaching the wall where the light switch was waiting for me. As I turned on the lights, I experienced what can only be described as what felt like a freight train running into me.

To say the least, I was caught off guard that day. I never saw it coming. In a matter of seconds, I went from being at total peace, waiting to help this woman, to the place of literally fighting with her for my life. The last thing I expected was a physical fight. I had never fought with anyone before, but on that day I didn't hesitate. It wasn't that I wanted to hurt her, but I wanted to keep her from hurting me.

When your life is at stake you will do things you never dreamed you would do. Even though she was stronger and bigger than me, outweighing me by fifty pounds, I didn't go down without a fight. I was horrified at the atrocious language that was coming out of her mouth as well as the different voices that would come and go. The longer we fought, I could feel my body getting weaker and weaker. The fight was stealing my strength.

Close to what I thought was the end, I found myself on the floor, pinned down by the weight of her body. As she wrapped her hands around my neck, to my horror I could feel her fingers pressing tighter and tighter, closing off the air that was trying to get through my windpipe. I tried to pry them off my neck, but there was no use — she was overpowering me. I couldn't breathe. She was choking the life out of me.

As I realized I couldn't fight her off any longer, thoughts started racing through my mind: "I am going to die; I am not going to make it," but then I thought about my two precious little boys who needed me. I knew I couldn't give up. In my mind I began to cry out to the Lord, asking Him to help me. As she was strangling me, I suddenly heard His voice say, "All your strength is gone now, isn't it Jenny?" As I answered in my mind, "Yes Lord," I heard Him say, "Now take Mine and start using My name."

At that moment I used what little breath that was left in my body to say, "In the name of Jesus I command you to get off of me." When I spoke those words, the most amazing thing happened. She threw herself off my body, screaming at the top of her lungs. When we first started, I knew something was desperately wrong with her, but I had no idea what was happening until the Lord began to tell me the name of the demons that were manifesting themselves through her.

As I heard Him speak their names, I just repeated what I heard Him say. His first words were, "Cast out the spirit of murder." As I continued to listen to His voice, I realized that I was "not fighting against flesh and blood, but principalities, against powers, against the rulers of darkness, against spiritual wickedness in high places" (Ephesians 6:12). For the next hour, the demons would come out with unearthly screams, and she would then lie on the floor lifeless, very still, until the next demon manifested itself in a different voice with different words. Some were angry. Some were violent, but each demon came out when I used the name of Jesus.

The longer I used His name I realized I didn't have to use my own strength any longer. I had His. I could feel my heart pulsating with the truth that there was power in the name of Jesus. The cycle of watching the demons manifest, calling for them to come out, and hearing them scream as they left her body went on for the longest time. Over and over, I saw the amazing power of His name.

I could also feel the power of the Holy Spirit rushing through my spiritual veins, strengthening me with the truth that I was going to live. This woman was demon possessed, but miraculously I learned on that day that even the demons have to obey at the very mention of His name.

You may have heard the story of the child who didn't know how to swim, but whose father just threw her in the water and said, "Swim." That's how I felt. Before that day I didn't know that I could cast out demons, but the Lord gave me on-the-job training. He told me to cast out the demons using His name, and miraculously, it worked.

After hours of coming face to face with the demonic, I tried to get up off the floor but I couldn't; my legs were too weak. They couldn't hold me up, so I began to crawl toward the doors in the back of the chapel. As I did, I felt her grab my right leg telling me that I wasn't going anywhere. She then stood between me and the doors in order to prevent me from leaving. I will always remember what happened next. I didn't see an angel or anyone else in the room, but someone lifted her up off her feet and threw her backwards through the chapel doors.

> *If you make the Most High your dwelling–even the Lord, who is my refuge- then no harm will befall you, no disaster will come near your tent. For He will command His angels concerning you, to guard you in all your ways.*
>
> Psalm 91:9-11

I watched as her body was hurled through the swinging doors, hitting the windows in the outside hallway. Realizing she was unconscious, I made my way up the stairs to the offices, telling the secretary to lock the doors. That was the last thing I remembered before passing out.

When I came to, my husband, my pastor, the paramedics and the police were standing over me. My first conscious thought was the realization of unbearable pain all over my entire body, and then I heard Mark's voice whispering in my swollen ear: "It's going to be okay Jenny. You are going to make it. You are strong, Jenny. You are going to be okay." As I listened to His voice, I didn't feel strong, but in my spirit I knew one thing without a shadow of a doubt, ...*His strength was made perfect in my weakness* (2 Corinthians 12:9).

If you had told on me that day that I would have been going into that room to fight for my life and exorcise demons, I would never have believed it. If I had known what was waiting for me in that room, I would never have had the courage to enter into one of the most difficult five-hour periods of my life. If you asked me today if it was worth it, I would definitely tell you that it was.

During those five hours I discovered with every fiber of my being that THERE IS POWER IN THE NAME OF JESUS. Before that day I knew in my head that there was power in His name, but on that day I got to experience it with my life. My season of struggle caused my roots to go down deeper into the presence of God, and my short season of adversity was the atmosphere that activated my faith in Jesus in a way that it had never been activated before. Later I heard James Taylor singing, "You've Got a Friend," and I thought about Him.

> When you're down and troubled and you need a helping hand
> and nothing, whoa, nothing is going right.

> Close your eyes and think of me and soon I will be there
> to brighten even your darkest night.

> You just call out my name, and you know wherever I am,
> I'll come running to see you again.

> Winter, spring, summer or fall, all you have to do is call
> and I'll be there
> yeah, yeah, you've got a friend.

The words to that song rang so true. I've got a friend, and all I had to do was call out His name—when I did He came running.

Winter is Just a Season-It Doesn't Last Forever

Before closing this chapter, both the wilderness wanderers and millions of trees whose wisdom comes from years of experience have one last very important secret to share with all of us who find ourselves in the middle of a difficult season in our lives. When the children of Israel were going through the wilderness, they never built houses. They always lived in tents. Why?

Even though it took a long time, they knew that the wilderness was a temporary place. They were just passing through. They knew their time there was not permanent. They knew they were headed to a better land. So many times when we are in difficult seasons we think the circumstances we are going through will never end, but we have to remember that our winters of adversities are just seasons.

Don't believe the lies of the devil when he tells you that your difficulty is going to last forever. God doesn't cause our winters, but He allows our winters to come knowing that when they have accomplished their purposes, they need to go. If you are in the middle of a winter season in your soul, remember, you are just passing through. Don't build a house in the middle of your season of adversity; just set up a tent and be ready to follow the cloud. In the fullness of time, the Lord will lead you out of there.

If trees could only talk, I am sure they would agree with the children of Israel giving a hearty, happy amen to the fact that winter doesn't last forever. Trees know that as surely as the sap goes down in the winter to work on their root system that the sap won't stay down forever. They know that spring is just around the corner, and the sap will rise again.

In the middle of our winters we need to remember the lessons that we learn from both the Israelites and the trees; our winter seasons of adversity won't last forever. The day will come in our all of our lives when, just like the king in Song of Solomon, we too will experience the thrill of saying, "THE WINTER IS PAST."

6

The Secret of His Kisses

May he kiss me with the kisses of his lips.

Song of Solomon 1:2a

Before I could even begin to look for the path to find out how to get to the place of becoming lovesick, I had to overcome the obstacle of the ten words that kept me from this book for years: "May he kiss me with the kisses of his lips." In the beginning, it never crossed my mind that these words could be painting a spiritual picture. When I would try to read them, I would cringe. I thought they were sacrilegious. Of course, to think that He would ever kiss me sounded ridiculous.

One day I decided to ask the Lord about that verse. My question to Him was, "Do You kiss, and if You do, how do You kiss?" I will never forget the day He answered my question. Mark and I had gone to the ocean to get away from the hustle and bustle of life for a few days. After we checked into our room, we hurriedly changed our clothes and headed straight for the beach to enjoy the last few hours before sunset.

As we took our shoes off, the waves rushed up to greet us while the sand embraced our bare feet as it squished up between our toes. The wind blew gently across our faces, inviting us to leave all our responsibilities behind and enjoy the invigorating freedom found in the fragrances that flooded our senses. My eyes gazed across the vastness of the ocean as the rays from the sun danced on top of the deep blue water. I loved everything I saw, but what truly captivated my attention were the waves washing up on the shore.

I watched them as they rolled toward us and then rolled back again, only to repeat the same cycle over and over and over. While watching the waves I was also overwhelmingly aware of the presence of the Lord. I had the distinct impression that He had something He wanted to say to me. I turned on my spiritual ears and was listening very intently when I heard Him say, "Jenny, what do you see?" I said, "I see the waves Lord." He said, "What are they doing?" I said, "They are rolling up on the beach and rolling back, only to roll up again and again and again and again. They just keep coming and coming and coming and coming."

The Lord said, "That is a picture of My grace. No matter what you ever do, or what you ever say, or what you ever think—nothing can keep My grace from coming toward you." As I wrapped my mind around His words, they warmed my soul. I said, "Thank You, Lord, for Your grace." I was privileged to sit under the teaching of Dudley Hall who laid a firm foundation in my life about the beauty of the grace of God, and even though I knew that I didn't deserve it and I certainly hadn't earned it, I received it because I knew it was His special gift to all of us who belong to Him.

Mark and I kept walking along the shore, enjoying the ambience of the evening. Finding ourselves at a jetty, we decided to walk out to the very end of the dock which was in a deeper part of the ocean. Sitting on top of one of the huge rocks that surrounded it, we leaned back and listened to the waves lapping gently against the rocks. It was just one of those wonderful moments in time when we didn't have to race to an appointment or clean the house or cook dinner—we could be still and drink in the beauty of God's creation.

After enjoying the peace that can only come from watching the sun setting on the horizon with nothing but miles and miles of deep blue water stretching out before us, with no warning whatsoever, a gigantic wave jumped up out of the ocean and saturated me. I was soaked through and through. I was shocked because I wasn't expecting it, but what shocked me the most is that I had the strangest sensation that I had been kissed by the Lord.

I knew that thought was absurd, and then I heard, "Psalms 45:2." My heart skipped a beat. I knew the Lord had something important He wanted to tell me. As Mark and I walked back to our room I didn't want to walk, I wanted to run. I wanted to get to my Bible and see what Psalm 45:2 had to say.

Mark and I have a private joke between us. He is the tortoise and I am the hare. I always want to move at a fast pace, and compared to me, he moves like a turtle. The truth is, at that moment I wanted to run to our room, but I contained myself and walked alongside Mark only because I didn't want to be rude and leave him behind. When we got to the door, I could hardly wait to hear the click of the lock. Still soaking wet, I grabbed my Bible.

> *You are fairer than the sons of men; Grace is poured upon*
> *your lips, therefore, God has blessed you forever.*
>
> Psalm 45:2

There it was. The very word He had been talking to me about, grace. In the margin I read that this entire chapter was a prophetic prophecy about Christ and His bride. The writer of that verse under the inspiration of the Holy Spirit was speaking prophetically about Jesus when he wrote, "Grace is poured upon your lips." The Lord had just been talking to me about the waves being a picture of His grace and as I felt my wet body, I was reminded that I had literally been saturated with it.

Now He was talking to me about His lips being moist with grace because grace had been poured out on them. At that moment the Lord said, "MY LIPS ARE MOIST WITH GRACE. ANYTIME YOU HAVE AN ENCOUNTER WITH ME, CONSIDER YOURSELF KISSED." I was immediately stunned and thrilled all at the same time. I thought about the fact that anytime I heard His voice I could consider myself kissed. Anytime He spoke to me through a dream, or vision, or a prophetic word, I could consider myself kissed. Anytime He showed up in any area of my life, I could consider myself kissed.

I laughed out loud as I realized the Lord really was a kisser. I was wrong to think the He would never kiss me. He would kiss me all right, but not on my lips. When He kissed me it would be my soul that He kissed, and His kisses would always be full of the beauty of His magnificent, unmerited, undeserved, grace.

We Get to Kiss Him Right Back

When it came to the subject of kissing, I was thrilled one day when I discovered that He was not the only one who got to do all the kissing.

> *But an hour is coming, and now is, when the true worshipers shall worship the Father in spirit and truth; for such people the Father seeks to be His worshippers. God is spirit, and those who worship Him must worship in spirit and truth.*   John 4:23

One of the words for worship in the Greek is "*proskuno*" which means, "to kiss toward." When we worship Him we are actually kissing Him in the realm of the spirit as we release our love to him with our words. I was so excited to discover that when He kissed me I didn't have to sit there unresponsively–I could kiss Him right back.

Why was I surprised?

I don't know why I should have been so surprised that the Lord wanted to have an intimate relationship with me, "that He wanted to kiss me with the kisses of His lips." Even from the very beginning, starting with Adam, God has always wanted to have encounters with us. He has always wanted to meet with us, speak with us, and reveal Himself to us.

> *And they heard the sound of the Lord God walking in the garden in the cool of the day, and the man and his wife hid themselves from the presence of the Lord God among the trees of the garden. Then the Lord God called to the man, and said to him, "Where are you!"* Genesis 3:8-9

The Garden of Eden was the first meeting place where God met with Adam and Eve. It was the place where He spoke to them, but one day when they heard God walking in the garden, they hid themselves from His presence. He was coming back to have fellowship with them, to have an encounter with them, but they were in hiding. From their hiding place they heard the voice of God say, "Adam, where are you?" Why were they hiding? They had fallen into the trap of sin, and because we were in Adam, when he fell, we fell.

Because of sin, God couldn't walk with Adam and Eve anymore. He couldn't have fellowship with them anymore because He is a holy God. Because of their sin He had to banish them from the garden, from the place of intimacy. At the very moment they sinned God could have walked away. He could have turned His back on Adam and Eve and us and never looked back. He could have washed His hands of us, and said, "It is over," but He didn't. Why?

It was because of His great love for us. He loves walking with us, talking with us, and revealing Himself to us. Instead of leaving us forever He had a plan to get back together, and the plan can be summed up in one word—Jesus. He would send His Son, His only Son, the Lord Jesus Christ, into the world to die on the cross and pay the price for our sins. He did it so we wouldn't have to hide from His presence anymore, so we could enjoy fellowship with Him and He could enjoy having fellowship with us once again.

Love

199

For God so loved the world, that He gave His only begotten Son, that whosoever believeth in Him should not perish, but have everlasting life.   John 3:16

Adam heard the same question God is asking all of us today, "Where are you?" Are you, like Adam, hiding from God? Has the enemy succeeded in breaking your intimacy with God like he broke Adam's? The enemy doesn't want us to have a close relationship with God. He wants us to think God would never want to have an intimate relationship with us. He wants to bring all of us to place of hiding, but the good news is we don't have to hide anymore.

There was a time in my life when I was just like Adam. I felt I needed to stay far away from God because of my sins. I thought He couldn't possibly ever want to be close to someone like me, but when I learned what He did because He loved me, and that my sins had been forgiven, it was then I knew I didn't have to hide anymore. I didn't have to stay away from Him anymore.

When I was a little girl I played hide and seek with the kids in the neighborhood. We would hide our eyes and count to twenty. We would then turn around and shout, "Come out, come out wherever you are." I think that is what the Lord is shouting to everyone that is hiding from Him today. "Come out, come out, wherever you are. Come out from your hiding place. You don't have to hide anymore." The price for our sins has been paid, and the Lord wants to walk with us, talk with us, have an intimate relationship with us, and kiss us with the kisses of His lips. He wants all of us to discover for ourselves that His lips are moist with grace.

Taco Bueno

God met with Adam in the Garden of Eden, and He shows up in many different places in our lives today. I remember a really wonderful encounter I had with the Lord at Taco Bueno in Hurst, Texas. That was one of the places the Lord and I met together all the time. When my boys were in school and Mark was at work, I would drive to the Taco Bueno which was just around the corner from my house, go through the drive-through and get my favorite lunch—a taco, and a diet coke.

One of the reasons I liked to sit outside in the car was because I could be alone with the Lord without distractions. The street that ran along the back side of this particular Taco Bueno was called Queens Way, and I liked to face my car toward Queens Way thinking that because He was my King and I was His bride, then surely I must also be His queen. When the weather was nice I always rolled down the windows to enjoy the combination of the fresh air along with my delicious lunch.

I remember sitting in my car, eating my lunch one day when I was aware that the Lord had something He wanted to tell me. I immediately put my lunch on the console of the car, giving Him my full attention. All of a sudden, I saw a little whirlwind outside my car. I watched it pick up a dead leaf, twirling it around and around. The wind carried the leaf through the window on the driver's side of my car, passing right in front of me and finally landed on the passenger side, right next to me.

I then heard the Lord say, "This is a picture of your life. Even as this leaf is dead and was carried by the wind, you have died and your life is hidden in Me. From this day forward I want you to always remember you are being carried by the Wind of My Spirit." I immediately thought about Colossians 3:3, *"For you have died and your life is hidden with Christ in God."* I knew He was right. I had died to my old way of life, and I had a secret, hidden life, with Him now.

I also thought about Job 38:1, *"God answered Job out of the whirl-wind."* It's amazing how God can use anything He pleases to speak to us, even dead leaves and strategically-placed whirlwinds.

Five Kisses

Years later, after being baptized in the Spirit, I remembered the Lord's words to me, "Anytime you have an encounter with Me, consider yourself kissed." As I thought about those words, five kisses that had taken place in my natural life came to my mind, and I compared them with different encounters I had with the Lord Jesus Christ in my spiritual life.

1. My first kiss.

Most of us remember our first kiss. I received mine when I was thirteen years old. All of my friends had been kissed, and I thought it was high time that I should be kissed, too. I was very curious about the subject of kissing, but just the thought of it made me very nervous. I went through the process of imagining what it was going to be like.

As I rehearsed an imaginary kiss in my mind, I realized that noses could be a problem. If I turned my head to the left at the same time he turned his head to the right, there was definitely going to be a collision. We wouldn't be mouth to mouth but nose to nose. I wanted to be kissed, but I was afraid that I wouldn't know how.

I went to church at First Baptist Church in downtown Fort Worth, and the pastor's son, David Richie, and I became friends. We were the same age, and because he couldn't drive, his dad would take us to the zoo or bowling or to the park to ride the rides.

One day while David and I were both at my cousin's house, my cousin told me that David wanted to kiss me. About that time, he walked into the room, reached down, gave me a quick peck on the lips and ran out of the room as fast as he could. At that moment, I realized that he probably didn't know any more about kissing than I did. It was awkward, and I was definitely disappointed. I decided there had to more to kissing than just a quick peck. I also remember wishing he had chosen a different place to kiss me than right in front of my cousin.

After thinking about my first kiss, I realized it was one-hundred percent opposite from every encounter I had ever had with the Lord Jesus Christ. His kisses have never been awkward. He has always known exactly when to have an encounter with me, where to have an encounter with me, and I have never — not even once — been disappointed. Because

He created me, He knows exactly how I like to be kissed in the realm of the Spirit.

2. A kiss for a thief.

The second kiss I thought about happened on my first date. I was fifteen. I had been in California visiting relatives, and when I got back I received a call from an old friend named Bruce Peak. He was the grandson of a neighbor who had lived next door to us, and we played together when he would come to visit his grandmother. I had not seen him for ten years, but I was excited when he called asking if he could come over.

When I first saw him I couldn't believe my eyes. He was so handsome. He had black hair, big brown eyes, and the color of his skin was a golden brown that had been tanned by the summer's sun. My mom had always told me I would not be allowed to have a car date until I was sixteen, but because Bruce was a friend of the family, she gave me permission to go on my first date with him.

I was thrilled. I can still remember the dress I wore. I made it myself. It was hot pink with a wide hot pink belt made out of the same fabric. The skirt was full with several white petticoats underneath causing it to stand out approximately five inches from my legs. Don't laugh. It was 1962, and that's what everyone wore.

There was only one problem. When the night finally came for our date, I had a huge fever blister right in the center of my top lip. It was gigantic. In my mind it felt like it stuck out past my nose. Even if I hadn't had the fever blister, I didn't think he would try to kiss me because I thought everyone knew you didn't kiss good girls on a first date. Anyway, who in their right mind would want to kiss a huge fever blister?

We decided to go to the drive-in movies, and I was relieved that he didn't go in for the kiss. When we got home, like a gentleman he walked me to the door. As we approached the front porch, I could see my two teenage cousins from California peeking out the window. I was horrified. I knew that if I could see them, he could, too.

Sure enough, when we got to the front door, my worst fears came true. Cousins and all, he reached down and planted a sloppy wet kiss right on my big fat fever blister. It really hurt. It was painful, and I didn't like it. After thinking about that kiss, I could see it was a spiritual picture of a kiss I had received in the spiritual realm from the Lord that hurt my flesh just like that kiss had hurt my lip.

My encounter with the Lord started out one night through a dream. In the dream I saw a thief sneak into a bedroom. I couldn't see the face of the thief because it was covered by a hood. He opened drawers and closed them until he found what he wanted, and as he got ready to leave I could suddenly see that the thief in the dream was not a man. The thief in the dream was me.

When I woke up, my heart was pounding. I instantly remembered the time in my life when I was a teenager, that I had gone to California to spend time with my mother's brother and his wife. While I was at their home I stole my uncle's ring. It had a gold band with a black onyx in the center. My aunt and uncle didn't have any children, and when I came to visit they were always wonderful to me. I was like the daughter they never had.

After I got back home, I took the ring to a pawn shop and sold it for just a fraction of what it was worth. I was horrified that the Lord had brought up that sin that I had kept hidden in the back of my mind for years. I immediately asked the Lord to forgive me. After the dream, the Lord spoke, telling me I was going to have to go back and make it right. He also told me an amount to send them in repayment.

I was devastated. I cried for days as I wrote a letter telling them what I had done and asking for their forgiveness. With the letter, I also included the check. After mailing the letter, I continued to cry for the next few days as I waited for their response. I was devastated.

When they got the letter, they called me. Hearing my uncle's voice on the other end of the line, I broke down and continued to sob. I couldn't contain myself. I was so humiliated. He told me that he definitely forgave me and tried to comfort me by saying there was a time in his life when he had stolen something, too.

After I talked with him, my aunt got on the phone. I was still crying as I told her how sorry I was. She then said the most amazing thing. She said, "Jenny, I have always wondered if there was a God, and now I know there is one. I was the one who bought that ring, and the amount of the check you sent was the exact amount that I paid for it." I was shocked. That was the last thing I expected her to say.

After the talk with my aunt and uncle, I realized the kiss the Lord gave me by sending me the dream hurt my flesh just as my flesh hurt when Bruce kissed me on my fever blister, but no matter how bad it hurt I realized the Lord had a plan to use it for good. I also realized that kiss was for His benefit, not mine. Even though it hurt, the pain I experienced was worth it because He had a great kiss waiting in the wings for me when I discovered how He used it in my aunt's life.

3. Weak in the knees.

It happened that when the priests came into the holy place, the cloud filled the house of the Lord, so that the priest COULD NOT STAND to minister because of the cloud, for the glory of the Lord filled the house of the Lord. 1 Kings 8:10-11

I then thought about another kiss that happened when I was in high school. The boy was a senior who had been voted most handsome, and I was a sophomore. I didn't know him very well, but I liked him and I was thrilled that he wanted to have a date with me. After the date, he walked me to the door, leaned in, and gave me a kiss.

How can I describe that kiss? There are no words. It was my very first passionate kiss. I had never been kissed like that before. It was a really good one. There was only one problem—my knees became weak and I could hardly stand up. I remember holding onto him as he slowly walked me over to the white iron bench that was sitting on my front porch. If he had not held on to me I would have fallen. I was so embarrassed. There is no telling what he thought. I can only imagine, since he never asked me for another date.

As I was thinking about that kiss I realized, unlike that kiss, when I have had an encounter with the Lord and have been weak in the knees and even fallen on my knees, I have never even one time been embarrassed. He doesn't mind at all when I fall on my knees. One of the first times I found myself on my knees before the Lord, I was at home in my bedroom standing by my bed when the Lord spoke, telling me He had given me a new name written on a white stone, and He told me my new name.

> *Whoever has ears, let them hear what the Spirit says to the*
> *churches. To the one who is victorious, I will give some of*
> *the hidden manna. I will also give that person a white stone*
> *with a new name written on it, known only to the one who*
> *receives it.* Revelation 2:17

Over the years, I have learned it is okay for us to get on our knees before the Lord. After all, we probably need the practice, because the day is coming when every knee shall bow and every tongue confess that Jesus Christ is Lord.

> *Therefore, God exalted him to the highest place and gave*
> *him the name that is above every name, that at the name of*
> *Jesus every knee should bow, in heaven and on earth and*
> *under the earth, and every tongue acknowledge that Jesus*
> *Christ is Lord, to the glory of God the Father.*
> Philippians 2: 9-11

4. My worst kiss.

I also thought about my worst kiss and my best kiss. I will go ahead, get it over with, and tell you about my worst kiss. When I was a senior in high school, a football player from another school invited me to go water skiing. I was not good at any sports, but one thing I could do well was water ski. I bought a new royal blue bathing suit, and I was so excited about the date.

When Saturday came, he pulled up with his parents' shiny new boat behind his car. When I got into the car, he introduced me to another couple who were sitting in the back seat. His car didn't have an air conditioner so we rode to the lake with all the windows down. The couple in the back seat almost sat on each other's lap, making out all the way to the lake. I couldn't have pried them apart if I'd wanted to.

When we reached the lake the other three skied first, and then it was my turn. To tell you the truth I wanted to show off a little bit and impress them with how good I was at skiing, so I extended my left leg horizontally across the water putting my foot in the loop on the rope. I then leaned back on the ski that was resting on the water with my right foot. Everything was great for a few minutes. I was gliding across the water with the greatest of ease. I was very proud of myself, but when I glanced up to see if they were watching I could see that my efforts to impress them were in vain. They were busy talking.

Suddenly, I slipped and fell and my foot was caught in the rope. Because I couldn't get it out, I received what was probably a twenty-five mile an hour enema. When they finally realized I was being dragged they stopped the boat, and helped me get in. My date quickly said, "Oh no, you must have hit the bottom of the lake because there is brown mud all over the bottom of your bathing suit."

The only thing they didn't know for just a few minutes was that it wasn't mud. My date grabbed a towel and tried to get the so called mud off of me. It didn't take long until they decided it was time to go.

When we got in the car and started home, I noticed that the couple in the back seat sat apart with one's head sticking out the right window, and the other had their head sticking out the left window. The only thing I was thankful for is that they didn't go to my school. I was so glad I would never have to see them again, and no one I knew would ever know what had happened. My date took the couple home and then told me he needed to take the boat by his parent's house before he took me home. I was horrified. All I could think about was getting home and getting in the shower.

When we got to his parent's house, he insisted that I should come in and meet his mother. I thought he surely had to be either an idiot or his nose wasn't working. He wouldn't take no for an answer. I still remember walking into their lovely home covered with poop. I am sure his mother must have been shocked as he introduced his date. After the nightmare of meeting his mother, he took me home.

As he walked me to the front door, I can still remember the tears streaming down my face. I tried to hold them back but I couldn't, and then to make matters worse, he reached down and kissed me. Yes, that's right—poop and all—he kissed me. I couldn't say a word. I was horrified. As I opened the door and ran to the shower, all I could do was sob out loud. I couldn't stop.

The shame of what I had been through had been too much. As I locked the bathroom door and touched the knob in the shower, I knew I would have to turn it on full force. I stood in that hot shower for what seemed like forever, hoping the force of the water and the antibacterial soap would wash away not only the poop but also the most embarrassing moment of my life.

After thinking about that date that ended with a kiss on my front porch as tears of shame ran down my cheeks, I thought about another front porch where the Lord kissed me years later. It was the night when I was born again. This time my tears of shame came from all the sins I had committed in my life. If I had the ability to wash away the stench of a lifetime of sin that night, I would have done it, but I couldn't.

Jesus was the only One who could wash me. He was the only One who could remove the stain of all my sins and make me clean. When I reached out to Him, asking Him to forgive me of my sins, He heard my cry and saw my tears, but unlike the young man He didn't just turn his back and walk away leaving me with my tears to wash myself. He lovingly reached down with His blood and washed away my sins, removing them from me as far as the east is from the west. He made me as clean as the wind driven snow. He didn't leave even one spot or blemish.

The shame is over now. It's gone. I don't have to worry about the stain of sin ever again. Today, I stand amazed at the way He loves me. It's true—He really loves me, and now that I am clean He kisses me any time He wants to.

> *And from Jesus Christ, who is the faithful witness, and the first begotten of the dead, and the prince of the kings of the earth; unto Him that loved us, and washed us from our sins in His own blood.*　　　　　　　　Revelation 1:5

5. My best kiss.

The last kiss I thought about that night was my best kiss. Mark and I have been married for forty-eight years now, but we got off to a really rocky start. I am surprised we ever made it. When I was in college, I had to have surgery and drop out of school for a semester. After my body healed, I had some extra time before getting back to school so I interviewed at Southwestern Bell and got a job in their marketing department.

I had four bosses, and one of the men I worked for was Mark Elder. He was quiet and shy, but I noticed by the board on the wall where all the sales results were posted, that every month he was always the top salesman in the department. It wasn't love at first sight, but the more I was around him the more I liked him. He had a great sense of humor, and he always made me laugh. I think he missed his calling in life. He should have been a comedian.

It was the policy in the department at that time that you couldn't date anyone in the office, but in spite of the policy, when I discovered he was single I decided I wanted a date with him. The only problem that stood in the way of dating him was that he would never ask me. Since he wasn't asking I decided to take matters in my own hands. I devised an elaborate lie, telling him that my cousin from California was coming to town and I wanted to fix him up on a date with her.

Now remember just for clarification, this elaborate scheme was for me in the year BC—before Christ. On the day of the supposed date, he called me to find out when he should come by and pick her up. On the other end of the line, I told him I was so sorry but she hadn't come in. I then told him how sad I was that I had ruined his evening, slipping in the fact I didn't have any plans either.

After a long silence on the other end of the line, he finally said, "Well, since neither of us have anything to do, would you like to go out?" I didn't want to appear too eager, so I paused and said very slowly, "Well, I guess so." I was so excited but suddenly very nervous. It dawned on me that He was six-and-a-half years older than me, and I had never dated an older man before.

I decided everything had to be perfect when he got there. I told my mother and dad they would have to get dressed in their best clothes. I told my dad, who was a carpenter, he needed to put his one and only suit on. I spent the entire afternoon on myself. Nothing was left untouched. I made sure I was ready from stem to stern. They had never seen me act like that before. I am sure they thought I was going overboard which, of course, I was.

Before Mark got there, I scanned the house to see if everything was in order only to notice that my beautiful sister's hair needed to be combed, so instead of asking her to comb it herself, I combed it. I then positioned her on the couch the way I thought she would look best. When I stood back to look at her I decided she would make a better impression without her glasses, so I removed them, leaving her sitting on the couch blind as a bat and very unhappy with me. In hindsight we all laugh about this story, but no one in my family was laughing about it on that day.

Then at the last minute, when I thought everything was just right, my little brother who had been out roaming the neighborhood came in covered with dirt. I immediately gave him money, bribing him to get lost until Mark and I left. I remember my Dad saying that day, "Jenny, I don't know this man, but obviously you have put him on a pedestal. He couldn't be that great—after all he puts his pants on one leg at a time just like the rest of us."

When Mark finally got there, I thought I had accomplished my goal to make him think we were the perfect family. I can still remember that warm summer night. Mark had just bought a 1963, split-window coupe gold corvette, and when I got in the car I remember smelling the newness of the leather and the wonderful fragrance of his cologne. He took me to a little club in Fort Worth, and we had a great time dancing the night away. Romance was definitely in the air. Mark was everything I thought he would be. The pedestal that I had put him on was intact.

On the drive home we continued to talk and laugh until something happened. Suddenly from the driver's side of the car many very, very— and I mean very—loud noises erupted. The sounds could have easily been the sounds you hear at a concert. They began with several deep drum rolls followed by rippling sounds from the trombone section. Then, if that wasn't enough, the piano just had to join in with the high notes only to have the drums ending out the concert lightly quivering on the driver's seat of the car.

When it was over, the smell from the thunderous sounds reached my nostrils, and in a split second Mark had fallen off the pedestal. All I was left with was an unpleasant, unwanted aroma in my nose. Mark was horrified. Having experienced one of the most embarrassing moments of his life, he rolled down the windows and said, "Excuse me." I was shocked. I couldn't even respond.

All I wanted to do was get home and get out of that car. It was several months before I reluctantly agreed to go out with him again after remembering that what Mark had done was minor compared to what I had done on the skiing accident. From then on Mark was on his best behavior. After I had dated him for two years, while he went to Cincinnati, Ohio, on a business trip, I realized I had fallen in love with him.

When he came back, he popped the question, "Will you marry me?" I was thrilled. There was only one problem. Before I answered him, the thought suddenly crossed my mind that if I was going to be getting married I would have to cook. A family member had just received an electric skillet and had been telling me how wonderful it was, so instead of the usual reply of, "Yes," I said, "If we don't get an electric skillet for a wedding present, would you buy me one?" I wish you could have seen the look on his face. He immediately said, "Yes!"

Our Wedding Day

The day we got married started off with a big surprise. We had relatives in from out of town. To make room for them, my sister Robin and I gave up our bedrooms, sleeping together in my brother's room while he slept at a friend's house. Before I opened my eyes that morning, I had an unusual sensation that something was different. I opened them to find my left arm resting on top of my head and my sister sound asleep, curled up against me with her nose nestled in my armpit.

About that time Robin woke up with the realization she had her nose in my armpit. When her eyes met mine, we both started laughing uncontrollably. We couldn't stop. We laughed until our sides hurt. It was a first for both of us. She had never had her nose in anyone's armpit before, and I had never had anyone's nose in mine. We have laughed about the armpit story for years, and I have used it as a spiritual picture about never invading someone's privacy by putting our noses where they don't belong.

If I thanked the Lord every hour of every day, I could never thank Him enough for the gift of my sister. There are no words to express how much I love her. She is not only full of wisdom, but she is the most giving, loving person I have ever met. She has walked through life with me and always been there when I have needed her. It is wonderful to be with someone that knows everything about you and still loves you in spite of everything they know.

Mark and I got married on June 8, 1968. Everything about that day was all I dreamed it would be. In my eyes, the dress was perfect. The flowers were perfect and the chapel was breathtaking as the light of the candles flickered against the stained glass windows. I still remember the moment when the preacher said, "I now pronounce you man and wife; you may kiss your bride." As Mark lifted the veil, and as his lips met mine it was the sweetest kiss I had ever experienced. My time of waiting for him was over. He was mine, all mine, and I was finally his, all his.

As we sealed the deal with a kiss, I realized all my earthly dreams had come true. We were one, and I was ready to begin the rest of my life with him by my side. As I thought about that kiss, I was reminded of my encounter with the Lord when He gave me the kiss of possession. It was the night His waiting for me was over. It was the night when I gave my life to Him. It was the night when He became mine, and I became His. It was the night I began my new life with Him. It was the night when He sealed the deal with a kiss as He placed His Spirit inside me, to live with me for the rest of my life. It was the night when all my heavenly dreams came true, because I would spend not only this earthly life but also my eternal life with Him by my side.

Till I Kissed Ya

In 1959, Don Everly wrote a song entitled "Till I Kissed Ya," sung by the Everly Brothers. The words to that song describe how have I felt over the years when the Lord has kissed me with a word, a dream, a vision, or a visitation.

> Never felt like this until I kissed ya
> How did I exist until I kissed ya
> Never had you on my mind
> Now you're there all the time
> Never knew what I missed till I kissed ya, uh-huh
> I kissed ya, oh yeah

Things have really changed since I kissed ya, uh-huh
My life's not the same now that I kissed ya, oh yeah
Mmm, ya got a way about ya
Now I can't live without ya
Never knew what I missed till I kissed ya, uh-huh
I kissed ya, oh yeah

You don't realize what you do to me
And I didn't realize what a kiss could be
Mmm, ya got a way about ya
Now I can't live without ya
Never knew what I missed till I kissed ya, uh-huh
I kissed ya, oh yeah

The words to that song were really true in my life. I had never realized what a kiss from the Lord could be like. I had never felt like I started feeling until I had been kissed by the King of Kings. Once He started kissing me by revealing Himself to me, I finally learned how to start kissing Him right back with my words of worship.

My spiritual life really did change—it wasn't the same anymore. I sometimes wonder how I ever existed on planet earth without those close encounters of the third kind, the Holy Ghost kind. I guess I survived because I just didn't know what I was missing. Now I can't live even one day without Him. I am ADDICTED to the kisses of His lips. I have to have them.

How Do You Like to be Kissed?

I saw the movie, "For the Love of the Game," starring Kevin Costner and Kelly Preston. At the beginning of the movie, Kevin's character asked Kelly's character a great question, "How do you like to be kissed?" I know exactly how I would answer that question when it comes to spiritual kisses. I like for the Lord to kiss me any way He wants to.

I want to ask you the same question? How do you like to be kissed? The Lord has many kisses for us in the streams of the Spirit, not only the kiss of possession but the kiss of revelation, the kiss of a manifestation, the kiss of intoxication, the kiss of jubilation, the kiss of communion, the kiss of inspiration, the kiss of illumination, the kiss of conversion, the kiss of sanctification, the kiss of compassion, and the kiss of a visitation, just to name a few.

He doesn't want us to just read about His kisses or be like my cousins who were peeking out the window, watching from a distance. He wants us to move into the place of intimacy with Him for ourselves. He wants us to remove the veils of doubt and unbelief that keep us from receiving what He wants to give us. He wants us to remove the veil of lies that tell us we are not worthy to receive His kisses. He wants us to remove the veils of the man-made shackles of religion that keep us from receiving everything He wants to give us. He wants us to remove the veils of comparison where we compare ourselves with ourselves. He wants to kiss all of us, not just some of us.

I want to encourage you to tell Him how you like to be kissed. He is just waiting for you to ask Him. He wants us to discover for ourselves that the words to that old song written by the Weavers and sung by Jimmie Rodgers are true: "He Has Kisses Sweeter Than Wine." He wants us to discover for ourselves that we were created for His pleasure and He takes great pleasure in kissing us. He wants us to discover for ourselves the secret from the secret place that HIS LIPS ARE MOIST WITH GRACE, and He also wants us to discover how much fun it is, when He kisses us, to kiss Him right back.

7

The Secret of the Song

The Song of Songs which is Solomon's Song of Solomon 1:1

When I was finally ready to enter into the Song of Solomon, I opened the book and focused on the first four words in the first verse, "The Song of Songs." As a new Christian, I had loved reading about the King of Kings, the Lord of Lords, and the Holy of Holies, but I didn't want to have anything to do with the Song of Songs until the Lord opened my heart to its splendor.

As I said those first four words over and over, I suddenly realized if God through Solomon had chosen to let us know it was the Song of Songs, then it wasn't just another ordinary song. I knew if Jesus was the King of Kings, He was the King above all the kings who had ever lived. If He was the Lord of Lords, He was the Lord above all the lords who had ever existed. If this was the Song of Songs, there must be something very special about this song. As I began to read through the song with new eyes, I suddenly felt like I was on holy ground. This song was a song that lovers sing, written in the language of love. It was a song of passion, a song of desire. I could hear the words of praise and adoration flowing back and forth between the two lead singers. It was almost like going to an opera and hearing the bridegroom unveiling his love to his bride and then hearing the bride unveiling her passionate love right back to him.

As I read the words of the bridegroom, singing his part over his bride, I thought about the words of Zephaniah:

> *The Lord your God is with you. He is mighty to save. He will take great delight in you. He will quiet you with His love. He will rejoice over you with singing.* Zephaniah 3:17

[handwritten note: One of my fav verses]

I loved the idea of the Lord Jesus Christ singing over me. As I read the words of the bride singing her part over her bridegroom, I thought about how much the Lord loves for us to sing our songs of worship to Him—but I had questions.

What was the Lord's purpose in writing this song? Did He want me to just read the words to this song, or did He have something else in mind? Was He trying to show me that He wanted me to sing love songs to Him? Did He want me to listen to Him, as He sang love songs over me? Was that even really possible? If I were going to enter into this song, what words would I sing?

Surely He wouldn't want me to recite words to Him that came from the heart of the Shulamite. Those words came from her heart—they didn't come from mine. Suddenly, I knew the answers to my questions. He did want me to enter into this eternal love song, and the words He wanted me to sing were not the words that came from the Shulamite or words that came from my head. He wanted me to sing words to Him that came from my heart.

It was at that moment I knew if I sang the words to Him that came from my heart, those words would flow into His heart and He would feel my love. The Lord wants all of us to enter into the ever growing, ever flowing Song of Songs. He wants to caress our souls with His love and allow the songs that are alive in our hearts to rise up from our innermost being and embrace His heart.

His Heartbeat *sing to beat of His heart*

As I continued to explore the song I realized, in order to enter into the Song of Songs, the words were not going to be a problem, but as everyone knows, every song has a different beat. In order to sing a song, you have to be able to hear the beat to the song. The same had to be true about this song. Would I ever be able to hear the beat on this side of heaven?

Then it happened. In the depths of my soul I knew, the songs He wanted me to sing to Him needed to be sung to the rhythm of His heart beating with love for me. I realized if I always sang in response to His heart of love beating for me, His love would spark my love, allowing my words to ride into His heart on the wings of love. With that realization, I knew nothing could hold me back. I was finally ready to enter in with my songs of love and sing them to the Lover of my soul.

The Power of a Song

We all know that there is something magical about the power of a song. A song has the power to stir our souls, lift us up when we are down, and to saturate us with a peace that passes all understanding. No wonder our Lord chose to set His words in this song to music. I think He wants us to understand that it thrills Him when we use our vocal cords to elevate our words of love for Him to the high places with our high notes, to the low places with our low notes, and allow our words of love to flow into Him from all the places in between.

He loves for us to worship Him with our songs. The Word of the Lord tells us that we were "created for His pleasure," and it gives Him great pleasure to hear our songs of worship. I will never forget one of the first times I accidentally stumbled into the beauty of singing a song to the Lord from my heart. It was so simple, yet the results were so profound. As I was lying on my bed, thinking about how much I was enjoying getting to know the Lord, I began to hear the words of a secular song in my mind.

At first the idea of singing a song that I hadn't learned in church to the Lord was foreign to my idea of what I should be singing, but the words to that song expressed exactly what I was feeling. I was all alone with no one else there, so right or wrong, I just jumped in and started singing the words to that song slowly out loud to the Lord. The name of the song was, "Getting to Know You."

> Getting to know You
> Getting to know about You
> When I am with You
> Getting to know what to say
>
> Haven't You noticed
> Suddenly I'm light and easy
> Because of all the beautiful and new
> Things I'm learning about You, day by day

As I sang, I could feel His presence. I then heard Him say, "Jenny, where did that song come from?" Hearing the sound of His voice startled me. I immediately felt chills all over my body as I thought about the answer to His question. The song I was singing was from, "The King and I." I didn't move a muscle as I allowed truth to sink into every fiber of my being.

Wow! The King was right there with me, listening to my words. From that moment in time, I have always been conscious of the fact that I am never alone. Wherever I go, the King is always with me. I also learned to never underestimate the power of singing words to the Lord from my heart no matter how simple they may be. They have a way of ushering me into His presence like nothing else can.

The words we sing don't have to be fancy. He doesn't care about fancy. We don't have to have a great voice to sing our songs of love to Him. It's not the greatness of our voices that move Him. What touches Him is when He knows that it is our love for Him that makes our hearts sing.

Chris

One of the greatest joys of my life is my son Chris. When he was just eight years old, the Lord spoke to me about him. It was on a weekday, and I had just finished teaching a Bible study in the chapel at church. When everyone had left, I walked into the main sanctuary. I can still remember exactly where I was standing when the Lord said, "I am going to use Chris for My glory to lead others into the place of worshipping Me with their songs."

After college, Chris moved to Austin and married the love of his life, Wendy. They found a church they enjoyed there, and because Chris played the guitar and loved to sing, he joined the worship team. After some time, he became one of the worship leaders in that church.

The first time I went to church with him in Austin, as Chris was leading the worship, I was overwhelmed with the presence of the Lord. As I looked around at all the worshippers, worshipping the Lord with their songs, I had a flashback. I remembered the day the Lord told me Chris would be a worship leader. I am so thrilled Chris worships the Lord with his songs, but I know the Lord is even more pleased than I am.

He Will Rejoice Over You with Singing

> *The Lord thy God in the midst of thee is mighty; He will*
> *save, He will rejoice over you with joy, He will rest in His*
> *Love, He will joy over you with singing. Zephaniah 3:17*

A.W. Tozer wrote in his book, "Mystery of the Holy Spirit," "The Holy Spirit is a living Person. And as He is a living Person, you can know Him and fellowship with Him, whisper to Him, and have His voice whisper back to you in some love text from the Bible or some love song."

I clearly remember the first time I heard Him "joying" over me with singing. I was in a flower shop buying some artificial flowers to make a flower arrangement for my kitchen table. I was busy loading my cart with flowers when I heard the Lord say, "Jenny, would you be willing to do the wedding march down this aisle?"

The store was packed with women, and my first reaction was to look around to see who would be watching. I was aware of the fact that if I did the wedding march down that isle I would definitely look like I was crazy, but then everything seemed to pale in the light of being obedient to the One I loved. I knew what He wanted me to do.

Do you remember how brides used to do the wedding march years and years ago? They would take one step with their right foot bringing their left foot up beside it and then stop. They would then take another step with their left foot bringing up their right foot alongside and then pause. They would continue doing this until they got to the end of the aisle where their bridegroom was waiting.

As I took the first step, I suddenly heard the sound of His voice again. To my surprise He was singing. There is no way to express on paper the beauty of the words or the beauty of the melody. I can still remember my heart racing with the knowledge that He was alive, singing over me, expressing His love to me through a song. To tell you the truth, if I hadn't held on to that cart I would have never made it down that aisle. When I got to the end of the aisle, there was a huge picture of a bride and a groom gazing into one another's eyes.

At that moment the Lord spoke to me and said, "Jenny, as you walk down the aisle of life, don't ever forget that I love you. Don't ever forget who you are. You are My bride. I have sent an escort, My Spirit, to escort you to the wedding. With every step you take, from this day forward, remember that you are one step closer to the wedding supper of the Lamb."

I learned on that day that the Word of the Lord is true. He really does, "rejoice over us with singing."

Tabernacle of David

After these things I will return, and I will rebuild the Tabernacle of David, which is fallen down, and I will build again the ruins thereof, and I will set it up.   Acts 15:16

It is impossible to write a chapter on how much the Lord loves our songs without looking at the Tabernacle of David. It is the key that reveals the magnitude of the Lord's passion for our songs. Years ago, I heard Rick Godwin preach a great sermon on the Tabernacle of David, and I want to share some of his insights as well as some of mine about this tabernacle.

In Acts 15:16, the Lord tells us He is going to restore the Tabernacle of David. He didn't say He was going to restore Tabernacle of Moses. He didn't say He was going to restore the Temple of Solomon. The only tabernacle He ever said that He would restore was the Tabernacle of David.

From the Word of God, we know that the only piece of furniture in the Tabernacle of David was the Ark of the Covenant, and above the Mercy Seat on that ark was the presence of God. The ark went on a long journey before David finally brought it to that tabernacle on Mount Zion. For forty years it traveled with the children of Israel through the wilderness. After leaving the wilderness and entering into the promised land, a terrible thing happened. God allowed the Ark of the Covenant, to be taken away from the Israelites by their enemy, the Philistines, because they started worshipping other gods. They fell into idolatry and ignored His presence.

When we read about this in the Bible, our first thought is to judge them. How stupid they were to ignore His presence by going after other gods, but before we judge them too harshly, we need to look at our own lives. Many of us do the same thing today. We ignore His presence, spending our time running after our own gods: the god of money, the god of prestige, the god of power, and the god of materialism. Amazingly, we act just like they did hundreds of years ago. The only difference is the names of our gods.

After the ark had been in captivity for many years, David was inaugurated as King of Israel and decided to bring it back to the nation of Israel where it belonged. When he went after the ark, someone once said it wasn't the gold he was going after. What he was going after was "the presence of God."

After making a mistake by trying to bring the presence of God back to Jerusalem on a manmade cart, David learned a valuable lesson that all of us need to remember today. You can never bring the presence of God in on anything manmade. We can't bring His presence in on a manmade program, a manmade idea, or a new gimmick. David discovered that the only way the presence of God could be brought into Jerusalem was on the shoulders of the priest. What a perfect picture.

Who carries the presence of God today? We do. His Spirit dwells in all of us who have been born again, and we are the ones who carry His presence. When David finally brought the ark back to Israel, he didn't place it on Mt. Gibeon where the Tabernacle of Moses had been set up. He placed it five miles away in a tent on Mt. Zion, the highest point in Jerusalem which of course is in the land of Judah. Keep in mind that the word Judah means praise.

The Exciting Part of the Tent

What took place in that tent that caused the Lord to love it so much He wanted to restore it? We find the answer to that question in 1 Chronicles 15:29; and 16:1-24. After placing the Ark of the Covenant into the tent, David appointed priestly singers along with the priests who played their instruments of music, harps, cymbals and trumpets to minister to the Lord. They all had their assignments, and they sang and played before the Lord in shifts.

The word of God tells us that they were in that tent, *"CONTINUALLY"* in 1 Chronicles 16:6. They didn't go into the tent to worship the Lord once

Raise & Worship

a week. They didn't go into the tent just on Sunday mornings, Sunday nights, and Wednesday nights. For twenty-four hours a day, seven days a week, three hundred and sixty-five days a year—day and night for almost thirty-six years—they took turns singing praises and worshipping the Lord with their songs and instruments in that tent.

If you passed by the tent at 4 a.m. you would have heard their songs flowing out. If you passed by at 7:15 p.m. you would have heard their songs flowing from that tent. You would never pass by that tent at any hour of the day or night without hearing the songs flowing out. They didn't go in once a year with the blood of a sinless lamb. No, what they brought in was their songs. Wouldn't it have been awesome to have heard their songs of worship?

Why did David institute worship to flow from that tent? I think he knew how much his Lord and his God loved his songs. I think he knew the power of the song that could minister to the heart of God like nothing else could. After Israel's sin of ignoring the presence of God for all those years, I think he wanted to please the Lord with the beauty of worshippers who would worship Him with their instruments and songs day and night.

The Lord said He would restore Tabernacle of David. Why? I think it is because the Tabernacle of David thrilled Him. In the Tabernacle of David, it wasn't the blood that flowed in His presence. It was the songs of praise and worship that flowed in His presence. After Jesus shed his blood on the cross, the blood never had to flow ever again. Now, what He loves to hear flowing is the sound of our songs.

When He says He is going to restore Tabernacle of David, there are those in the body of Christ who don't think He meant He was going to set up another tent on a dirt hill in Israel and fill it with singers. They believe that we are the tent. We are the covering in which His presence dwells. 1 Corinthians 3:16, *says, "Do you not know that you are the temple of God and the Spirit of God dwells in you."* We are the place His Spirit dwells in today. When the song is flowing from our tents, some believe we could be part of the restoration of Tabernacle of David.

God's Pattern of Restoration

It is important to remember that anytime God restores anything the thing restored is always greater in quantity and quality. The latter is always greater than the former. After God gave Satan permission to devour Job, He restored everything that was taken from him two-fold. Samson lost his anointing. He lost his strength, but at the end of his life, God restored his strength and Samson destroyed more Philistines who were the enemies of God than he ever did in the beginning. The later was greater than the former. When Ezra rebuilt the temple of the Lord, he rebuilt it double the original dimensions.

Look around at all the dwelling places of God today. Listen to all the songs flowing out of our tents. At any hour of any day, somewhere all over the world there are hundreds of songs flowing from the tents of the saints. The latter is greater than the former. How do you think the Lord feels as He listens to our songs flowing from our tents? I think He loves them.

The Enemy Will Try to Rob Us of Our Song

As surely as the Lord loves for us to sing our love songs to Him, the enemy will try to rob us of our song. He will try to kill our song. He will tell us that we are not worthy to sing our songs—but the devil is a liar. When the enemy tries to destroy our song by telling us how sinful we are and telling us that God is not interested in hearing our songs, we need to remember the one whom God used to establish tabernacle of David.

David was not a perfect man. He was an adulterer who slept with another man's wife. He was the one who planned the murder of Uriah, Bathsheba's husband. He didn't have a perfect family. Not everyone loved him. He had a wife who despised him. He had rebellious, immoral kids. He had faults and problems just like we do.

What qualified David to be the one to establish this tabernacle that God loved so much? In 2 Samuel, we find the answer. David was described as the "Sweet Psalmist of Israel."

> *Now these are the last words of David. David, the son of Jesse saith, and the man who was raised on high saith, The anointed of the God of Jacob, And the SWEET PSALMIST OF ISRAEL, the Spirit of Jehovah spake by me, And his word was upon my tongue.* 2 Samuel 23:1-2

David was a worshipper. He knew how to worship his Lord and his God with his song. As a young boy tending the sheep, he would play his harp and sing songs to the Lord. I think his songs must have vibrated from his heart in such a powerful way that they ascended out of his mouth into the very heart of God.

When his son, Solomon was given the opportunity to ask for anything he wanted, he asked the Lord to give him wisdom. He was after God's mind, but David was after God's heart. His heart pulsated with passion for his Lord and his God, and out of the overflow of all that was in him he worshipped his God with his songs. David was a sinner, who made mistakes, but in spite of all his faults God loved his songs. We find many of the songs that he wrote in the Psalms.

When the enemy tries to steal our song, we need to remember that no one is perfect. If God was waiting for someone to be perfect in order to worship Him, worship would never happen. He is not looking for someone who has never sinned to worship Him. All He is listening for are words that come forth from a heart that is beating with love for Him. When the enemy tries to rob us of our song, we need to remember, that we have been forgiven. The blood of Jesus has cleansed us, and Jesus can hardly wait for us to bless Him with our songs.

I've Got You, Babe

One day as I was in the shower, I heard a song rolling around in my head. You know how you sometimes hear a song and you can't get it off your mind. That is exactly what happened, so I just started singing it. It was the old Sonny and Cher song, "Babe." Remember the words to the chorus?

Cher would sing to Sonny,
> "Babe, I've got you babe.
> You've got me and baby I've got you! Babe."

Sonny would sing right back to Cher,
> "Babe, I've got you babe.
> You've got me and baby I've got you. Babe."

I sang the chorus over and over because that was all I could remember. While I was singing, I just decided to change the words and sing it to the Lord. I sang, "Lord, I've got you, Lord. You've got me, and Jesus I've got You! Lord, I've got you Lord." As I sang those words over and over to the Lord they made me feel happy. I thought about the fact that He had me. The One who created me had me securely in His hands, and no one could ever take me out. I thought about the fact that I had Him. Since I had Him, I had everything I could ever want or need! It couldn't get any better than that.

I was having a great time singing when I suddenly felt the presence of the Lord. I stopped singing and listened intently. Then I heard Him sing those fourteen words right back to me. "Babe, I've got you babe, you've got Me and, Jenny, I've got you, Babe." That was it. He only sang it one time. Then I heard Him say "Luke 10:21."

As I scrambled out of the shower, grabbing my New American Standard Bible, I read these words, *"In that hour Jesus rejoiced in spirit and said, I thank thee Father, Lord of heaven and earth, that thou hast hid these things from the wise and prudent, and hast revealed them unto*

BABES." There it was, written in His Word, the very word that He had just called me, "babe." My heart started beating so hard I thought it was going to beat out of my chest. He called me babe. What was He saying?

I backed up and read the preceding verses. The seventy disciples had just returned from ministering saying, *"Even the devils are subject to us in your name. And Jesus said, Rejoice not that the spirits are subject unto you, but rather rejoice because your names are written in heaven."* The revelation that demons were subject to them in the name of Jesus is what had made the disciples rejoice, but Jesus assured them that it was more important to rejoice that their names were written in heaven.

Jesus was rejoicing over the fact that this truth had been hidden from those considered to be wise and prudent, but this deep eternal truth had been revealed to those who were just babes. The wise and intelligent didn't get the revelation. The Pharisees and Sadducees were the ones who were considered to be the wise and intelligent of that day. They were the ones who had a thorough knowledge of the scriptures, but when Jesus actually came He didn't live up to their preconceived ideas of how He should act, or what He should say.

They didn't receive Him because He didn't live up to their false expectations. Their minds were so clogged up with the letter of the law they didn't recognize Him when He stood right in front of them. He didn't reveal this truth to those who thought they had all the answers and didn't want to listen to Him. He revealed this truth to His disciples, to those who were like babes, who were willing to just follow Him, listen to His voice, receive what He told them, and believe what He told them was true.

I realized to receive revelation from the Lord, He doesn't want us to come to Him with our minds all puffed up with head knowledge. He wants us to come to Him like a babe with an attitude of being willing to just listen, believe, and receive. When I thought about the fact that He called me His babe, it made me happy because I knew there were times in my life I had certainly not acted like a babe. There were times when all I was after was head knowledge, but now I knew what I wanted more than anything else in this world was to be His babe.

Today, when I hear that old song sung by Sonny and Cher it makes me smile because of that day in the realm of the spirit He sang over me and called me His babe!

THE VISITATION

In the summer of 1999, I had a visitation from the Lord. We read in John 14:21 the words of Jesus:

> *The person who has my commands and keeps them is the one who loves me, and whoever loves me will be loved by my Father, and I will love him, and I WILL MANIFEST MYSELF TO HIM*   John 14:21

The word manifest in the Greek is *emphanizo*. It is pronounced em-fan-id-zo, and it means to reveal oneself, to appear, to show oneself, to allow oneself to be clearly seen. That is exactly what happened in 1999. He revealed Himself to me in a vision. The light of the glory of His presence flooded my room. He walked up to me, extending His right hand saying, "Come with Me."

My heart leapt at the sound of His voice. Suddenly, I was caught up in the Spirit. I was in the heavenly city. The brilliance of the beauty of the colors were breathtaking, but the sounds, oh, the sounds—there are no words. I was overwhelmed with the awesomeness of what I was hearing. The Lord said, "Listen closely."

I immediately heard a man singing from the depths of his soul Randy Travis' song, "I'm Going to Love You for Ever." He was singing and dancing before the Lord with such unbridled passion. I was shocked because this was a secular song. I thought when we got to heaven we would be very refined, standing in rows like a church choir, but this wasn't anything like I thought it would be. Then I heard a woman singing Celine Dion's song, "I'm Everything I Am Because You Loved Me." She sang,

For all the times You stood by me
For all the truth that You made me see
For all the joy You brought to my life
For all the wrong that You made right
For every dream You made come true
For all the love I found in You
I'm everything I am because You loved me.

You were my strength when I was weak
You were my voice when I couldn't speak
You were my eyes when I couldn't see
You saw the best there was in me
Lifted me up when I couldn't reach
You gave me faith when I couldn't believe
I'm everything I am because You loved me.

I then heard the voice of a man singing John Denver's "Annie's Song" lyrics "You fill up my senses," while another woman worshipped Him in the dance. I saw another woman singing, "Shout to The Lord" originally sung by Australia's Hillsong. Another woman was singing Whitney Houston's song "I Will Always Love You." A man was singing the lyrics of Rod Stewart's song, "Have I told you lately that I love you?" I heard him continue the song singing, "Have I told you there's no one else above You?" It went on and on and on.

I heard some singing the wonderful old hymns we used to sing. One man was singing, "Amazing grace, how sweet the sound that saved a wretch like me." What I was hearing was beyond magnificent. Some were singing secular songs. Some were singing spiritual songs, but when their voices rose up before the Lord it sounded like they were all singing one beautiful love song in perfect harmony. Suddenly, there was complete silence. There was a holy hush in heaven. Everyone stood as if they were just waiting for something, and then it happened.

The Lord started singing a love song over the saints. I had never heard anything so beautiful in all my life. I was overcome. All I could do was cry. Tears of joy ran down my face. I knew the saints would sing their songs, but for some reason it had never crossed my mind that He would sing, too. The magnitude of His glorious voice blew me away. I was undone.

After the song was over, the Lord spoke to me and said, "You didn't think the saints would be the only ones to get to sing in heaven, did you? After all, you were made in My image. Why do you think you like to sing? It is because I like to sing." The Lord laughed and said, "You thought when you got here you were going to have to memorize songs. That's not true. You can sing a secular song, songs you learned in church, or songs birthed from your own heart. The only thing I care about is that the words you sing express what is in your heart."

He then said, "I have been listening to you sing secular songs to Me for years, and I just wanted you to know I am pleased." He said, "Would you be willing to go back and tell them what you heard?" I wanted to stay in that place forever, but I knew He had given me an assignment. I came back from my visitation with a word from the Lord, "Whatever is in your heart, whether it is considered to be secular song, a spiritual song or a song that springs up from your own soul—as long as it comes from your heart, open your mouth wide and sing it. Go ahead, worship the One who died for you with your song! Caress His heart with your words of love.

After the visitation, I started thinking about all the places I had been in the world, and how nothing could compare with what I had seen and heard in the heavenly city. I wrote a poem about what I was feeling.

I've Seen Another City

I've seen the wonders of the world
Their beauties to behold
I've seen their hills and valleys
Heard their stories all unfold

I've see Egyptian pyramids
From along the River Nile
I've seen Paris in the springtime
With her Mona Lisa smile

I've seen the Queen of England
Her crown jewels shimmering on her shore
I've seen Rome's Sistine Chapel
Michaels masterpiece we all adore

I've sailed the deep blue ocean
As she glistened streaks of silver
I've seen the sun's glory glide the sky
Seen her set upon the rivers

I've seen Hawaii's lush green land
Topped with brilliant color
I've seen Mexico's shimmering sand
Where warmth does love to hover

I've seen San Francisco's golden gates
Bridge land across the water
I've seen New York's first lady
Hold torch higher ever hotter

I've gazed across Arizona's canyon
I've felt her west winds blow
I've seen Colorado's rocky highs
Capped with fresh fallen snow

But listen, my children, listen
I've got another story to unfold
I've seen another city
Where streets are paved with gold

The King unveiled her beauty
As glory filled my soul
Now I know it's really true
One day we will behold

After seeing this heavenly city
The world no longer lures
I no longer hear her calling me
Of that you can be sure

I've seen what flesh calls beauty
Their grace and style and form
But nothing can compare
With the heavenly city's charm

For I've seen another city
The only one I want to see
The reason for her beauty?
The King who reigns there is in love with me

The Secret of the Song

Lord, help us remember the secret of this song. Keep reminding us that You don't want us to just read this song or just think about this song, just memorize this song, or even just talk about this song, but You are longing for the power behind the words of this song to usher us into a divine love affair. Keep reminding us that You want all of us to enter into this ever growing, ever flowing, eternal love song and sing our part from our hearts to You, our King, our Beloved Savior, the Lover of our souls.

8

The Secret of the Dance

Why should you gaze at the Shulamite, as at the dance of
the two companies?   Song of Songs 6:13

I n this verse, the King compares gazing at the Shulamite to watching the "dance of the two companies." Even though there is no way to know for sure exactly what kind of dance he was talking about, we can look at Genesis 32:10 to see what the words "two companies" might represent.

Jacob said, *"I crossed over the Jordon with my staff, and now I have become 'two companies.'"* In other words, He crossed over with nothing but a stick in his hand, but God blessed him and he came back a very rich man surrounded with cattle, servants, and family. He came back in a place of victory over a life of defeat.

The dance of the "two companies" could be a picture of the dance that someone does when they have been down, in a place of defeat, and have experienced the Lord bringing them through a difficult time to a place of victory. We are not sure exactly what kind of dance the king was describing, but one thing we do know for sure from His Word is that our King loves for us to worship Him in the dance.

Let them praise His name in the dance.   Psalms 149:3

Praise Him with the timbrel and the dance. Psalms 150:4

Miriam Danced

When the children of Israel crossed the red sea and experienced the Lord delivering them from their enemies, Miriam and the women worshipped the Lord in the dance. They were celebrating with their bodies what they were feeling in their hearts. They were celebrating what the Lord had done. You might say, they were doing the "victory" dance.

> *Miriam the prophetess, Aaron's sister, took the timbrel in her hand, and all the women went out after her with timbres and with dancing.*   Exodus 15:20

You Make Me Feel Like Dancing

Dancing has always been part of my life. When I was in high school, my Mom and Dad bought a brand new stereo system which we put in our living room. It was in the olden days when our music consisted of the forty-five and seventy-eight rpm vinyl records. The system also had a radio in it that played all the current popular songs.

In my junior year, I had a boyfriend who was a great dancer. When he came over, we would always head for the living room, put on the oldies but goodies, and dance. He taught me all the latest moves including the watusi, the alligator, and the bop. One Friday night we went to a school dance and to our surprise, we won the prize for the best dancers.

Mark is a good dancer too. We have always had fun dancing together. We have danced in many places, but probably the most fun place we have ever danced is on the bottom of the ocean floor. Of course we didn't have any music, but we didn't need the music of the world in order to dance—we made our own music. When my boys were young we always had music and dancing going on in our house, and even today when my grandchildren come over we are always dancing.

In hindsight, I think all the dancing I have ever done was in preparation for the time when I discovered that the Lord loves for us to worship Him in the dance. That must have been one of the reasons He put the desire to move to the music in our bones. When the Lord and I are all alone, I love to put on my favorite songs and worship Him in the dance.

In 1977, the song "You Make Me Feel Like Dancing" by Leo Sayer, became a number one hit song in the United States. I love the words to the chorus of that song. They describe exactly how I feel when I think about the Lord. He makes me feel like dancing.

> You make me feel like dancing
> I want to dance the night away
> You make me feel like dancing
> I'm gonna dance the night away
> You make me feel like dancing
> I feel like dancing, dancing, dancing the night away

David Danced Before the Lord with all His might

> *David danced before the Lord with all his might.*
> ***2 Samuel 6:14***

After David was inaugurated as King of Israel, he went after the ark of the covenant that had been in captivity in the hands of the Philistines and brought it back to Jerusalem. When he entered the city with the ark, the Word of the Lord tells us that, *"David was dancing before the Lord with all of his might."* To celebrate the return of the nation's most precious possession, he threw restraint to the wind and celebrated with every fiber of his being.

Instead of rejoicing with him, Michal, David's wife, stood at her window and watched her husband from a distance. The Word of the

Lord tells us she didn't like it; she *"despised him in her heart."* When he returned from the day's celebration, she chastised him. In response David said, *"It was before the Lord, who chose me above your father and above all his house, to appoint me ruler over the people of the Lord, over Israel; therefore, I will celebrate before the Lord"* (2 Samuel 6:21). David made it clear he wasn't dancing to entertain the people. He was dancing before his Lord and his God.

Dancing Allows Our Bodies the Freedom to Express What is Going On in our Spirits

Many Christians think dancing before the Lord is a ridiculous thing to do. It is a foreign concept that makes no sense to our natural minds. Most of us have not been raised to understand the power of allowing our bodies the freedom to release what is going on in our spirits through the power of the dance. If the truth be told, we have all seen others dance before the Lord, and just like Michal we didn't like it.

The question that has to be answered when we watch someone dance, worshipping the Lord, is "What is their motive?" Is their motive to impress others, or are they truly worshiping the Lord in the dance? If their motive is to dance for their own benefit, to draw attention to themselves, the dance will be offensive, but there is nothing more beautiful than to watch someone dancing out of a heart that is truly overflowing with love for their Lord and their God.

One of the most beautiful sights I have ever had the privilege to witness was a precious friend of mine, Mary Alice White, who has now gone home to be with the Lord. When she danced before Him, I am sure all the angels stood in awe at the way she exuded her love for Him in the dance.

We can choose to stand at the window of disdain like Michal and make fun of those who have chosen to enter in, or we can make the choice to enter into the dance for ourselves. I know what you are thinking. There is no way that you would ever dance before the Lord in the presence of anyone else. I totally understand. I feel the same way, but you don't have to be in church to dance before the Lord. You can dance before Him in the privacy of your own home. If you ever find yourself all alone, in a place of being overwhelmed with what the Lord has done, I want to challenge you to put on your favorite music and allow your body the freedom to express what is going on in your spirit.

I Could Have Danced All Night

I still remember the time when I, like David, couldn't contain myself. I had to enter into the dance. Mark and the boys had gone to the ranch for the weekend, and I was all alone in my home getting ready to teach at a women's retreat with the overwhelming thought that I didn't want to serve leftovers. I wanted a fresh word from the Lord. I wanted something hot off heaven's grill.

As I was reading the Word, it suddenly came alive and did high kicks in my spirit. The Lord was giving me exactly what I had asked Him for, fresh manna from heaven. I was beside myself with joy. I can still remember setting the Bible down with the knowledge that I had to release the joy that was bubbling up on the inside of me with my body. I wanted to thank Him. I wanted to worship Him with every part of my being. I wanted to celebrate.

I remember putting on my favorite worship songs and beginning to dance. It was truly a time where I worshiped Him in the dance, releasing what I was feeling in my spirit. At some point the dance changed from overwhelming thanksgiving, celebrating what the Lord had done, to the slow dance of expressing my overwhelming love to the Lover of my soul.

You may remember the old movie, "My Fair Lady" starring Julie Andrews. It was one of my favorites. I think I loved it because Liza Doolittle was such a picture of me. There were so many things that she couldn't do well. Like me she didn't speak well, and like me she didn't measure up to the standards set by the world of what a real lady should be. In the movie a very educated man took Liza under his wing with the goal in mind to change her.

That is exactly what happened to me. The Lord drew me unto Himself, and started changing me. In the process, I fell progressively deeper and deeper in love with Him. At the end of the movie as the teacher realized he had also fallen in love with Liza, he took her in his arms and they began to dance. As she reflected on that night, she sang the song, "I Could Have Danced All Night." Do you remember the words to the song?

I could have danced all night. I could have danced all night
And still I beg for more.
I could have spread my wings and done a thousand things
I'd never done before.

I'll never know what made it so exciting,
But all at once my heart stood still.
I only know when He began to dance with me,
I could have danced, danced, danced, all night.

That song reflects exactly how I felt the night of my first dance with the Lord. I could have danced all night. I can still remember it just like it was yesterday. What I know for sure about that night is that the Lord brought me to the place where I began to hear the heartbeat of the Divine Drummer, and I could no longer sit on the sidelines. I could no longer watch from the window. I had to enter in to the place of worshipping the Lord in the dance.

Since then, whenever I find myself all alone at the place where words are not enough to express my gratitude or my love, I turn on the music and allow my body the freedom to express to the Lord my God those things that are exploding in my spirit. I like to put on songs that say what my heart is feeling.

Many times they are secular songs. When I want to express my love, I like to dance before Him to Haley Reinhart singing, "Can't Help Falling in Love", or the Desperation Band singing "Amazed." Sometimes when words are not enough, I dance my prayer to the Lord as Charlotte Church and Josh Groban sing, "The Prayer." Other times when I think about the future, I even dance to Eva Cassidy singing "Over the Rainbow." When

I want to praise Him in the dance, I like the song, "Your Love Keeps Lifting Me Higher" by Jack Wilson.

No matter what song I choose, one thing I always know is when I dance, the One who created me is pleased. He is pleased because I am doing what He created me to do, worship Him, and when I worship Him in the dance I always feel His pleasure.

She Doesn't Dance There Anymore

When I was women's minister of our church several years ago, a friend of mine, Jackie Holland, who was on staff at the church, felt called to minister to women who worked at strip clubs in the area. One night she asked me to go to a local club with her and another friend. She wanted to give the dancers gift baskets to let them know that Jesus loved them. I had never been to a club like that before and I wasn't sure how I was going to feel when I saw the women, but I knew the Lord wanted us to go.

We loaded up the old church van with around twenty baskets. There were only two seats in the van, so I sat in a folding chair in the back of the van with the baskets. When we pulled up to the club, Jackie said, "There is one thing you have to remember before we go in. There is a possibility we might see someone we know."

She continued to tell us that if we did, we could not tell anyone. She said we were not there to uncover sins, but we were there with the goal in mind to cover sin. She then looked at both of us very seriously and said, "We won't tell anyone, but if we do see anyone we know, we will wait outside and when they come out we will beat them up." We all started laughing.

We probably looked strange when we walked in carrying all the baskets. As I looked at the naked women on the stage my heart welled up with compassion. I wondered what roads they had traveled to bring them to this place. I have learned from life that it is best never to judge someone unless I have walked a mile in their shoes. Even though the spotlights were shining on the women as they danced, I knew they carried internal wounds that none of us could see. Someone, somewhere had hurt them.

All I could think about was that they were a picture of me, of my own nakedness before Jesus covered me with His robe of righteousness. I thought about the Lord's words in Ezekiel 16:8, "*I passed by you and saw that you were at a time for love, so I spread my skirt over you and covered your nakedness.*" I knew that they desperately needed to know they were loved, and I prayed that Jesus would cover their nakedness with His precious blood.

Sometimes we tend to put sins in categories. We think that some sins are worse than others, but that is not true. In the eyes of God all sins are the same. They may have taken their clothes off, but I had done other things that were equally as sinful in the eyes of God.

We were ushered to the back room. After the women danced, one by one they came into that well-lit room where they put on their clothes and then came over to see what we had for them. They loved the baskets and were eager to see what was in them. I was amazed how some of them opened up and sincerely wanted to talk. Most of them welcomed us and were not offended by our visit or our invitation to come to church. We left that night knowing we had been obedient to the Lord, but not knowing if anything we said or did would have a lasting impact.

We will never know all that the Lord accomplished, but one of the women that was at the club that night doesn't dance at clubs anymore. Her story has changed. Instead of dancing in a place of shame to please the audiences of the world, when she chooses to dance, she now dances alone in a place of purity, to please an audience of ONE. Those who have been forgiven much love much, and there is nothing more beautiful than to watch someone who has been forgiven much express their love for our Lord in the dance.

The Toyi Toyi

Years ago, I listened to a tape recorded by a woman who told an exciting story about the dance. I wish I could remember her name to give her credit, but I can no longer find the CD. She said she had gone to South Africa at a time when Nelson Mandela had just been released from prison and set in as president of the nation. She had gathered in a convention center with a large group of Christians. Nelson Mandela and Bishop Tutu were on a stage with a huge choir standing behind them. The choir was worshipping the Lord with their voices, celebrating what God had done.

She said as this choir began to sing, the presence of the Lord fell in the place. The audience began one by one to stand until the entire crowd was on their feet. Everyone in the room knew that they were standing on holy ground. It is the culture in South Africa for Christians to celebrate the Lord with the dance. The crowd began to do a dance called the *toyi toyi*. At one time in South Africa it was used in times of oppression to express how the people were feeling, but today, it is used as their dance of celebration.

She said Nelson Mandela and Bishop Tutu stood on the stage very erect, very stoic, very British, watching the crowd as they broke out in the *toyi toyi*. As she was watching Mandela's face, she saw the tears began to flow. The revelation of what God had done seemed to saturate his soul. He had been in a place of defeat, but God hadn't left him there. God had lifted him out of that "miry clay and set his feet on a Rock."

His rigid posture began to relax. He started moving his body back and forth, swaying to the music. His feet began to move in slow motion as the joy that had been contained in his soul was seeping into his body. Suddenly to the amazement of everyone in the room the *toyi toyi* took over. He began to dance before the Lord with all of his might. Everyone knew he wasn't doing the *toyi toyi* for their benefit. He was *toyi toying* before the Lord from a place of overwhelming thanksgiving for what the Lord had done in his life.

The speaker on the CD said as Tutu watched Mandela something happened. He started dipping and jumping and dancing before the Lord. She said it was amazing to watch Tutu do the *toyi toyi*. Their bodies were expressing what their spirits were feeling. We will never know what was going on in Mandela's mind as he was *toyi toying*, but he could have been thinking:

Look What the Lord has Done

Once I was in bondage. Now I have been set free...*Toyi Toyi*
Once I was down. Now I am up...*Toyi Toyi*
Once I was rejected. Now I have been accepted...*Toyi Toyi*
Once I was lost. Now I have been found...*Toyi Toyi*
Once I was a prisoner. Now I am a President...*Toyi Toyi*

Break Out of Your Shell

If the truth of what the Lord has done in your life and the passion with which He loves you ever saturates your soul, let me encourage you, like Nelson Mandela, to break out of your shell and experience the joy of worshipping the Lord with your entire body. You don't have to be a professional dancer like those on "Dancing with the Stars" to please the Lord with your dance.

When we are dancing, He is not looking to see if our bodies are moving to the beat of the music with beauty and perfection. He is looking at our hearts. If our bodies are moving out of a heart that is filled with thanksgiving and love, He will always be pleased. We can worship Him in the dance any way we want to. We can just move to the music doing whatever feels right to us. We can worship Him by just patting our feet or swaying back and forth to the music. We can rejoice in Him by jumping up in the air and twirling around. We can enter into the dance by just lifting our hands and shuffling our feet all at the same time.

We don't need to copy anyone else. We can just move to the music, doing what feels right to us. Dancing is a magnificent way of expressing our love to our Lord through our bodies. Something powerful is released when we throw caution to the wind and step into the place of worshipping the Lord Jesus Christ through the dance.

Thank You, Lord

Thank You Lord for creating us with the desire to worship You in the dance. Just the very thought of You makes us feel like dancing!

9

The Secret of Hearing His Voice

Oh, you who sit in the gardens, my companions are listening for your voice. Let me hear it.

Song of Solomon 8:13

As the king sat in his garden his bride said, *"My companions are listening for your voice. Let me hear it."* She made it very clear; she wanted to hear his voice. Not only did the bride and her companions want to hear the voice of their king, we want to hear the voice of our King.

Before I was born again, if you had told me I would ever hear His voice, I would have never believed it. The minute anyone started talking about hearing God I was immediately skeptical. Why would the God who created the universe ever want to talk to me? With my natural mind, I thought hearing God was impossible. I had no idea the Lord was speaking to His people today. That thought sounded like foolishness to me.

The natural man receiveth not the things of God for they are foolishness to him.　　　　1 Corinthians 2:14

In high school we all remember voting for those who were most beautiful, or most handsome, or most likely to succeed. If there had been a category in my high school for least likely to hear from God, I think I could have easily won. Yet when the day came that I finally heard Him speak I realized it was not only possible, but it was the greatest experience I would ever have while encased in this earthly body. Nothing brings me to the place of ecstasy and satisfies my soul like hearing His voice.

Who Has the Ability to Hear His Voice?

> *He that has ears to hear, let him hear.* Matt. 11:15

Fifteen times in the New Testament Jesus said those exact nine words. The question we need to ask ourselves is who has "ears to hear." There is a lie out of the pit of hell that tells us we can't hear the voice of God, but nothing could be further from the truth. Jesus said, *"My sheep hear My voice, and I know them, and they follow Me"* (John 10:27).

Those of us who belong to Jesus are His sheep. We are the ones who have the ability to hear the Good Shepherd's voice. It is not what we do that gives us the right to hear His voice—it is who we are. Some Christians think God only talks to the super-spiritual, to those who pray an hour a day, or read their Bibles every day, or go to church three times a week. They think God only speaks to a certain, select few, but that isn't true. The minute we are born again He gives all of us the capacity to hear His voice. Hearing His voice is the privilege and right of every born again believer.

How God Speaks

It would be ridiculous to make a list of the ways God speaks to us, because no matter how detailed we made the list it wouldn't be complete. We can't put Him in a box or confine the ways He speaks to a list because He is God, and He can speak to us any way He wants to. One of the major ways He speaks to us today is through His Word. There are also many examples in the old and new testaments where God spoke through dreams and visions, and He still speaks to us through dreams and visions today.

Someone once said a picture is worth a thousand words, and I am sure God agrees with that statements because of all the pictures He has sent to us through dreams and visions. He speaks to us in so many different ways. When He got ready to let Peter know He was bringing the Gentiles into His kingdom, He put him in a trance and spoke to him through a vision. When He wanted to let Cornelius know the very same thing, He sent a vision of an angel who gave him instructions to go to Peter's house where Peter gave him the good news. He does what He pleases.

Very few people have received a message from an angel, but we know from the Word of God that it has happened. There are also times when He communicates with us through an inner witness, and other times when He speaks through inanimate objects like burning bushes. I am sure Moses was surprised when he saw a bush burning in the desert that was not being consumed by the fire, but I am equally sure he was more surprised when he heard the voice of God speaking to him from that bush telling him to take off his shoes; he was standing on holy ground.

I will forever remember exactly where I was standing several years ago in a card shop in Hurst, Texas, when the words to a card jumped up off the pages, and I could hear the Lord speaking the same words that were on that card to me. He said, "Wild thing, I think I love you." I laughed out loud because I knew He was playing with me. I am sure the other people in the store thought I was laughing at the card, but I was actually laughing at how much fun the Lord is to be with, surprising me with a word through a card when I least expected it.

There are also reports in the Bible when He has spoken not only through inanimate objects, but also through an audible voice and some have said they have heard His audible voice today, but one of the most common ways He speaks is in what the Bible describes as a still, small voice. The Hebrew word for "still" is *dmamah*, which means quiet, calm. When we hear His voice, it is not a loud, overwhelming voice that shakes us to the very core of our being. The volume of His voice is much like the volume of our own voice that we hear in our heads. I'm sure He knew if He spoke to us in a loud, booming voice we couldn't handle it. When He speaks He usually uses a still, quiet, calming voice that speaks to us from within.

> *The Lord said, "Go out and stand on the mountain in the presence of the Lord, for the Lord is about to pass by." Then a great and powerful wind tore the mountains apart and shattered the rocks before the Lord, but the Lord was not in the wind. After the wind there was an earthquake, but the Lord was not in the earthquake. After the earthquake came a fire, but the Lord was not in the fire. And after the fire came a still, small voice. When Elijah heard it, he pulled his cloak over his face and went out and stood at the mouth of the cave. Then a voice said to him, "What are you doing here, Elijah?"*   1 Kings 19: 11-14

Our Spirit is the Organ by Which We Apprehend Divine Things

> *May God Himself, the God of peace, sanctify you through and through. May your whole spirit, soul, and body, be kept blameless at the coming of our Lord Jesus Christ."*
> *I Thessalonians 5:23 NIV*

This passage reminds us that we have a spirit, we have a soul, and we have a body. Our soul, which includes our mind, will, and emotions, is the essence of who we are. It is the part of us that will live after our bodies die. God is Spirit. When His Spirit comes into our bodies, He comes into our spirit. Proverbs 20:27 tells us, "The spirit of man is the candle of the Lord." He enlightens us through our spirits. That is why when we hear His voice, we usually hear Him speaking from the inside, from our inner man, because that is where He lives. In His wisdom, He has created a communication system far superior to anything on today's market. He has set up a system where the sound of His voice doesn't have to travel over the airwaves. When He speaks to us, He speaks Spirit to spirit. A. W. Tozer wrote in his book, "Mystery of the Holy Spirit," "our spirit is the organ by which we apprehend divine things."

In the movie "Two Weeks' Notice" with Sandra Bullock and Hugh Grant, there was a scene when Sandra's character left Hugh's character. While she was gone, he could hear the words she had spoken when she was with him being played back, echoing in his mind. At the end of the movie when he was trying to get her back, he said, "You have become the voice in my head." The voice in our head is sometimes an echo of things the Lord has said in the past, but it is also the voice in our head that is fresh, alive, speaking words to us in the here and now. His voice is the voice we hear in our head that is not our voice. His voice is the voice that we hear in our heads in the same place we hear our own thoughts.

How do we know the difference between His voice and ours? Before we had caller ID when someone we knew called us on the phone we didn't see them, but the minute they opened their mouths and spoke we knew exactly who was on the other end of the line. Because we knew them, we recognized their voice. The same thing happens when Jesus speaks today. When He speaks, we know it is Him because we are His sheep and we know His voice.

His Spirit Bears Witness With Our Spirit

> *The Spirit Himself, bears witness with our spirit that we are the children of God.*　　　　　　　　　Romans 8:16

How do we know we are children of God? We have an inner witness, the Holy Spirit, bearing witness with our spirit that we belong to Him. When we are born again we don't always hear Him say the words that we are His, but we know we are because His Spirit bears witness with our spirit. We know that we know that we know, deep down in our inner man. There is an inner knowing.

> *I say the truth in Christ, I lie not, my conscience also bearing me witness in the Holy Ghost*　　　Romans 9:1

There are times when the Lord communicates with us through His inner witness in other areas of our life. Sometimes when we are doing something we know is wrong, He doesn't wave a red flag in front of us and speak to us in an audible voice saying "Stop," but we have a clear inner knowing which is the Holy Spirit convicting us of sin. There are other times He speaks to us by a check in our spirit.

If we are ever in the midst of trying to make a decision, it is important to let the peace of God rule. Colossians 3:15 NIV says, *"Let the peace of God rule in your hearts, since as members of one body you were called to peace."* If we don't have a peace about something, it is often God's way of saying, "Don't do it."

When His Spirit is bearing witness with our spirit, there are also times when suddenly we know something we didn't know just a few minutes earlier. We didn't hear Him speak it but we know, and His Spirit bears witness with our knower that the information came from Him. Forty-four years ago, as a brand new Christian, Bill Anderson, my pastor at the time, came by our home for a visit. While he was there, suddenly, without hearing anything, I knew I was going to teach the word of God. Since I knew nothing about the Bible, it didn't make sense that I would ever teach, but often the things God says doesn't make since to our logical minds.

I wish you could have seen the look on his face when I told him I was going to be a Bible teacher. I think, in his compassion, wanting to let me down easy and ensure that I didn't get too excited about teaching something I knew nothing about, he said, "Jenny, before you are ready to teach you are going to have to get into the Bible and spend a lot of time studying. You are going to have to crawl for a while before you can walk."

He was right. I crawled for a very long time, but I am walking now, and the word the Lord dropped in my spirit that day came true. I became a teacher of the Word of God.

Alison Krauss sings a song, called "When You Say Nothing at All." In the first four verses she sings:

> It is amazing how you can speak right to the heart
> Without saying a word, you can light up the dark
>
> Try as I may, I could never explain
> What I hear when you don't say a thing.

Like the song says, it is amazing how the Lord Jesus Christ can speak right to our hearts without saying a thing. It is very difficult to try to explain His inner witness, but when we experience His Spirit bearing witness with our spirits we know it is Him. Sometimes, He also speaks to us through a strong impression.

In the early morning hours in June of 1974, I was awakened with a strong impression to get up and write a letter to my grandmother who lived in Graham, Texas. I didn't hear His voice telling me to write the letter, but I knew in my inner man I needed to get up and write it. I felt like I needed to thank her for all the things she had done for me and the spiritual impact she had had on my life. I wanted to go back to sleep but I couldn't, so I got out of bed, found paper and pen, and wrote her a three-page letter.

As I was writing, for some reason I felt like it would be my last opportunity to talk to her so I made sure I told her everything I wanted her to know. I thanked her for walking me down the street to the little church in our neighborhood when I was just a little girl. I thanked her for living her life in such a way that she gave me a great example of how to walk with the Lord. I thanked her for all the times she took the little bit of money she had and bought me a hamburger and coke and took me to the drive-in movies. In my mind I went down memory lane and realized even though she was poor and on welfare, she had left me with such a rich heritage.

The next morning, I mailed the letter. Three days later she had a stroke and went into a coma. When I got to the hospital, I found out from some of her friends she had received the letter before she had the stroke, and she had shown it to everyone because it meant so much to her.

I had the privilege of being alone with her when she died. When I was a little girl, she often told me how she had sat with people who were dying and she would hear what she called the "death rattle." That night, sitting in her hospital room, I heard "the death rattle" for the first time, and I knew what it was the minute I heard it. The Lord was ready to bring her home.

I am so grateful for that strong impression from the Lord to write that letter. Before we were born, God knew the exact number of days we would live on this earth. I believe He spoke to me through that strong impression because He knows the end from the beginning, and He knew her appointed time to die was at hand.

Your eyes saw my unformed substance, and in Your book all the days of my life were written before they ever took shape, when as yet there was none of them. Psalm 139:16

From one man he made every nation of men that they should inhabit the whole earth, and He determined the times set for them, and the exact places where they should live. God did this so that men would seek Him and perhaps reach out for Him and find Him, though He is not far from any one of us. Acts 17:26-27

Remember the former things of old: for I am God, and there is none else; I am God, and there is none like me, DECLARING THE END FROM THE BEGINNING, and from ancient times the things that are not yet done, saying, My counsel shall stand, and I will do all My pleasure.

Isaiah 46:9-10

We Grow in Our Ability to Hear His Voice Through the Different Ways He Speaks

When babies are born they have the ability to hear, but they don't understand everything that is being said to them. When we are born again we have the ability to hear, but we grow in ability to hear from God through the many ways He speaks to us. Our ability to hear and understand the ways He speaks is also much like the process of lifting weights. At first, when we start lifting weights our muscles may only be strong enough to lift five pounds, but then after exercising they grow into the ability to lift ten pounds and then twenty pounds, and then thirty pounds. Just like our muscles that grow and get stronger and stronger with use, over time our spiritual muscles grow stronger and stronger in their ability to hear from God through the many ways He speaks.

The story of the prophet Samuel as a boy in the Old Testament is a perfect example. In the beginning when Samuel first started hearing the voice of God, he didn't fully understand what was happening. Eventually, his ability to hear grew to the place that He became so skilled at listening to His voice that he was used by God as His mouthpiece to speak to the nation of Israel, delivering messages to her kings.

Developing the Art of Listening

Jesus said,

> *Consider carefully how you LISTEN. Whoever has will be given more; whoever does not have, even what they think they have will be taken from them.*　　Luke 8:18

In this day and age, we are bombarded with voices. We walk into our front doors turning on our televisions, filling our homes with the voices of strangers. We sit in front of our computers and listen to the many voices that come over the air waves. We carry our cell phones with us at all times, constantly pushing that little green button to listen to the flood of voices coming from our families and friends.

We fill our ears with many voices, but the problem is those voices often drown out the voice of God. There is hardly a moment in the day when we are not in a storm of activity listening to the voices of the world, but when was the last time we took the time to tune in and listen to the voice of Jesus? One of the best kept secrets to increasing the frequency of hearing His voice is developing the art of listening. Sometimes we need to stop and have the courage to sit in a place of silence, lean into Him, and just listen.

I have noticed when I consciously turn my thoughts to Him, giving Him my undivided attention, those are the times when the thrill of hearing His voice seems to increase. Many times when I want to hear His voice, if I find a quiet place, turn on my spiritual antennas, and press into Him with listening ears, I find He has something He wants to say to me. There are also times when I focus on Him with listening ears and He says nothing at all. I wish I could be the one in charge of when He speaks, but unfortunately, I'm not. When He isn't talking I realize His timing is perfect, and when He has something to say to me He will say it.

When it comes to listening, have you ever noticed we listen to the things we consider to be important? Joyce Meyers told a story about listening that is a great picture of how we should live our lives. She was on a car trip with her husband, and because the weather was bad, she turned on the radio to get a weather report. She was in the process of working on several projects, but she kept one ear tuned to the radio. The minute she started hearing the weather report, she separated herself from what she was doing and gave her full attention to what was being said on the radio. That is exactly how the Lord wants us to live our lives. He wants us to go through our days with one ear always tuned in, listening for His voice.

Cindy Langley

There is nothing more wonderful than to be going through the day and suddenly hear the sound of His voice. Years ago after a Bible study, I had a meeting with a woman named Cindy Langley who had been coming to our church for a few weeks. The first time she came to church, a friend of hers asked some of us to meet her telling us her husband wanted to join our church, but she was not happy about it. As she shared her heart with me that day, I could certainly relate to what she was saying. It was hard for her to leave her friends of many years behind. There had been a time in my life when I changed churches and had to experience the same emotional turmoil.

As I listened to her speak, I was also tuned in, listening for the voice of the Lord. Right in the middle of our conversation, I heard His voice. He said, "Cindy is going to be one of your best friends." I thought she would probably think I was crazy because she didn't know me, but I went ahead and told her what I was hearing. I love how the Lord knows things long before we do. I also love it when He tells us ahead of time what is going to happen in the future.

For the last twenty-five years she has been one of my very best friends. We have shared laughter and tears and have had the privilege of seeing the Lord answer many of our prayers with miracles. We have spent years together, along with Betsy Hall, decorating each others' Christmas trees at Christmas time, and we have taken trips together every year for over twenty years now. I can't imagine my life without her. She has enriched my days far greater than words could ever say.

Chirp Chirp

Peter Lord, a wonderful preacher who lives in Florida, told a story one day that captivated my attention. He said his family and some friends were having a get-together at his home, and during the evening he stepped outside only to discover one of the guests standing by his shrubs with his head leaning in as if he were looking and listening for something. When Peter asked him what he was doing, the man asked him if he knew he had eighteen different kinds of crickets living in his bushes.

Peter was surprised because he had lived in that home for years and had never even one time consciously heard a cricket. The young man, who was a graduate student from the University of Florida getting his doctorate in entomology, told Peter that he had learned to distinguish the difference in the voices of over two hundred different types of cricket calls because he was writing his final term paper about crickets.

Just like the young man who had developed the art of listening to the sounds that different crickets make, we need to develop the art of listening to better hear and understand the ways God speaks. Peter had passed by those shrubs hundreds of times and no doubt there were times when those crickets were making noises, but Peter wasn't listening. I think that is a great picture of how we live our lives today. God is speaking, but we are not listening.

Why did the young man develop the art of listening to crickets? The ability to hear the crickets became important to him when getting his doctorate depended on learning everything he could about those crickets. Because it was important to the student to listen to crickets, he heard them, but because Peter had no interest in hearing from the crickets, after years of passing them he didn't hear them. We listen for the things that are important for us to hear. We need to walk through our lives with our ears tuned in, listening for the sound of our Lord's voice.

Mary Sat at His Feet, Listening

Jesus made it very clear about the importance of choosing to listen to His voice.

> *As Jesus and his disciples were on their way, He came to a village, where a woman named Martha opened her home to him. She had a sister called Mary, who sat at the Lord's feet*

257

LISTENING to what He said, but Martha was distracted by all the preparations that had to be made. She came to Him and asked, "Lord, don't you care that my sister has left me to do the work by myself. Tell her to help me! Martha, Martha, the Lord answered, you are worried and upset about many things, but only ONE THING IS NEEDED. Mary has CHOSEN what is better, and it will not be taken away from her.   Luke 10:38-42

Jesus told Martha only ONE THING was really needed, and it was the ONE THING Mary was doing; LISTENING to the voice of Jesus. Like Martha, we get so distracted, so worried and bothered by the things of life that we don't make it a priority to press in and listen for His voice. Jesus said Mary had chosen the best part. We are all given twenty-four hours in a day, and we choose to do the things that are important to us. What we do every day is always a result of our choices, and when it comes to listening for His voice, compared to everything else, it is the best thing we can ever do.

Luke

I have a wonderful grandson named Luke who is in the fourth grade. I love to spend time with him. Not only is he smart and a great athlete, he is so much fun to be with. He lives in Austin, and when I visit I like to go to school to have lunch with him. Last year I went to his school and sat between Luke and another classmate at their lunch table. The minute I sat down, his friend started talking to me nonstop. I soon realized He was totally consuming the time I had to spend with Luke. I hated to be rude, but I had a choice to make.

I decided I could sit there for the entire thirty minutes and listen to his friend, missing my time with Luke, or I could turn away from his friend and give my full attention to Luke, who of course is one of the most important people in my life. Because I choose to listen to Luke, we ended up having a great lunch together and I found out something very important that he wanted to tell me. The same thing is true in our lives with the Lord. There are times we need to tune out all the other voices and just listen for the sound of His voice.

How Can We Be Sure What We Are Hearing Is From God?

1. The voice of the Lord is always full of grace, and truth and love. When He speaks, His words bring not only a peace that passes all understanding but an unspeakable joy to our souls. His voice is always encouraging us to be all He created us to be, and giving us guidance and wisdom as we walk through our lives.

    And thine ears shall hear a word behind thee, saying, this is the way, walk ye in it, when ye turn to the right hand, and when ye turn to the left   Isaiah 30:21

2. When the Lord speaks, He will never contradict His written Word. Anytime we are hearing anything that is contrary to His Word, we can be sure it is not God.

3. If we ever hear a voice that tears us down or causes us to feel unworthy or discouraged or makes us think He doesn't love us, that voice is not God.

4. If we hear a voice that causes us to worry or causes confusion, it is not God.

5. If we ever hear a voice that causes us to feel condemnation, leaving us with the feeling we are bad but not sure why, that voice is not the voice of God. God tells us, *"There is therefore, no condemnation to those who are in Christ Jesus"* (Romans 8:1a). He will convict us of sin but with conviction He always puts His

finger on the sin, letting us know exactly what we need to confess and turn away from.

6. If we ever hear a voice that says anything that produces fear, it isn't God. 2 Timothy 1:7 tells us, *"For God has not given us a spirit of fear, but of power and love, and a sound mind."* Over and over when Jesus appeared to His disciples, He would say, "fear not." Fear does not come from God. He is the Comforter, and His words always bring comfort.

Years ago, the Lord spoke to me one day, and I still remember His words infusing my soul with comfort. I grew up in a home where my father was a carpenter. After I was born, he built a home for us in an area in south Fort Worth, Texas, called Poly. It was a small framed home, painted white, with reddish brown shutters. I loved that little house so much that I told my mother and father when I grew up I was going to marry a rich man and buy it.

Because my dad was a carpenter, there were times he had work and also times when he didn't. When I would hear my Mom and Dad argue over the lack of money, I was left with a feeling of insecurity. Even though all our basic needs were met, I would often worry if we were going to be able to buy food or get to stay in our house. When I met Mark, he worked for Southwestern Bell. When we got engaged, in the back of my mind, I thought I would never have to worry about money again because he received a regular paycheck. It was wonderful to know that just like clockwork, twice a month we would have the money we needed to pay our bills. I loved it. His job made me feel so secure.

I didn't realize it at the time, but I put my faith in Southwestern Bell to meet our needs. After working for the company for twenty-six years, they were downsizing, offering a severance package to those who would be willing to leave and Mark decided he would branch out and go into business for himself. On the day he told me he was leaving Southwestern Bell, my heart sank as those old feelings of insecurity raced to the surface.

The fear of what would happen in the future without Southwestern Bell caused me to believe I was going to have to spend the rest of my life walking on the tightrope of uncertainty.

As my heart started wrestling with fear that day, I heard the Lord speak to me. He said, "You have trusted in a broken cistern that can hold no water. I am now going to show you that you can trust in Me, the FOUNTAIN OF LIVING WATERS." His words brought so much comfort that day, replacing the security blanket that had just been yanked out from under me with the truth. Even though Southwestern Bell was gone, the Fountain of Living Waters, the One who created the universe, would be the One who would supply all of my needs.

> *For my people have committed two evils; they have forsaken Me, the Fountain of Living Waters, and hewed them out cisterns, broken cisterns, that can hold no water.*
> Jeremiah 2:13

Show Me the Money

No matter how old we are, without the money to meet our needs fear can try to rob us of our peace. We all have funny stories in our families, and one of our family stories happened years ago on a cold, wintery afternoon in January when Nate, my oldest grandson was seven years old.

On this particular day we decided to go to Mac's Restaurant. As usual Nate ordered his favorite meal, chicken fettuccine, and I ordered soup and salad. I remember him raving about how Mac's fettuccini was better than all the other restaurants in the area. He was certain the secret to its superiority was the whole kernel corn they added to the dish. He enjoyed every bite to the fullest until the end of the meal when the waiter brought the ticket.

At that time in my life, I had the bad habit of keeping my credit cards and money in my bra. After the waiter brought the ticket, Nate watched me intently as I searched the interior of my bra for the money to pay the bill. After a thorough investigation of my bra, I realized I had left all my money and credit cards at home. In my mind, I knew I was going to call Mark to come to the rescue, but before telling Nate my plan I decided to tease him, telling him I didn't have any money to pay the bill, and we were probably going to have to go to their kitchen and wash dishes.

I will always remember the unhappy look on his handsome little face and how upset he was with me for not making sure I had the money to pay for our meal. In his angriest little voice, he said, "Gigi I will never go out with you again unless I watch Granddad stuff your bra with money." All I could do was laugh, knowing his grandfather would be delighted to fill my bra with money, but Nate wasn't laughing. Whether the lack of money is just a joke or the circumstances are real, it is never a laughing matter.

When fear comes we need to remember our promise from the Lord,

> *...and my God will supply all your needs according to His riches in glory, in Christ Jesus*   Philippians 4:19

What Kind of Ears Do You Have!

The Bible talks about many different kinds of ears. There were those who had ears to hear but they didn't hear. There were also those who had ears that refused to listen. Others had ears that were dull of hearing, itching ears, uncircumcised ears, ears that were attentive to His voice, and still others had ears that had been awakened. In my life, I have had ears to hear, but I didn't hear. I have had ears that were dull of hearing. I have also had ears that were attentive to His voice, but my favorite ears are the ones that have been awakened. What kind of ears do you have?

1. They had ears to hear, but they didn't hear.

In my early Christian life when I read through the Bible, one phrase would always leap up and speak to me, *"They have ears to hear, but they do not hear"* (Ezekiel 12:2). Every time I read those words I knew they were describing me. I knew I had ears to hear because I had been born again, but I seldom heard from the Lord. What was keeping me from hearing His voice? Why did other people seem to hear His voice, but not me?

I am ashamed to tell you this, but one time I was so exasperated, and so frustrated, I exploded and told the Lord exactly how I was feeling. I told Him I was unhappy because He seemed to talk to everyone but me. I had just been sitting on the floor of my prayer room reading the Word where I came across story after story about how He had spoken to so many of the saints that had gone before me. The more I read, the unhappier I became. I guess I was just jealous.

I reminded Him, as if He didn't already know, of how He talked to Abraham, telling him his descendants would be like the stars in the sky, and how He spoke to Moses, giving him the ten commandments and all the details about how to build that tabernacle in the desert. I also reminded Him of how He spoke to Noah and told him how to build that ark.

In hindsight, I know I was acting just like a child. I felt like it wasn't fair that He spoke to others when I didn't hear Him speaking to me. I told Him I didn't know what I was doing wrong, but I begged Him to let me hear His voice. In hindsight I realize now He was using His Word and His Spirit to draw me to the place of longing to hear His voice. Even though that experience caused turmoil in my heart, it also caused me to press in and start asking the Lord for my heart's desire.

2. Hearts that have been hardened by unbelief have ears that are "dull of hearing."

> *...we have many things to say, and hard to be uttered, seeing ye are DULL of hearing.*   Hebrews 5:11b

In Acts 28:26-27, we find Paul preaching to a crowd of people. Some in the crowd believed and some were full of unbelief. Paul reminded those who didn't believe the words from God spoken through Isaiah the prophet, "*Go unto this people, and say, 'Hearing, ye shall hear, and shall not understand, and seeing ye shall see, and not perceive: For the heart of this people is waxed gross, and their ears are dull of hearing, and their eyes have they closed; lest they should see with their eyes, and hear with their ears, and understand with their heart, and should be converted, and I should heal them.'*"

3. Some have ears that are attentive to His voice.

> *And He taught daily in the temple, but the chief priests and scribes and the chief of the people sought to destroy Him and could not find what they might do, but all the people were very attentive to hear Him.*　　　Luke 19:47-48

Some have ears that are attentive to hear his voice. Attentive ears are ears that are eager to listen because hearing what He has to say is important. They are not easily distracted.

4. Some have ears that have been awakened.

It wasn't until October of 1973 when I was baptized in the Spirit that my ears were truly awakened to hear the sound of His voice with greater frequency. It was on that day a paradigm shift took place in my spiritual life and I was never the same again.

> *The Lord God has given me the tongue of a disciple that I may know how to sustain the weary one with a word. He awakens me morning by morning. He awakens my ear to listen as a disciple.*　　　Isaiah 50:4

What Happens When We Hear from God?

It is very difficult to adequately describe how we feel when we hear His voice, but one of the things that often happens is found in the words spoken by the Shulamite.

1. Leaping Hearts!
My heart leaped as He spoke. Song of Songs 5:6

Of course, the bride was talking about her king, but when our King speaks to us there are times when that is exactly how we feel. It feels like our hearts are doing high kicks, leaping with exhilaration at the sound of His voice. I remember the day I was standing at my kitchen sink washing dishes not even thinking about the Lord or the fact that He was watching me, when He showed up right in the middle of my day and surprised me.

I lived in Hurst, Texas, at the time. It was a verse from Song of Solomon spoken by the king to his bride that I knew well but had never thought about it ever applying to me. When He spoke I heard Him say, "Jenny, one glance from you makes My heart beat faster."

> *You have made my heart beat faster, my sister, my bride. You have made my heart beat faster with a single glance from your eyes.*   Song of Songs 4:9

It was just a few simple words, but I was undone. I was so shocked I stopped what I was doing and sat down on the kitchen floor. I couldn't believe He just said that to me. When I stood back up, I looked out my kitchen window and glanced up at the heavens just to play with Him. Of course, I knew my glancing His way with my physical eyes was not what He was talking about. He was just letting me know how much He loves it when I turn to Him in the realm of the spirit and glance His way with my spiritual eyes.

I have learned over the years, I can just relax and be myself with Him. I don't have to use fancy words or try to be something I'm not. His words to me that day just reinforced the truth I already knew. Not only did my love for Him make His heart beat faster, leaping with joy in the realm of the Spirit, but when I hear the voice of my Bridegroom speaking words of love to me, the sound of His voice makes my heart leap and beat faster too.

2. Burning Hearts!

Many times when we hear Him speak the same thing happens to us that the two disciples experienced when they were on their way home on the road to Emmaus after the crucifixion of Jesus. The Bible tells us these two men were walking along, talking about what had just happened. As they were walking, Jesus Himself, came along and started talking with them. At first they didn't recognize Him. They told Him their version of the day, and for the rest of their walk He spent time explaining to them that everything that happened was a fulfillment of the Old Testament prophesies about what would happen when the Messiah came.

When they reached their destination, they invited Him to eat with them, but before they began to eat, Jesus gave thanks and broke the bread, and when He did their eyes were opened and they recognized Him. At that moment the Word of God says, *"Jesus disappeared."* They then asked each other,

> *Were not our hearts burning within us while He talked with* *us.*   Luke 24:32

That is exactly what often happens to us when Jesus is speaking. There is what can only be described as a BURNING in our spirits. We have burning hearts!

3. Changed Hearts!

I saw the science fiction movie, "Contact," released in 1997 with Jodie foster and Matthew McConaughey. In the movie, Jodie played a girl named Ellie. It was not a spiritual movie, but as I watched the movie I was riveted because I could see it was a huge spiritual picture of not only how to hear the voice of God, but what happens when we hear Him.

In the movie, when Jodie was just a little girl her father planted a seed in her heart, telling her there was more in the universe than she could see with her natural eyes. He also told her if she would just listen she could hear from that unseen realm. He not only told her she could hear from the unseen realm, but he also taught her to put on a headset, which became her second pair of ears, and listen for a message from outer space. He taught her that the key to hearing was listening. If she would just press in and listen, she would hear from the realm of the unseen.

Because her father told her it was possible to hear, she expected to hear and she listened. In the movie, Ellie became obsessed with an unshakable, relentless pursuit to hear from a realm she had never heard from before. Day in and day out, night after night, she listened. In the beginning she didn't hear anything, but she refused to give up. She went to college and learned everything she could, becoming an astrophysicist. She ended up using the most advanced technology with giant dishes and the largest antennas in the world. They allowed her to listen with even greater clarity for a word from outer space.

Almost every time you saw her in the movie she had her headset on, listening. She was always listening, listening, listening. Skeptics were quick to tell her she was a fanatic. They told her what she was doing was useless and she was wasting her time. They told her it was never going to happen, but she refused to give up. One day as she was listening, a signal came in from outer space. It finally happened. She reached her goal. She heard from someone in the realm of the unseen who gave her a special message about how to get where they were. She followed the instructions and ended up making contact.

At the end of the movie when she was trying to explain what had happened, she said because of her encounter, "SOMETHING IN ME CHANGED FOREVER, AND I WAS NEVER THE SAME AGAIN." In the movie Ellie was not listening to hear the voice of God. She was listening for contact with extraterrestrial beings, but what she did was an example of what we need to do in order to hear the voice of God. Like Ellie, our father has told us it is possible to hear from the unseen, and He has given us the equipment, His Holy Spirit, to hear His voice.

Just like in the movie, there are always skeptics who tell us we are wasting our time; hearing His voice is never going to happen, but like Ellie we need to ignore their voices. In order to hear His voice, we need to follow her example 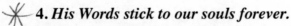and develop the art of listening. We need to develop the art of tuning in, of pressing into Him and focusing on Him with our spiritual antennas up, ready to hear whatever He wants to say.

I have discovered when I press into Him, diligently seeking Him, He is always right there waiting on me to turn to Him so we can make CONTACT. And just like Ellie in the movie, every time I hear His voice something in me changes forever, and I am never the same again. Nothing in this world compares with the thrill of hearing His voice.

4. *His Words stick to our souls forever.*

When we hear His voice, not only are we left with changed hearts, or burning hearts, or leaping hearts, but His Words also have a way of sticking to our souls forever. There are times in our lives when people say things that we forget, but when we hear Him speak we never forget it. His Words never leave us. They become part of our spiritual existence.

5. *The sound of His voice always leaves us wanting more.*

As for me, I have also discovered, without fail, after I hear the voice of my Bridegroom, the same thing happens over and over—HE ALWAYS LEAVES ME WANTING MORE. His voice whets my appetite. It leaves me with a sense of anticipation as I eagerly await the next time when He chooses once again to bless me by bestowing on me the privilege of hearing His majestic, magnificent, life-changing voice.

Speak, Lord, Your Bride is Listening

Lord, thank You for letting us hear Your voice. Speak to us again, sweet Jesus. We are listening.

Develope the art of listening — pressin, focus on Him — And get ready —

10

Secrets from the Secret Place

> *Oh my Dove, in the cleft of the rock, in the secret place of*
> *the steep pathway, let me see your form. Let me hear your*
> *voice, for your voice is sweet and your form is lovely.*
>   Song of Songs 2:14, NASB

Your Voice is Sweet

The king begins this passage with words of endearment, calling the
Shulamite "my dove." He also told her he wanted to hear her voice,
and then he described how he felt about her voice saying *"Your voice is
sweet."* That is exactly how our King feels about our voices today; He
wants to hear them, and He thinks our voices are sweet.

Someone once said the reason He thinks our voices are sweet is
because He has played a love song on the strings of our hearts, and our
hearts have been sweetened by His love. He loves to hear the sound of our
voices talking to Him, no matter what we have to say. One of the words
we use for talking to Him is prayer. When we pray, I think He leans in
to listen to every word. Whether our prayer is one of thanksgiving, or
praise, or a declaration of our love, a cry for help, or a petition on behalf
of others, He loves to hear the sound of our voices.

Parker

I have a beautiful granddaughter whose name is Parker. I call her my beauty, not only because she is beautiful on the outside but especially because she is so beautiful on the inside. The depth of her inner beauty astounds me. She is thoughtful, always thinking of others, smart, funny, and so much fun to be with. She is fifteen years old now, but when she was very young and I would go to Austin to visit with her we slept together on a trundle bed. There was only one problem—Parker insisted I sleep on the crack, the area between my side and hers.

In the early days, after she would go to sleep, I would move off of the crack hoping to relieve my back from the uncomfortable persistent pain, but Parker would always wake up and insist I get back on the crack. One night I asked her why she wanted me to sleep on that crack, and she finally told me she was afraid she would fall through the crack. Of course I knew there was no way she could fall through that crack, but to appease her I never moved off that crack again because I wanted to make sure she felt secure.

As I laid on that crack, night after night, I began to pray for her. I prayed that she would come to know the Lord. I prayed for her to have a close relationship with Him. I prayed for her to have eyes to see, and ears to hear in the realm of the Spirit. I prayed the Lord would give her wisdom and revelation in the knowledge of Him, and the eyes of her understanding would be enlightened. I prayed for her future husband, and I prayed for her unborn children.

As I prayed I knew the Lord was listening. I knew He was pleased to hear my voice on Parker's behalf, and "Parker, I have a message for you: Don't ever worry about falling through the cracks because I have prayed for you, my darling. I've got you covered."

Cleft in the Rock

In this passage, after the king lovingly called the Shulamite "my dove," he revealed the place where he found his dove. She was in the cleft of the Rock. Christ is portrayed in scripture, not just once, but over and over as our Rock.

> *He is my Rock and my Salvation. He is my defense. I shall*
> *not be moved.*   Psalms 62:2

> *For I don't want you to be unaware brethren that our fore-*
> *fathers were all under the cloud and all passed through the*
> *sea, and all ate the same spiritual food, all drank the same*
> *spiritual drink, for they were drinking from a spiritual Rock*
> *and that Rock was Christ.*   1 Corinthians 10:1-4

If Christ is our Rock, where is the cleft in the Rock? The definition of cleft is "an opening made by a split, a hollow between two parts." On Calvary, the soldier took his sword and drove it through the side of Jesus, putting a cleft in the Rock. His side was opened by a sword, just as Adam's side was opened by the hand of God. And just as Eve came forth from Adams's side, we were birthed from the blood that flowed from the cleft in the Rock, from the pierced side of the Lord Jesus Christ.

Do you remember the old hymn, "Rock of Ages, Cleft for Me?" Jesus is the Rock that was cleft for you and me. When we were born again, the Holy Spirit, the Dove, was placed inside each one of us, and we were placed in Jesus, the Rock. The good news is once we get into the Rock, no one can ever take us out. When He places us into the cleft of the Rock, I think He sits on the edge of His chair just waiting to hear the sweet words flowing from our hearts to His ever-listening ears. Before we can ever get to the "secret place" we have to enter into the cleft of the Rock.

How Do We Get to the Secret Place Today?

The pathway to the secret place was described by the king as a "steep pathway;" therefore, we know it was a pathway that led to higher ground. All who have chosen to follow the pathway to the secret place in the realm of the Spirit today have discovered the same thing. You may be one of those who are afraid of heights and are not certain whether or not you want to take this path, but have no fear—there is no danger on this path. It is a road well-traveled.

Many have taken this path before us, and the exciting news is it has been paved with His love. "The secret place of the steep pathway" is a spiritual picture of the place where secrets flow, found within the cleft of the Rock. It is the place where the Lord reveals secrets to his bride. Daniel 2: 28 tells us, *"There is a God in heaven who reveals secrets."* The secret place is the place where the Lord tells us things we have never heard before.

There are some things we can't get at Yale, or Harvard or from the internet. There are some things we can only get from the secret place, from God Himself. Everyone loves to hear secrets. Inquiring minds want to know, but in order to hear secrets from God we have to first be willing to get into the cleft of the Rock. If we are willing to explore all that is in the Rock, we will find the secret place where divine revelation flows.

In order to find a clue of where we need to be in order for secrets to flow from the heart of the Lord to our hearts, we need to look at one of the men that God used to bombard the world with divine secrets. John, the disciple who followed Jesus, discovered the secret of how to get to the secret place. He wrote the entire book of Revelation which was filled with divine revelation from the secret place, and it was from the secret place that God revealed to him what was going to happen in the future.

Where was he when he received this divine revelation? He was in the very same place that all of us have to be in order to receive secrets from God today. We discover in the first chapter of Revelation, exactly where he was.

I, John, your brother and fellow partaker in tribulation and kingdom and perseverance which are in Jesus, was on the Island called Patmos, because of the word of God and the testimony of Jesus. I was in the Spirit on the Lord's day and I heard behind me a loud voice, like the sound of a trumpet, saying, "Write in a book about what you see and send it to the seven churches."　　　　　Revelation 1:9-11a

When John received divine revelation he was on the Island of Patmos. We could get on a plane and fly to the Island of Patmos in the Aegean Sea, and we may or may not receive a word from the Lord. The physical place where we stand has nothing to do with receiving secrets from God. The answer we are looking for is not in the Island of Patmos. There is only one place we can go to receive secrets from God, and John revealed the place. He said, *"I was IN THE SPIRIT."* How did he get to the place called, *"IN THE SPIRIT?"*

Let's look at John's life and do a little detective work. We know that the place where John first met Jesus was at the Sea of Galilee. It was there that Jesus called him to be a disciple, but he didn't get into the secret place from the Sea of Galilee. We know that John traveled with Jesus for three years and saw Him transfigured on the Mount of Transfiguration.

It was there he also heard the voice of God say, "this is My Beloved Son in whom I am well pleased," but he didn't enter into the secret place, that place called "in the Spirit" from the Mount of Transfiguration. We can only imagine how John must have felt as he stood at the foot of the cross with Mary, the mother of Jesus, and watched Him die. It was a life changing place, but he didn't get to that place called "in the Spirit" from Calvary.

John was also on the Mount of Olives and heard the last words of Jesus before he ascended into heaven. We read those words in the first chapter of Acts. In Acts 1:4 Jesus told His disciples, that they should not depart from Jerusalem, but wait for the promise of the father. Then in the next verse, Acts 1:5 Jesus said, *"John baptized you with water, but you shall be BAPTIZED WITH THE HOLY SPIRIT not many days from now,"* and with His final words in Acts 1:8 Jesus said, *"You shall receive POWER when the Holy Ghost comes on you, and you shall be my witnesses both in Jerusalem and in all Judea, and Samaria and even the remotest part of the earth."*

After Jesus spoke from the Mount of Olives, John saw Him being lifted up and a cloud receive Him out of his sight. We know that John's experience on the Mount of Olives was a mountain-top experience, but he didn't get into that place called "in the Spirit" from the Mount of Olives. John left that mountain and went to the upper room in Jerusalem to do what Jesus told him do. It is interesting to note that Jesus didn't tell the disciples to go to Jerusalem and tell everyone what they had seen. He told them go to Jerusalem and wait until they got the power.

In Acts 2:1-4 while waiting for the power, we read what happened. *"When the day of Pentecost had fully come, they were all in one accord, in one place. And suddenly there came a sound from heaven as a rushing mighty wind, and it filled the whole house where they were sitting. Then there appeared to them divided tongues as of fire, and one sat upon each of them, and they were all filled with the Holy Spirit and began to speak with other tongues as the Spirit gave them utterance".* If John had not been baptized in the Spirit, he would never have received divine revelation from his Lord and his God.

How did John get to the secret place? He got there the only way all of us get there today—by being baptized with the Holy Spirit. Today we can't see the secret place with our natural eyes, but it is more real and more thrilling than anything we will ever see with our physical eyes. From the Island of Patmos, in the secret place, John received divine prophetic secrets from God about things that would happen in the future.

What is a Prophet?

The word prophet in Hebrew is *nabiy* which means inspired by God. It comes from the root word, *naba*, which means inspired to speak.

Prophets and prophetesses in the old and new testaments were men and women who were inspired by God to speak on His behalf. They prophesied about many things that would happen in the future, including facts about the coming Messiah.

Hundreds of years before Jesus was ever born they described His life in detail. The prophet Micah prophesied when the Messiah came He would be born in Bethlehem. Isaiah prophesied when the Messiah came he would be born of a virgin, He would become a sacrifice for our sins, He would be silent before His accusers, He would be crucified with criminals, He would be spit upon and struck, and He would be buried in a rich man's grave.

Zechariah prophesied when the Messiah came he would be betrayed for thirty pieces of silver, the money would be used to by a potter's field, and He would be pierced. David prophesied when the Messiah came He would be given vinegar to drink, His hands and feet would be pierced, and soldiers would gamble for His garments. There were forty-four prophecies prophesied by the prophets in the Old Testament about the coming Messiah, and Jesus fulfilled them all.

Of course, there was also the prophet Samuel whom God used to anoint David when he was just a boy telling him one day he would be king of Israel. In the natural no one could have known when David was young that he would one day be king of Israel, but God did. He knows the end from the beginning, and He used His prophet Samuel to reveal that secret to David.

God also spoke through other prophets revealing other secrets about what would happen in the future to the nation of Israel. In the Old Testament there were approximately forty-eight male prophets and seven female prophetesses. God didn't just use the men; He also used the women. Miriam, Deborah, and Huldah were the most famous women prophetess in the Old Testament.

We can also look through the New Testament and see other men and women who God used to reveal divine truth to His people. John the Baptist, Zacharias, the father of John the Baptist, Anna, Elizabeth,

Agabus, the four daughters of Phillip, and Silas were all prophets and prophetesses in the New Testament.

Is Prophecy Alive and Well Today

> *And it shall come to pass in the last days, saith God, I will*
> *pour out My Spirit upon all flesh, and your sons and daugh-*
> *ters shall prophesy, and your young men shall see visions,*
> *and your old men shall dream dreams, and on My servants*
> *and on My handmaidens I will pour out in those days of*
> *My Spirit; and they shall prophesy.* Acts 2:17-18

In Ephesians 4:11 we see one of the three lists of the gifts that God gave to the church. He said some would be apostles, some prophets, some evangelists, some pastors and teachers. It is interesting today how we highly esteem and receive the evangelists, pastors, and teachers, but we often brush the apostles and prophets under our church house carpets because we think the need for them has gone away. We don't understand their purpose, but God does. He was the One who gave them to us. Prophecy is one of the gifts given to the New Testament church by God. Paul gave us a glimpse of the importance of the gift of prophecy to the New Testament church:

> *Follow after charity, and desire spiritual gifts, but rather*
> *that you may prophesy. For he that speaketh in an unknown*
> *tongue speaketh not unto men, but unto God; for no man*
> *understandeth him; howbeit in the spirit he speaketh mys-*
> *teries. But he that prophesieth speaketh unto men to edi-*
> *fication, and exhortation, and comfort. He that speaketh*
> *in an unknown tongue edifieth himself, but he that proph-*
> *esieth edifeith the church. I would that ye all spake with*
> *tongues, but rather that you prophesied; for greater is*
> *he that prophesieth than he that speaketh with tongues,*

*except he interpret, that the church may receive edifying
Now, brethren, if I come unto you speaking with tongues,
what shall I profit you except I shall speak to you either by
revelation, or by knowledge, or by prophesying, or by doc-
trine?*

I Corinthians 14:1-6

There are times when the Lord speaks prophetically today, revealing His will for our lives though prophets and those who have the gift of prophecy. There is a difference in the two. The prophet usually has a stronger word for the church at large, whereas those operating in the gift of prophecy usually have a word that strengthens and encourages individual believers. A word of prophecy will always line up with the Word of God, and a personal word of prophecy often confirms something that is already in our hearts.

For many years I was skeptical about the gift of prophecy. To tell you the truth there was a time I thought it only existed in the men and women I read about in the pages of the Bible. It didn't make sense to my natural mind that anyone today could actually hear from God so clearly that they could give a word to someone else from God. The thought of the gift of prophesy always made me feel uneasy. It sounded like hocus pocus to me. I thought maybe those who said they had the gift of prophecy just made things up. Just the thought of that gift was something I wanted to run away from.

I never dreamed in my wildest imagination I would ever have a prophetic word for anyone, but a few years after I was baptized in the Spirit, the Lord woke me up one night with a simple word for a brother in the body of Christ. I learned that night, that God's ways are not our ways, and the gift of prophecy is nothing to be afraid of. It is simply one of His gifts. I didn't expect it. I didn't ask for it, but in His sovereignty, He just decided to give it to me, just like He has given it to so many others in the body of Christ.

My First Prophetic Secret from the Secret Place

It seems like just yesterday when I received my first prophetic word from the Lord. It was one of the biggest surprises of my life. As I dozed off to sleep that night I wasn't prepared for what was about to happen. In the early morning hours while it was still dark outside, I was awakened to the sound of the Lord's voice saying, "I am sending a man." He said it several times, and when I was fully awake, He went on to say, "The fields of the earth are ripe for harvest. I am sending a man. His name is James Robison. I am going to expand his borders and send him to the world to reap many souls for My kingdom."

The minute I heard the word I was in a state of shock. It wasn't the fact that the word for James was so profound that shocked me. It was the fact that the Lord had entrusted me with a special assignment to deliver a word on His behalf, and I thought it was probably the most important thing I would ever do in my spiritual life. I immediately sat straight up in bed, walked over to the light switch, turned on the overhead light, and started putting on my clothes. I had never had any teaching on the gift of prophecy. I had no idea that you didn't have to go immediately when the Lord gave you a word for someone.

In hindsight, I am sure the Lord must have been laughing. While I was putting on my clothes, Mark, who had been lying beside me sound asleep, woke up with the light in his eyes saying, "What are you doing?" I said, "Mark, I have heard from God, and He has given me a message to deliver to James Robison." Mark said, "It is 2:30 in the morning, and James is probably sound asleep." I said, "If I had a word from God for you, wouldn't you want me to wake you up and give it to you? Mark said, "I would want you to give it to me, but not at 2:30 in the morning. Come here and lie down beside me, and in the morning you can give James the word."

I didn't want to lie down because the thought that God would entrust me with a word for someone was overwhelming. I didn't want to let Him down, but I was obedient to my husband. I remember him wrapping his arms around me, holding me as I stared out the window for the rest of the night, waiting for the sun to come up.

The next morning, I got the boys off to school and found out James was having a Bible conference in Irving. I knew one of my best friends, Betsy Hall, was at that conference, so I called her and asked her to arrange a meeting with him. When I finally met with James, he was very gracious. When I told Him the word the Lord had sent me to deliver, he said the Lord had told him the same thing. I found out later when you receive a word from the Lord for someone, it is often a confirmation of something He has already told them.

I am so grateful Mark made me get back in bed that night. When we first receive a gift in the natural realm, like a new computer or a new oven, we don't always immediately know all the ins and outs of how to use it. We often have to spend some time with it before using it becomes second nature. The same thing was true about my first time using the gift of prophecy. I had much to learn. I never again tried to deliver a message at 2:30 in the morning.

Later the prophecy about James came true. The Lord expanded his borders, opening the door for his television ministry to reach into the homes of millions of viewers not only in America, but Europe, Australia, New Zealand, Cambodia, Thailand, India, and the Ukraine. Today he is going into the world through television, reaping souls for the kingdom.

Supernatural Gifts

Nate, my oldest grandson, is fifteen now. He is not only loving, kind, and tenderhearted, but he excels as an athlete, in the academic arena, and in the knowledge of the power of prayer.

When he was young he loved to dress up in costumes. He had a Superman costume, a Spiderman costume, a Hulk costume, and many others. On any given day you could see him running through my house clothed in one of his many costumes, hands outstretched with a cape flying behind him. I still remember the day he stood on my stairs all dressed up as Superman, telling me how strong Superman was and how he had the ability, unlike normal men, to fly.

In the midst of his conversation he asked me if I had supernatural gifts like Superman. As I was assuring him I didn't, I suddenly realized even though I'm not faster than a speeding bullet or more powerful than a locomotive, or able to leap tall buildings in a single bound, when it comes to the spiritual world, I along with thousands and thousands of others in the kingdom of God, have been given supernatural gifts from the Lord Jesus Christ. The dictionary defines the word supernatural as, "some force beyond scientific understanding of the laws of nature." The gifts of the Spirit are all beyond scientific understanding of the laws of a natural man, but thankfully the King of another kingdom has bestowed them on us to help us operate in His kingdom.

There are different kinds of gifts, but the same Spirit distributes them. There are different kinds of service, but the same Lord. There are different kinds of working, but in all of them and in everyone it is the same God at work. Now to each one the manifestation of the Spirit is given for the common good. To one there is given through the Spirit a message of wisdom, to another a message of knowledge by means of the same Spirit, to another faith by the same Spirit, to another gifts of healing by that one Spirit, to another miraculous powers, to another prophecy, to another distinguishing between spirits, to another speaking in different kinds of tongues, and to still another interpretation of tongues. All these are the work of one and the same Spirit, and he distributes them to each one, just as he determines. 1 Corinthians 12:4-11

Prophetic Words for My Family

Over the years the Lord has given me words for different ones in His kingdom. In the month of October of 2005 He gave me a word for each of my children, their wives, and three of my four grandchildren. In June of 2014 he gave me a word for my youngest grandson, Gabriel. I want to share the words He gave me for each member of my family for their edification, exhortation, and comfort.

> *He who prophesies speaks edification, and exhortation, and comfort to men.*   1 Corinthians 14:3, NKJV

Kevin and Brandi's Word from the Lord

In a vision I saw the hand of the Lord, and in His hand was a solid gold, old fashioned pocket watch. It had a long gold chain attached to it, but instead of being attached to the timepiece at the top, both ends of the chain were attached to the timepiece on each side of the watch, making it look like it could be worn as a necklace. I was surprised as I looked at the hands of this timepiece, because instead of moving separately they were tied together by a cord moving like one hand instead of two.

As I watched the hands on this timepiece move, they would both be at 1:00 at the same time; then they would move directly to 2:00, missing all the minutes. They were moving together from one hour; to the next hour to the next hour simultaneously. I then saw the Lord take a knife and cut the cords that bound the hands of the clock together; and suddenly they were free to move like they had been created to move.

The Lord spoke to me and said, "This timepiece is a picture of Kevin. Tell him to always remember that even as this timepiece was in My hand, his times are in My hand, too. He said, "To Kevin it looks like his hands are tied for now just like the hands are tied on this timepiece, but tell Kevin what he is doing right now may not look like eternal purposes, but I am the One who has tied him to this place with cords of love.

The reason that I have tied him here is because he is in preparation for the appointed time."

He continued, "The hands on the timepiece were not moving accurately because the time was not yet right, not yet ripe, not yet ready. It is not time for Me to cut the cords and move him into the fullness of time. However, when the appointed time comes, I will cut the cords and his hands will be free to be used by Me in the next phase of eternal purposes. Time will pass quickly for Kevin in the grand scheme of things, but tell him that he is not spinning his wheels. The time he is spending now is very essential to prepare him for his destiny. At the set time, at the appointed time, in the fullness of time, I will untie his hands and he will be released to move in the next phase of eternal purpose for Me."

My times are in His hands.   Psalms 31:15

He said, "The reason the chain is tied to the timepiece on both sides is because I have a special purpose for this chain." I saw the Lord take this chain with the timepiece attached and hang it like a necklace around Brandi's neck. He said, "Brandi is not a ball and chain to Kevin. The reason he hangs around her is because he enjoys her, and he loves to be with her."

It was as if a magnifying glass zoomed in on the face of the timepiece, and I saw that right in the center of the timepiece was the most beautiful, breathtaking pearl. The Lord said, "This pearl is a picture of Brandi. I placed Brandi in Kevin's heart, just like that pearl was placed in the heart of this timepiece, causing the heart of the pearl to be together with the heart of the timepiece. Brandi is heart to heart with Kevin. I knew Kevin would need someone strong, who was grounded, not flighty. He needed someone he could respect, someone who could walk side by side through life with him. I placed Brandi in Kevin's heart because she has the ability to see things from his perspective."

Next, I saw a safe, and the Lord took the timepiece and put it in the safe. He said, "The safe is also a picture of Brandi. When Kevin feels weathered by the world, she is the place he likes to run to. Not only is Brandi a safe place for Kevin, but other people can trust her with the things that are valuable to them. She is trustworthy. She is a safe place in My kingdom for the weary to run into."

He said, "Brandi is a Ruth in My Kingdom. Even as Ruth was a caregiver to Naomi, Brandi is a caregiver. She cares for the things that others care about. They can trust her with their cares. Brandi is My pearl of great price; when I saw her, I knew I had to have her, so I gave up My very life's blood to purchase her. Brandi is very valuable to me, to Kevin, and to My kingdom."

> *The kingdom of heaven is like a merchant seeking fine pearls, and upon finding one pearl of great value, he went and sold all that he had, and bought it.* Matthew 13:45-46

Nate's Word from the Lord

In a vision, I saw a baby eagle and three chickens. The Lord said, "The baby eagle is a picture of Nate." Each chicken had a box. Each chicken loved their box, and every time they saw the baby eagle they beckoned him to come join them in their boxes.

The name on the first chicken's box was "Religion." He had taken much time to decorate his box by putting beautiful bars all around it. The first chicken said to the baby eagle, won't you please come and join me in my box. The baby eagle said, thank you, but I have other plans for my life. I am going to spend my life flying high up in the sky. I am going to fly in heavenly places. I am going to see things from a heavenly perspective."

The chicken promptly said, "No way; that is impossible. There was a day years ago when eagles did fly high up in the sky, but not today; don't waste your time trying something that will never happen. Come and get in my box with me." As the eagle examined the box more closely, he asked the chicken where he got those bars. The chicken proudly said,

"These bars are strong and beautiful because they came from man. They are manmade bars."

As the eagle looked at the bars he had a strange feeling if he got into that box, the chicken would try to keep him locked up with manmade rules and regulations that he would never be able to live up to. The baby eagle graciously refused to get in the box labeled "Religion" because he had no intention of letting anything keep him from fulfilling his destiny.

The second chicken's box was labeled, "Pack of Lies." As the baby eagle walked past this chicken's box he said, "I can fly high up in the sky. I'm going to be able to fly in heavenly places. I am going to look down and see things from a heavenly perspective." The chicken promptly replied, "No way. You can't fly high up in the sky, let alone be able to see things from a heavenly perspective. Just look at yourself. You are not as good as all the other eagles. You are full of flaws. You will never be able to fly high up in the sky like other eagles. Won't you please come and get in my box with me?"

The baby eagle had a feeling if he got into the box with that chicken he would keep him from fulfilling his destiny by filling his life with lies. He quickly refused the invitation.

As the eagle walked along, the sun was setting on the horizon and it was suddenly nighttime. There was darkness over the earth. The eagle then heard the third chicken calling out to him from a place of darkness. "Good morning," said the chicken. The eagle was puzzled. He knew it wasn't morning, because they were in the dark. He then saw the name on that chicken's box. It was "Lack of Knowledge." The eagle quickly realized this chicken didn't know the difference between day and night. It thought it was living in the light, but it was actually living in darkness. It didn't know the truth. The chicken asked the eagle to come and join him in his box. He told him if he did he could be just like him. He wouldn't have to spend his life, wasting his time studying, learning about things that weren't important. He told the eagle he could spend his days living it up, having fun playing with him.

The baby eagle said, "No thank you, I am going to fly high up in the sky. I am going to look down from the high places and see things from a heavenly perspective. The chicken promptly said, "No way. You will never be able to fly high in the sky and see things from a heavenly perspective. Don't you know that eagles can't fly? Come get in my box with me." The baby eagle knew he didn't want to live his life not knowing the truth. He knew it would take time and energy to learn the truth, but it would be time well spent. As he walked away, he was grateful he didn't have to spend his life living in a box with that chicken.

When he got home, his father was waiting for him. He said, "Son, the time has come. You are ready to fly." The baby eagle followed his father to a tall cliff. As he looked down from the top of the cliff, he felt a little queasy. They were really high up in the sky. The father eagle said, "Watch me and do what I do. If you do what I tell you to do you will be able to fly high up in the sky just like me."

He watched his father as he jumped off the cliff and began flapping his wings. He flapped, and flapped, and flapped. As the baby eagle watched, his father suddenly quit flapping and just spread his wings, but to the baby eagle's amazement, instead of falling his father began to soar, rising higher and higher and higher in the sky. The baby eagle yelled out asking his father, "How can you fly without flapping?" His father looked at his son from the high places and said, "It is easy, son. You just ride on the current of the wind. Don't worry, you won't fall. The wind will carry you."

The father eagle than called out to the baby eagle and said, "Come fly with me." At first the baby eagle was hesitant. It was a long fall to the ground, but he knew his father would be right by his side to catch him in case he had any problems, so he jumped off the cliff and started flapping his wings. He flapped and flapped and flapped. Sure enough, after a few minutes, he felt something warm beneath his wings. His father was right. It was the wind. He extended his wings, just like his father told him to do, and the wind took over. He was soaring.

As he looked down, he realized everything he believed was true. He could see earthly things from a heavenly perspective now. As he felt the wind beneath his wings, he began to just relax and trust the wind as it carried him higher and higher and higher. He was thrilled to know he wasn't earthbound any more. He knew that he would never be earthbound again. He was so glad that he didn't get in the box with those chickens. If he had he would have missed the ride of a lifetime. The moral of this story is—don't be a chicken. Don't let anyone put you in their box. Don't be afraid to believe the truth. Don't let anyone tell you that you can't do what you were created to do.

The Lord then said, "Tell Nate he is an eagle in My kingdom. The gravity of the world, the gravity of religion, the gravity of lies of the enemy, nor the gravity of lack of knowledge will be able to pull him down to their level. He will know the truth, and truth will set him free to fulfill his destiny. Many will never experience the thrill of riding with the Wind of My Spirit. They will never feel the warmth of My Wind beneath their wings, but Nate will.

"In My body some are ears. Some are hands. Some are feet; and some are mouths. I will set Nate into My body as an eye. I will give him eyes that see. At the set time, in the fullness of time, at the appointed time he will hear Me calling him. When he does, he will start flapping. When he feels the warmth of My Wind beneath his wings, it is then that he will experience the thrill of soaring. Once he feels the Wind of My Spirit beneath his spiritual wings there is nothing in this world that will ever be able to keep him from mounting up and soaring in heavenly places with Me."

> *You will know the truth and the truth will set you free.*　　　　　　　　　　　　　　　　John 8:32

> *Blessed are the Eyes that see.*　　　　　　　　Luke 10:23a

*Just as a body, though one, has many parts, but all its many parts form one body, so it is with Christ. For we were all baptized by one Spirit so as to form one body, whether Jews or Gentiles, slave or free- and we were all given the one Spirit to drink. Even so the body is not made up of one part but of many. Now if the foot should say, "because I am not a hand, I do not belong to the body," it would not for that reason stop being part of the body. And if they should say, "Because I am not an eye, I do not belong to the body," it would not for that reason stop being part of the body. If the whole body were an eye, where would the sense of hearing be? If the whole body were an ear, where would the sense of smell be? But in fact God has placed the parts in the body, every one of them, just as he wanted them to be. If they were all one part, where would the body be? As it is there are many parts, but one body.*1 Corinthians 12:12-20*

Gabe's Word from the Lord

I saw a dog who looked like he was hungry. He was searching for something to eat. I watched him find a T-bone steak, and the minute his eyes met the steak he didn't' hesitate. He devoured the meat, gnawing on the bone until nothing was left. The Lord said, "This dog is a picture of Gabe. Just like the dog devoured the meat on the bone, in the fullness of time, Gabe will be a Word man, who will devour the meat of My Word. The milk of the Word will not satisfy Gabe's spiritual palate. He will be a meat lover.

Just like the dog who had no intention of stopping until all the meat was gone, Gabe won't stop short. He won't give up. He will be a man with spiritual tenacity, who will go after the meat of My Word with all of his heart. He won't be like those who always wait on others to feed them. He will get into My Word and learn to feed himself. As a spiritual man, Gabe won't be weak or anorexic. He will be strong. My Word will give him strength to move past the shallow into the deep things of My Spirit. He will learn to walk in a place of wisdom, understanding, and intimacy with Me.

The meat he eats will strengthen his spiritual body enhancing his ability to hear, enhancing his ability to see, and enhancing his ability to set his mind on things above. He will discover the meat of My Word is not tough, or hard to swallow, but it is tender, delicious, and pleasing to his spiritual palette. He will discover as he eats My Word that nothing can satisfy the longing in his soul but Me.

> *You have been believers so long now that you ought to be teaching others. Instead, you need someone to teach you again the basic things about God's word. You are like babies who need milk and cannot eat solid food. For someone who lives on milk is still and infant and doesn't know how to do what is right. Solid food is for those who are mature, who through training have the skill to recognize the difference between right and wrong.*

Hebrews 5:12-14

Chris and Wendy's Word from the Lord

I saw the Lord's hand, and in His hand was a solitaire diamond. A spotlight was shining on the diamond. The Lord said, "This is Chris." As I looked closer I could see that the diamond was many-faceted. He said, "Chris is many-faceted. There are many sides to him. Chris is a father, a family man, a builder, a hunter, a husband, an artist, a musician, a singer, a writer, and a worshiper. He does many things and he does them well."

He continued, "The spotlight is on Chris right now as a worshiper, but the stage is small. Tell Chris that he has only just begun. Tell him his future is bright. He has weathered the storm and he weathered it well, coming out on the other side much stronger. Tell him I have a plan for his life." He said, "Give Chris a message from Me, 'Just relax and wait.

In the fullness of time I will execute My plan, and you will bear much fruit in My kingdom for Me.'"

Well done, good and faithful servant: thou hast been faithful
with a few things, I will put in in charge of many things.

Matthew 25:23

I saw the Lord, and in His hand was a band of gold. On top of the band were four gold prongs. As I looked at the prongs I could see that they were empty. They were just sitting on the band waiting for a solitaire diamond to take its place. The Lord said, "This four-pronged band of gold is Wendy. There was a time in her life I saw her sitting in a place where she felt empty, wondering if she would ever find the right man to fill her life. At the appointed time, I placed Chris, the solitaire diamond, into Wendy's life, into her arms to have and to hold."

"Everyone knows the purpose of the prongs on the band of gold. They are of great value to the diamond. They are the place where the diamond rests. They support the diamond and they lift the diamond up. Even though when people look at a diamond ring they don't usually say, 'Aren't those prongs beautiful?' Without the prongs no one would be able to see the true beauty of the diamond."

The Lord said, "Even as there are four prongs on this ring, there are four aspects in Wendy as a wife. The first prong represents a place of rest. When Chris found Wendy he found his place of rest. He rests in Wendy. The second prong represents support. She is a strong support in Chris's life. She keeps him from being lost, from losing his way. The third prong represents the fact that Wendy always lifts Chris up. Even as she was a cheerleader in high school and college, she is now Chris's cheerleader in life. She encourages him by building him up with her words. The fourth prong represents value. No one understands the value of the prongs like the diamond itself, but Chris understands Wendy's value in his life because in her he found, his place of rest and strong support. In

Wendy he found the place that allows him to shine like he was created to shine."

The Lord then said, "I love My Wendy. Even as gold has great value in the world, Wendy has great value in My kingdom. She not only encourages and uplifts Chris, but she is an encourager in My kingdom who lifts others up with her encouraging, supportive words. I have given Wendy the gift of exhortation, and she executes her gift well. Tell Wendy I take great delight in her. She is My heart's desire."

I then saw the Lord with a crown in His hand. It was one of those crowns that kings and queens wore in the days of old. Instead of many stones in the crown there was just one. It was the most breathtaking, beautiful red ruby that I had ever seen. I couldn't take my eyes off of it. The Lord took the crown and placed it on Chris's head. He said, "Chris is a king in My kingdom.

"The jewel in his crown is Wendy. She is also a jewel in My kingdom. Oh how she sparkles, and oh how she shines. She carries the aroma of My presence, and when others look at her they can see a reflection of Me. Tell Wendy, at the appointed time; the set time; in the fullness of time; I will bring her forth, shine My spotlight on her, and put her on display for My glory."

> *An excellent wife, who can find? Her worth is far above rubies. The heart of her husband trusts in her.*
>
> Proverbs 31:10

Parker, The Chip Off the Old Block

I saw the Lord, and in His hand was a big block. He took His knife and chiseled a chip off of it. He then took the chip and whittled it into the shape of a block. It was just a smaller version of the big block. The Lord said, "The big block is you, Jenny. The smaller block is Parker. Parker is a chip off the old block. Even as you are a listener in My kingdom, Parker will learn to listen to Me in the same way. She will have ears that hear."

He that has ears to hear, let him hear.   Luke 14:35

I then saw a vision of a train with four boxcars. The Lord said, "Each car on this train represents an aspect of the way Parker will function in My kingdom. The name, "Follow Me" was written on the first car of the train. The Lord said, "Parker will be a leader in My kingdom. Because she will follow Me, she will have the confidence to be able to turn around and say to others, 'follow me because I am following after Him.' As a leader, Parker will always be full of confidence, not in the flesh because she will put no confidence in the flesh, but her confidence will be in the invisible leadership of My Spirit."

The second car on the train was named, "Good Job." The Lord continued, "Parker will be an encourager in My Kingdom. She won't tear others down with words of destruction; she will build them up with words of encouragement and praise. She will not only look after her own interests in life, but she will also look at the things that interest others.

Do not merely look out for your own personal interests, but
also for the interests of others.   Philippians 2:4

The third car on the train was named, "Full of Faith." "Parker will walk in a great measure of faith. She will have the faith of a grain of a mustard seed that can move mountains. Parker will always believe if I have said something, I will do what I said I would do. If I have said it, then Parker will believe it and that will settle it for her. Parker knows that nothing is too difficult for Me."

Nothing is too hard for You!   Jeremiah 32:17

The last car on the train was named, "I Can Do It." "'Can't' will not be a word in Parker's vocabulary. She will be like the little red caboose behind the train in fairy tale land that said, 'I think I can, I think I can, I think I can.'" She will not say, 'I can't.' She will be my Can, Can Girl.

Parker will know as she walks through life that she CAN do all things through Me because I am the One who strengthens her."

> *I can do all things through Christ who strengthens me.*
> Philippians 4:13

Luke's Word from the Lord

In a vision, I saw Luke running with a ball in his hands. It was a football like many in the world have carried. Luke then looked up and saw the Lord with His arms open wide. They were outstretched in a parallel position, and His hands were nailed to a tree. The Lord said to Luke, "Red rover, red rover, let Luke come over." When he heard the call, he grinned, dropped the ball and started running toward the Lord, never taking his eyes off of Jesus, and never looking back.

The Lord said, "What you saw was a picture. Luke will be a red rover in My kingdom. As he travels through life, he will always be conscious of the color red. The color of My blood will be at the forefront of his life. One day at the appointed time, Luke will look up and see Me with My arms outstretched, parallel to the earth, nailed to that old rugged cross. When he sees My hands nailed to that tree because of My great love for him, he will drop everything and start running. When he starts running nothing in all of this world will keep him from running after Me."

> *Therefore, since we have so great a cloud of witnesses surrounding us, let us also lay aside every weight, and the sin which so easily entangles us, and let us run with endurance the race that is set before us, fixing our eyes on Jesus, the author and finisher of our faith.* Hebrews 12:1-2

I then saw the Lord with a ball in His hands. It wasn't a ball like we see in this world. It was a supernatural ball. He took the ball and threw it to Luke. When He did, Luke reached up and caught it. The Lord said,

"This ball is the Good News of what I did on the cross. Luke will carry this ball in his heart everywhere he goes. He will hold on to this truth, and he won't drop the ball. As he carries the ball, he will be like a parrot who listens and repeats what he hears. He will have ears that hear My voice. He will listen to My words and repeat the things he hears to others."

"I will give him the supernatural ability to take the things of mine and repeat them in such a way that others will want to catch the same ball, and start running after Me, too. Luke will repeat the story of My great love that took Me to the cross. He will tell them how I took the punishment for their sins in their place. He will tell them if they will just put their faith and trust in Me, I will forgive them of their sins and give them the free gift of eternal life."

11

The Secret of the Spirit and the Bride

I have discovered from our Bridegroom, the Lord Jesus Christ, that He is in a position of readiness, by the power of His Spirit, to prepare every Bride who is willing to enter into the Divine romance. Of course we need to remember that the Bride in the body of Christ is His church, which includes all of us, both male and female.

> *For as many of you as have been baptized into Christ have put on Christ. There is neither Jew nor Greek, there is neither bond nor free, there is neither male nor female: for ye are all one in Christ Jesus.* Galatians 3:27-28

The Wind of the Spirit

What is the Wind of the Spirit doing to prepare the bride? He is moving throughout the earth calling, wooing His Bride. Just like the wind that roams the earth, we can't see Him but we can feel His presence and hear His voice.

The call we are hearing in the Wind of the Spirit today is the voice of our Bridegroom. He is the One calling us to come to the deep. He knows we have splashed around in the shallow waters long enough. He is calling us to come to the "secret place." He is calling us to come to the place of intimacy. The good news is the secret place is not for just a select few. Whosoever will can come.

The River of Living Water

What is the River of Living Water doing today? Oh yes, He is still flowing. There is an old worship song that says, "There is a River, who is a King." He is the River of Living Water that is running through our spiritual veins. He is alive, living inside all who have been born again. He is waiting on us to ask Him to fill us up. He is longing to fill us with Himself.

He not only wants to fill us; He wants us to enjoy the River. He wants us to enjoy Him. He wants us to feel free to splash around and have fun in His presence. Just like the river bed was created to relax, lean back and receive the river, He wants us to lean back in a position of rest and just receive His river of love.

The Oil and the Wine of the Spirit

What are the Oil and the Wine of His Spirit doing? Both are still flowing from heaven's throne room in abundance. The Oil of the Spirit is waiting to saturate the eyes and ears of every bride who wants eyes that can see and ears that can hear with greater clarity in the realm of the Spirit. Jesus started pouring the New Wine more than two thousand years ago, and He is still serving that same New Wine today. He wants to intoxicate us with the New Wine of His Spirit. He wants us to loosen up so we will quit being so stiff, so rigid, so religious around Him.

The Divine Physician, like the good Samaritan, wants to pour the Oil and Wine of His Spirit into our wounds, into the deep recesses of our souls. He wants to heal our heartbreaks and our hurts. There are certain places in all of us that only He can reach. He wants to saturate the hard, rough places that keep us from receiving His love. He wants to soften us, making us more pliable in His nail-scarred hands.

Fresh Fire

What is His Fire doing? He is still burning with a holy passion. He is ready to release Fresh Fire to replace the lukewarm flame that has been flickering in the hearts of His Bride. In this very hour He is ready to ignite hearts that have grown cold, so they can get hot and start burning with passion for Him once again.

Just like the two on the road to Emmaus whose hearts were burning because they had been with Him, He wants our hearts to burn because of the revelation of His presence with us. You may be asking, "What is He waiting for? Why doesn't He just go ahead and set my heart on fire?" The answer is simple — He is a gentleman. He will never by pass our will. He is waiting on us to give Him the go-ahead.

Our Bridegroom

What is our Bridegroom doing while the bride is busy allowing His Spirit to make her ready? When my youngest son Chris, got married something happened that was a picture of what Christ is doing today. The guests that had been invited to the wedding were all seated. Mark and I had been seated by our assigned usher. Wendy's mother and father had been seated. As I noticed the crowd stirring, I realized the time when everyone thought the wedding should start had come and gone. I looked at my watch thinking Chris was late. Where was he? He should have already come to the front to receive His Bride.

As I scanned the room I saw him, and to my surprise he was looking directly at me. When my eyes met his, I saw a big smile cross his face. He had one last message for me before He stepped up. I could clearly read his lips as he silently mouthed the words, "I love you." He then made his way to the front to receive his bride.

Like Chris, Jesus is waiting in the wings. He wants to make sure that everyone has the opportunity to hear those three all- powerful words, "I love you." When the last person hears the message that He loves them so much He was willing to die for them, He will step out from behind the wings of heaven and receive His bride.

Our Bridegroom is longing for a lovesick bride who will be willing for the Fire, the Wine, the Oil, the River and the Wind to have their way with her. He wants us to respond to the call of His Spirit and allow Him to take us into His Banqueting House. He wants us to see that there is a banner flying over us in the Wind of the Spirit and that banner over us is love. He knows when we begin to comprehend the way He loves us, the passion He longs for will spring up from the depths of all that we are.

The last chapter of the last book of the Bible says, "...*the Spirit and the bride say, Come*" (Revelation 22:17). With His final, closing, written words, the Lord places the spotlight on the Spirit and His Bride. The Spirit brings the Bride of Christ to center stage for one purpose, to invite all who are thirsty to come to Jesus. He knows when the world sees the passionate way His bride loves Him they will be enticed to know the One she loves.

Notes

Letter from the Author

1. Deuteronomy 29:29 NIV
2. John 14:26 KJV
3. Habakkuk 2:2a NIV
4. Acts 16:9 KJV
5. Ezekiel 2:9 NIV

Introduction

1. Mark 12:30 NASB
2. *All of Me*, written by Seymoor Simons and Gerald Marks and sung by Willie Nelson
3. Revelation 21:9b NASB
4. *Burning Love*, written by Dennis Linde, sung by Elvis Presley
5. Song of Solomon 2:4-5 AMP
6. 1 Corinthians 1:27 KJV
7. 2 Timothy 3:16 NASB
8. Matthew 13:1-9 NIV
9. Matthew 13:18-23 NIV
10. Galatians 4: 22-31 AMP

11. Galatians 4:24a AMP
12. www.yourdictionary.com/allegory
13. Song of Solomon 6:13 KJV
14. Galatians 3:26-28 KJV
15. Song of Solomon 4:12-16 KJV
16. Galatians 5:22 NASB
17. 2 Corinthians 2:15-16 AMP
18. John 7:38 NASB
19. Dudley Hall, "the words were silently sitting on white pages, all dressed up in black"
20. Song of Solomon 7:10 AMP
21. Song of Solomon 2:16 KJV
22. Daniel 2:28b KJV
23. Song of Solomon 5:1 NASB

Chapter 1

1. Song of Solomon 1:1-4 KJV
2. Psalms 42:1 NASB
3. Isaiah 26:9 AMP
4. Philippians 3:8 KJV
5. Proverbs 3:32 NASB
6. Romans 11:36 NASB
7. Ephesians 3:17-19 NASB
8. John 14:20-21 NIV
9. Song of Solomon 1:4 KJV
10. Ecclesiastes 12:8 KJV
11. Hebrews 12: 1-2 KJV
12. Jeremiah 12:1-2 KJV
13. Philippians 3:12 NIV
14. John 3:3 NASB
15. Ephesians 2:8-9 KJV
16. John 6:44 NASB

17. Romans 8:16 ASB
18. Revelations 21:9 KJV
19. Exodus 25: 1-2, 8-9 KJV
20. Hebrews 8:1-5 NIV
21. Exodus 27:1-8 NIV
22. Exodus 38:1-7 NIV
23. Leviticus 1:1-13 NIV
24. Hebrews 9:22 NASB
25. 2 Corinthians 5:21 NASB
26. (Altar) *The New Strong's Exhaustive Concordance of Bible*, James Strong, LLD, STD, copyright 1995, Thomas Nelson Publishers
27. John 1:29 NAS
28. Exodus 30: 17-21 NIV
29. Exodus 38:8 NIV
30. Exodus 40: 7, 30-32 NIV
31. Ephesians 5:26 NIV
32. Exodus 25: 31-40 NIV
33. Exodus 27: 17-24 NIV
34. Leviticus 24: 1-4 NIV
35. Peter 2:9 NIV
36. Ephesians 5:18 NIV
37. Exodus 25: 23-30 NIV
38. Exodus 37:10-16 NIV
39. Leviticus 23:13 NIV
40. Leviticus 24: 5-9 NIV
41. Numbers 28: 7-10, 14-14, 24, 31 NIV
42. John 6:51 NIV
43. Exodus 30: 1-10 NIV
44. Exodus 40: 34-38 NIV
45. Exodus 37: 25-29 NIV
46. Hebrews 7:25 KJV
47. Exodus 25: 10-22 NIV
48. 2 Samuel 5-7 NIV

49. Exodus 25:22 AMP
50. Numbers 7: 89 NIV
51. Exodus 33: 9-11 NASB
52. John 10:27 NKJV
53. www.cbumgardner.wordpress.com, *Hebraic Literature; Translations from the Talmud, Midrashim and Kabbala,* (M. Walter Dunne, 1901)
54. Matthew 7:50 NASB

Chapter 2

1. John 16:23b-24 NASB
2. John 14:13-14 NASB
3. Matthew 7: 7-8 NASB
4. I John 5: 14-15 NASB
5. Exodus 33:18 KJV
6. James 4:2b ASV
7. 2 Corinthians 11:2-3 NIV
8. Jeremiah 2:5b NASB
9. Psalm 16:11b AMP
10. Song of Solomon 1:4 ASV
11. (Chambers) *The New Strong's Exhaustive Concordance of Bible*, James Strong, LLD, STD, copyright 1995, Thomas Nelson Publishers
12. Jeremiah 31:3 NASB
13. Ephesians 1:13 NASB
14. 1 Corinthians 12:13a NASB
15. John 14:20 NASB
16. Jeremiah 33:3 NASB
17. Mark Twain, www.goodreads.com/quotes/505050 the-two-most-important-days-in-your-life
18. Isaiah 46: 9-10 NASB
19. Acts 13:36 NIRV

20. Jeremiah 29:11
21. Acts 2:17-18 KJV
22. Job 33:14-17 NASB
23. 2 Timothy 2:25-26 NASB
24. 1 Kings 19:19 NASB
25. (Oxen) www.dictionary.reference.com/browse/oxen
26. 1 Kings 19: 21 NASB
27. Hebrews 12:1 KJV
28. 2 Kings 2:9 NASB
29. 2 Kings 13:20-21 NASB

Chapter 3

1. Song of Solomon 2:4 NKJV
2. (Banqueting) *Yayin*, wine, *The New Strong's Exhaustive Concordance of Bible*, James Strong, LLD, STD, copyright 1995, Thomas Nelson Publishers, Hebrew
3. Acts 2:2-4 NKJV
4. Acts 2:13 KJV
5. Acts 2:15 KJV
6. Acts 1:8 NASB
7. Luke 3:16 NIV
8. 1 Corinthians 12:13 KJV
9. Matthew 3:11 KJV
10. Mark 16:16 KJV
11. 1 Corinthians 14:18 NASB
12. 1 Corinthians 13:8 NASB
13. 1 Corinthians 14:39 NASB
14. Mark 16:17 KJV
15. 1 Corinthians 14:2 KJV
16. 1 Corinthians 14:14 KJV
17. 1 Corinthians 14:4 KJV
18. Jude 1:20 KJV

19. Romans 8:26-27 NKJV
20. Luke 11:9-13 ASV
21. I John 4:16 NASB
22. (Lovesick) www.yourdictionary.com
23. *You Were Made for Me*, song written and sung by Sam Cooke, 1959
24. Revelation 4:11 KJV
25. www.brainyquotes.com/quotes/authors/oliverwendallholmes
26. Acts 2:4 KJV
27. Acts 2:6-11 ASV
28. (6500) www.infoplease.com/askeds/many-spoken-languages
29. *The Beauty of Spiritual Language*, Jack Hayford, copyright 1996 by Jack W. Hayford, Published in Nashville, Tennesse, by Thomas Nelson, Inc.
30. *Annie's Song* written and sung by John Denver, 1974
31. Ephesians 5:18 KJV
32. John 1:15 AMP
33. 1 Corinthians 2:14 KJV
34. Colossians 3:2a ASV
35. Exodus 4: 10-12 NIV
36. 1 Corinthians 15::46 NIV
37. 2 Corinthians 2:15-16 NIV
38. Galatians 5:16-17 NKJV
39. Matthew 4:1 KJV
40. Ephesians 6:11-18 KJV
41. Luke 10:30, 33-34 NIRV
42. Acts 2:17a KJV
43. Acts 10:44-46 AMP
44. Acts 9:6 NASB
45. Cotton Mather, www.christianitytoday.com/ch/news/2002/oct14.html
46. Johnathan Edwards In 173 www.christianitytoday.com/ch/news/2002/oct14.html

47. A. B. Simpson, www.enwikipedia.org/wiki/ albert_Benjamin_Simpson

48. D. L. Moody, 1832-1899 www.christianitytoday.com/ch/ news/2002/oct14.html

49. Charles Finney, www.modernreformation.org

50. Charles Parham, www.enwikipedia.org/wiki/charlesfoxparham

51. William Seymore, 1870-1922, www.enwikipedia.org/wiki/ williamseymore51.

52. Smith Wigglesworth, www.healingandrevival.com/ BioSWigglesworth.htm

53. *Mystery of The Holy Spirit*, A. W. Tozer, copyright 2007, by Bridge-Logos

54. *John G. Lake, His Life, His Sermons, His Boldness of Faith*, 1994 Kenneth

55. Copeland Publications, xx-xxi

56. Father Dennis Bennett, www.http://digitalcommons.liberty.edu/ cgm_missions/7 en.wikipedia.org/wiki/charismatic-Christianity 500 Million

Chapter 4

1. Song of Solomon 4:1 NASB

2. Ezekiel 16:14 NASB

3. Song of Solomon 1:5 NASB

4. 1 Kings 8:10-11 NASB

5. *Nothing but the Blood,* written by Robert Lowery, copyright Public Domain

6. Romans 4:7-8 NIV

7. Daniel 2:26-28 NLT

8. Jeremiah 15;16a NASB

9. Romans 12:2a NIV

10. Ephesians 1:18-19 NASB

11. www.space.com25303howmanygalaxiesinuniverse

12. Song of Solomon 7:10 KJV

13. *Alphabet Song,* written Buddy Kaye, Sidney Lippman, Fred Wise
14. Grenzbegriff, www.google.com/search?german-word-grenzbegriff
15. Song of Solomon 5:1 NASB
16. 2 Corinthians 2:11 NASB
17. Matthew 18:21-35 AMP
18. Matthew 18:32-35 AMP
19. Manna, *The New Strong's Exhaustive Concordance of the Bible,* James Strong, LLD, STD, copyright 1995, Thomas Nelson Publishers
20. Ezekiel 16:14 NASB
21. Zechariah 2:8 NASB
22. Ephesians 1:6 NASB
23. 2 Corinthians 5:20 NASB
24. Psalm 91:11 NASB
25. Luke 10:19 NASB
26. Revelation 21:9 NASB
27. 1 Corinthians 6:20 NASB
28. Ezekiel 16:14 NASB
29. Song of Solomon 2:4 NASB
30. Isaiah 61:3 NASB
31. Revelation 4:11 NASB
32. 2 Timothy 1:9 NASB
33. Acts 9:15 NASB
34. Colossians 2:10 NASB
35. 2 Corinthians 3:18 NASB
36. Isaiah 62:4 NASB
37. Song of Solomon 7:10 NASB
38. Colossians 1:13 NASB
39. Luke 24:49 NASB
40. Ephesians 1:18 NASB
41. 2 Peter 1:4 NASB
42. 1 John 2:12 NASB
43. Colossians 5:1 NASB

44. 1 John 4:4 NASB
45. Titus 3:7 NASB
46. Deuteronomy 28:13 NASB
47. 1 Peter 2:24 NASB
48. 2 Timothy 1:14 NASB
49. Ephesians 1:18 NASB
50. Titus 3:7 NASB
51. Malachi 3:17 NASB
52. 1 Peter 1:35 NASB
53. Romans 8:38-39 NASB
54. Psalm 40:2 NASB
55. Romans 8:37 NASB
56. 1 Corinthians 2:16 NASB
57. Revelation 2:17 NASB
58. 2 Corinthians 5:17 NASB
59. Revelation 12:11 NASB
60. 2 Peter 1:4 NASB
61. 1 Peter 2:9 NASB
62. Galatians 3:13-14 NASB
63. Ephesians 3:16 NASB
64. 1 Corinthians 1:2 NASB
65. 2 Timothy 1:7 NASB
66. Ephesians 1:13 NASB
67. Romans 12:2 NASB
68. Psalm 139:17-18 NASB
69. 2 Timothy 2:20-21 NASB
70. 2 Timothy 2:20-21 NASB
71. Revelation 21:9 NASB
72. Ephesians 2:10 NASB
73. Hebrews 13:5 NASB
74. Song of Solomon 6:3 NASB
75. Acts 22:3 NASB

Chapter 5

1. Song of Solomon 2:10-13 NIV
2. Jeremiah 5:21 NASB
3. Hebrews 13:5 NKJV
4. Psalm 139:17-18 NIRV
5. Psalm 31:15 KJV
6. 1 Peter 5:8-10 NASB
7. 2 Peter 1:4 NASB
8. Galatians 5:1 NASB
9. Hebrews 11:1 KJV
10. Jeremiah 1:12 NASB
11. Luke 1:37 AMP
12. Matthew 19:26 KJV
13. Genesis 50:20 AMP
14. Romans 8:28 NASB
15. Deuteronomy 8:2 NIV
16. Deuteronomy 8:15-16 AMP
17. Philippians 1:6 KJV
18. Psalm 91:9-11 NIV
19. 2 Corinthians 12:9 KJV
20. *You've Got A Friend*, written and sung by James Taylor

Chapter 6

1. Song of Solomon 1:2a NASB
2. Psalm 45:2 NKJV
3. John 4:23 KJV
4. (*Proskuno*) to kiss toward, Greek, *The New Strong's Exhaustive Concordance of the Bible*, James Strong, LLD, STD, copyright 1995, Thomas Nelson Publishers
5. Genesis 3:8-9 NASB
6. John 3:16 KJV

7. Colossians 3:3 KJV
8. Job 38:1 KJV
9. 1 Kings 8:10-11 NAS
10. Revelation 2:17 NIV
11. Philippians 2:9-11 NIV
12. Revelation 1:5 KJV
13. *Till I Kissed You,* written by Don Everly, sung by The Everly Brothers, 1959
14. *Kisses Sweeter than Wine,* written by the Weavers, sung by Jimmie Rodgers

Chapter 7

1. Song of Songs 1:1 NASB
2. Zephaniah 3:17 NIV
3. *Getting to Know You,* (The King and I), written by Oscar Hammerstein, composer, Richard Rogers, Marni Nixon, dubbed for Deborah Kerr in 1956
4. A. W. Tozer, *Mystery of the Holy Spirit*
5. Acts 15:16 NASB
6. 1 Chronicles 15:16 NASB
7. 1 Chronicles 16:4-6 NASB
8. 1 Corinthians 3:16 NASB
9. Rick Godwin, sermon on Tabernacle of David
10. 2 Samuel 23:1-2 KJV
11. Psalm 42:1 NASB
12. *I've Got You Babe,* sung by Sonny and Cher, written by Sonny Bono
13. Luke 10:21 NASB
14. John 14:21 NIV
15. (*Emphanizo*) Manifest Greek, *The New Strong's Exhaustive Concordance of the Bible*, James Strong, LLD, STD, copyright 1995, Thomas Nelson Publishers

Chapter 8

1. Song of Solomon 6:13 NASB
2. Psalm 149:3 ASV
3. Psalm 150:4 ASV
4. Exodus 15:20 NASB
5. *You Make Me Feel Like Dancing*, written and sung by Leo Sayer
6. 2 Samuel 6:12-23 NASB
7. Ezekiel 16:8-14 NASB
8. *I Could Have Danced All Night*, (My Fair Lady) sung by Julie Andrews written by Alan Jay Lerner
9. Ezekiel 16:8 NASB
10. www.newyorktimes/1994toyitoyi

Chapter 9

1. Song of Solomon 8:13 NASB
2. 1 Corinthians 2:14 KJV
3. Matthew 11:15 KJV
4. John 10:27 NASB
5. Revelation 3:20 KJV
6. Proverbs 3:32 NASB
7. Proverbs 20:27a NASB
8. 1 Corinthians 2:9-10 KJV
9. *Two Weeks Notice*, written by Mark Lawrence
10. 1 Kings 19:11-14 NIV
11. *(Dmamah)*, Hebrew, *The New Strong's Exhaustive Concordance of the Bible, James Strong*, LLD, STD, copyright 1995, Thomas Nelson Publishers
12. Romans 8:16 KJV
13. Romans 9:1 KJV
14. Colossians 3:15 NIV

15. *When You Say Nothing At All*, written by Keith Whitley, sung by Alison Krause
16. Psalm 139:16 AMP
17. Acts 17:26-27 NIV
18. Isaiah 46:9-10 KJV
19. I Samuel 3:2-10 NASB
20. Luke 8:18 NIV
21. Luke 10:38-42 NIV
22. Romans 8:1 KJV
23. Isaiah 30:21 KJV
24. II Timothy 1:7 KJV
25. Jeremiah 2:13 KJV
26. Ezekiel 12:2 NIV
27. Hebrews 5:11b KJV
28. Acts 28:26-27 KJV
29. Luke 19:47-48 KJV
30. Isaiah 50:4 NASB
31. Song of Solomon 5:6 NASB
32. Song of Solomon 4:9 NASB
33. Luke 24:32 NIV
34. *Contact,* written by Carl and Ann Druyan

Chapter 10

1. Song of Songs 2:1-4 NASB
2. Matthew 3:16 NKJV
3. Psalm 62:2 KJV
4. 1 Corinthians 10:1-4 NASB
5. www.yourdictionary.com/cleft
6. Daniel 2:28 NLT
7. Revelations 1:9-11a NASB
8. Acts 1:5 NASB
9. Acts 1:8 NASB

10. Acts 2:1-4 NASB
11. (*Nabyi*), Hebrew Prophet Inspired by God, *The New Strong's Exhaustive Concordance of the Bible*, James Strong, LLD, STD, copyright 1995, Thomas Nelson Publishers
12. Acts 2:17-18 KJV
13. Ephesians 4:11 KJV
14. 1 Corinthians 14:1-6 KJV
15. 1 Corinthians 14:29-31 KJV
16. Supernatural www.oxforddictonaires.com
17. 1 Corinthians 12:4-11 NIV
18. Psalm 31:15 NIV
19. Matthew 13:45-46 NASB
20. John 8:32 NIV
21. Luke 10:23a NIV
22. Hebrews 5:12-14 NLT
23. Matthew 25:23 NIV
24. Proverbs 31:10 NASB
25. Luke 14:35
26. 1 Corinthians 12:12-20 NIV
27. Hebrews 5:12-14 NLT
28. Matthew 25:23 NIV
29. Proverbs 31:10 NASB
30. Philippians 3:3 NKJV
31. *I Will Follow Him*, (Sister Act) written by Franck Pourcel and Paul Mauriat
32. Philippians 2:4 NASB
33. Matthew 17:20 NIV
34. Jeremiah 32:17 NKJV
35. Philippians 4:13 KJV
36. Hebrews 12:1-2 NASB

Chapter 11 Spirit and the Bride

1. Revelation 22:17a ASV
2. Galatians 3:27-28 KJV

Graphics

Image01.jpg – Cover of Book, Godolphin Woods, Cornwell by Midlander, tonyarmstrongphotography.com

Image02.jpg – Seeing Christ in the Tabernacle, Ervin N. Hershberger, Vision Publishers

Image 03.jpg – Back of Book, Picture of the Author, Bludoor Studios, info@bludoorstudios.com

Page 315 !

- Trust only in the Fountain of Living Waters —
- The best kind of ears are ears that have been awakened to Gods Verse — ears to hear!
- There were many women prophets who prophesied about the coming Messiah and Jesus fulfilled all of them —
- Jesus is calling us to come to the deep, the secret place, a place of intimacy with Him —

CPSIA information can be obtained
at www.ICGtesting.com
Printed in the USA
FSOW01n1309240417
33490FS

9 781498 491242